ANNUAL EDITIONS

Human Resources 09/10

Eighteenth Edition

SO-AFC-824

EDITOR

Fred H. Maidment

Western Connecticut State University

Dr. Fred Maidment is associate professor of management at Western Connecticut State University in Danbury, Connecticut. He received his bachelor's degree from New York University and his master's degree from the Bernard M. Baruch College of the City University of New York. In 1983 Dr. Maidment received his doctorate from the University of South Carolina. He resides in Connecticut with his wife.

McGraw Hill **Higher Education**

Boston   Burr Ridge, IL   Dubuque, IA   New York   San Francisco   St. Louis
Bangkok   Bogotá   Caracas   Kuala Lumpur   Lisbon   London   Madrid   Mexico City
Milan   Montreal   New Delhi   Santiago   Seoul   Singapore   Sydney   Taipei   Toronto

Higher Education

ANNUAL EDITIONS: HUMAN RESOURCES, EIGHTEENTH EDITION

Annual Editions® is a registered trademark of The McGraw-Hill Companies, Inc.

Annual Editions is published by the **Contemporary Learning Series** group within the McGraw-Hill Higher Education division.

1 2 3 4 5 6 7 8 9 0 QPD/QPD 0 9

ISBN 978–0–07–352853–3
MHID 0–07–352853–6
ISSN 1092–6577

Managing Editor: *Larry Loeppke*
Senior Managing Editor: *Faye Schilling*
Developmental Editor: *Dave Welsh*
Editorial Coordinator: *Mary Foust*
Editorial Assistant: *Nancy Meissner*
Production Service Assistant: *Rita Hingtgen*
Permissions Coordinator: *DeAnna Dausener*
Senior Marketing Manager: *Julie Keck*
Marketing Communications Specialist: *Mary Klein*
Marketing Coordinator: *Alice Link*
Project Manager: *Sandy Wille*
Design Specialist: *Tara McDermott*
Senior Production Supervisor: *Laura Fuller*
Cover Graphics: *Kristine Jubeck*

Compositor: Laserwords Private Limited
Cover Image: © BananaStock/PictureQuest/RF (both images)

Library in Congress Cataloging-in-Publication Data
Main entry under title: Annual Editions: Human Resources. 2009/2010.
 1. Human Resources—Periodicals. I. Maidment, Fred H., *comp*. II. Title: Human Resources.
658'.05

www.mhhe.com

Editors/Advisory Board

Members of the Advisory Board are instrumental in the final selection of articles for each edition of ANNUAL EDITIONS. Their review of articles for content, level, currentness, and appropriateness provides critical direction to the editor and staff. We think that you will find their careful consideration well reflected in this volume.

EDITOR

Fred H. Maidment
Western Connecticut State University

ADVISORY BOARD

Preface

In publishing ANNUAL EDITIONS we recognize the enormous role played by the magazines, newspapers, and journals of the public press in providing current, first-rate educational information in a broad spectrum of interest areas. Many of these articles are appropriate for students, researchers, and professionals seeking accurate, current material to help bridge the gap between principles and theories and the real world. These articles, however, become more useful for study when those of lasting value are carefully collected, organized, indexed, and reproduced in a low-cost format, which provides easy and permanent access when the material is needed. That is the role played by ANNUAL EDITIONS.

The environment for human resource management is constantly changing. The events of September 11, 2001 are just a preview of the global environment that may be developing for human resource managers. This terrorist act is certain to change the role of human resources in the future. At the very least, what has transpired will make the practice of human resources more difficult and more challenging. Meeting those challenges will be the task human resource managers will face in the future; and this task will play a key factor in the success of any organization.

Management must respond to these forces in many ways, not the least of which is the effort to keep current with the various developments in the field. The 43 articles that have been chosen for *Annual Editions: Human Resources 09/10* reflect an outstanding cross section of the current topics in the field. This volume addresses the various components of HRM (human resource management) from compensation, training, and discipline to international implications for the worker and the employer. Articles have been chosen from leading business magazines such as *Forbes* and journals such as *Workforce, HR Magazine*, and *Supervision* to provide a wide sampling of the latest thinking in the field of human resources.

Annual Editions: Human Resources 09/10 contains a number of features designed to be useful for people interested in human resource management. These features include a Table of Contents with abstracts that summarize each article with bold italicized key ideas and a Topic Guide to locate articles on specific subjects. The volume is organized into seven units, each dealing with specific interrelated topics in human resources. Every unit begins with an overview that provides background information for the articles in the section. This will enable the reader to place the selection in the context of the larger issues concerning human resources. Important topics are emphasized and key points that address major themes are presented.

This is the eighteenth edition of *Annual Editions: Human Resources.* It is hoped that many more will follow addressing these important issues. We believe that the collection is the most complete and useful compilation of current material available to the human resource management student. We would like to have your response to this volume, for we are interested in your opinions and recommendations. Please take a few minutes to complete and return the postage-paid Article Rating Form at the back of the volume. Any book can be improved, and we need your help to continue to improve *Annual Editions: Human Resources.*

Fred H. Maidment
Editor

Contents

UNIT 1
Human Resource Management in Perspective

The concepts in bold italics are developed in the article. For further expansion, please refer to the Topic Guide.

UNIT 2
Meeting Human Resource Requirements

The concepts in bold italics are developed in the article. For further expansion, please refer to the Topic Guide.

UNIT 3
Creating a Productive Work Environment

The concepts in bold italics are developed in the article. For further expansion, please refer to the Topic Guide.

UNIT 4
Developing Effective Human Resources

UNIT 5
Implementing Compensation, Benefits, and Workplace Safety

The concepts in bold italics are developed in the article. For further expansion, please refer to the Topic Guide.

UNIT 6
Fostering Employee/Management Relationships

The concepts in bold italics are developed in the article. For further expansion, please refer to the Topic Guide.

UNIT 7
International Human Resource Management

The concepts in bold italics are developed in the article. For further expansion, please refer to the Topic Guide.

Part B. Managing International Human Resources

The concepts in bold italics are developed in the article. For further expansion, please refer to the Topic Guide.

Correlation Guide

The *Annual Editions* series provides students with convenient, inexpensive access to current, carefully selected articles from the public press. **Annual Editions: Human Resources 09/10** is an easy-to-use reader that presents articles on important topics such as *the future of marketing, developing marketing strategies,* and *many more.* For more information on *Annual Editions* and other *McGraw-Hill Contemporary Learning Series* titles, visit www.mhcls.com.

This convenient guide matches the units in **Annual Editions: Human Resources 09/10** with the corresponding chapters in three of our best-selling McGraw-Hill Human Resource textbooks by Bernardin, Ivancevich, and Cascio.

Annual Editions: Human Resources 09/10	Human Resource Management: An Experiential Approach, 5/e by Bernardin	Human Resource Management, 11/e by Ivancevich	Managing Human Resources: Productivity, Quality of Work Life, Profits, 8/e by Cascio
Unit 1: Human Resource Management in Perspective	**Chapter 1:** Strategic Human Resource Management in a Changing Environment	**Chapter 1:** Human Resource Management **Chapter 2:** A Strategic Management Approach to Human Resource Management	**Chapter 1:** Human Resources in a Globally Competitive Business Environment **Chapter 2:** The Financial Impact of Human Resource Management Activities
Unit 2: Meeting Human Resource Requirements	**Chapter 5:** Human Resource Planning and Recruitment **Chapter 6:** Personnel Selection	**Chapter 5:** Human Resource Planning and Alignment **Chapter 6:** Job Analysis and Design **Chapter 7:** Recruitment **Chapter 8:** Selection	**Chapter 5:** Planning for People **Chapter 6:** Recruiting **Chapter 7:** Staffing
Unit 3: Creating a Productive Work Environment	**Chapter 7:** Performance Management and Appraisal **Chapter 8:** Training and Development **Chapter 9:** Career Development	**Chapter 6:** Job Analysis and Design **Chapter 9:** Performance Evaluation and Management **Chapter 13:** Training and Development **Chapter 14:** Career Planning and Development	**Chapter 8:** Workplace Training **Chapter 9:** Performance Management **Chapter 10:** Managing Careers
Unit 4: Developing Effective Human Resources	**Chapter 7:** Performance Management and Appraisal **Chapter 8:** Training and Development **Chapter 9:** Career Development	**Chapter 9:** Performance Evaluation and Management **Chapter 13:** Training and Development **Chapter 14:** Career Planning and Development	**Chapter 8:** Workplace Training **Chapter 9:** Performance Management **Chapter 10:** Managing careers
Unit 5: Implementing Compensation, Benefits, and Workplace Safety	**Chapter 10:** Compensation: Base Pay and Fringe Benefits **Chapter 11:** Rewarding Performance	**Chapter 10:** Compensation: An Overview **Chapter 11:** Compensation: Methods and Policies **Chapter 17:** Promoting Safety and Health	**Chapter 11:** Pay and Incentive Systems **Chapter 12:** Indirect Compensation: Employee Benefit Plans **Chapter 15:** Safety, Health, and Employee Assistance Programs
Unit 6: Fostering Employee/ Management Relationships	**Chapter 7:** Performance Management and Appraisal **Chapter 12:** Managing the Employment Relationship	**Chapter 9:** Performance Evaluation and Management **Chapter 16:** Managing Employee Discipline	**Chapter 9:** Performance Management **Chapter 14:** Procedural Justice and Ethics in Employee Relations
Unit 7: International Human Resource Management	**Chapter 2:** The Role of Globalization in HR Policy and Practice	**Chapter 4:** Global Human Resource Management	**Chapter 1:** Human Resources in a Globally Competitive Business Environment **Chapter 16:** International Dimensions of Human Resource Management

Topic Guide

This topic guide suggests how the selections in this book relate to the subjects covered in your course. You may want to use the topics listed on these pages to search the Web more easily.

On the following pages a number of Web sites have been gathered specifically for this book. They are arranged to reflect the units of this Annual Editions reader. You can link to these sites by going to *http://www.mhcls.com.*

All the articles that relate to each topic are listed below the bold-faced term.

Labor relations

Minorities in the workplace

Motivating employees

Outsourcing/Offshoring

Sexual harassment

Staff development

Internet References

The following Internet sites have been selected to support the articles found in this reader. These sites were available at the time of publication. However, because Web sites often change their structure and content, the information listed may no longer be available. We invite you to visit http://www.mhcls.com for easy access to these sites.

Annual Editions: Human Resources 09/10

General Sources

Accountantsworld.com
http://www.accountantsworld.com

An online site dedicated to the field of accounting. Also included in the site are links to financial resources, including business, careers, e-commerce, insurance, and human resources.

American Psychological Association
http://www.apa.org

This site contains important information on workplace topics including revitalization of business and restructuring.

Bureau of Labor Statistics
http://stats.bls.gov:80

The home page of the Bureau of Labor Statistics (BLS), an agency of the U.S. Department of Labor, offers sections that include Economy at a Glance, Keyword Searches, Surveys and Programs, other statistical sites, and much more.

Economics Statistics Briefing Room
http://www.whitehouse.gov/fsbr/esbr.html

Easy access to current federal economic indicators is available at this site, which provides links to information produced by a number of federal agencies. Subjects are Output, Income, Employment, Production and Business Activity, Prices, Money, Transportation, and International Statistics.

Human Resource Professional's Gateway to the Internet
http://www.hrisolutions.com/index2.html

This Web site has links to other human relations locations, recruiting-related Web sites, HR–related companies, and search tools.

National Bureau of Economic Research Home Page
http://www.nber.org

The National Bureau of Economic Research does specialized research on every aspect of economics. These projects include, but are not limited to, pricing, labor studies, economics of aging, and productivity.

Society for Human Resource Management (SHRM)
http://www.shrm.org

SHRM is the world's largest association devoted to human resource management. Its mission is to serve the needs of HR professionals by providing essential and comprehensive resources. At this site, you'll find updates on methods, laws, and events as well as career information.

United States Department of Labor
http://www.dol.gov

This site provides a wealth of information on a number of labor-management issues. It has statutory as well as regulatory information and more.

United States Small Business Administration
http://www.sba.gov

The Small Business Administration encourages the establishment and development of small businesses through subsidized loans, business advice, and other forms of assistance.

UNIT 1: Human Resource Management in Perspective

Corporate Social Responsibility
http://www.aplink.net/~mikegree/career/social.htm

This article discusses balancing bottom line concerns with social responsibility.

Employment and Labor Law
http://www.lectlaw.com/temp.html

This site offers wide-ranging Web resources and articles covering electronic privacy rights, sexual harassment, discrimination, Americans with Disabilities (ADA) statutes, the Fair Labor Standards Act, and employment law.

Institute of Industrial Relations
http://www.iir.berkeley.edu

The Institute of Industrial Relations of the University of California, Berkeley, has links to research by the Center for Culture, Organization and Politics, the Center for Organization and Human Resource Effectiveness, and the Center for Work, Technology and Society.

Law at Work
http://www.lawatwork.com

From this site you can not only look at current labor laws, such as OSHA, but consider drug testing at work, unemployment questions, sexual harassment issues, affirmative action, and much more.

School of Labor and Industrial Relations Hot Links
http://www.lir.msu.edu/hotlinks

Links to newspapers, libraries, international intergovernmental organizations, as well as government statistics are provided here.

United States Equal Employment Opportunity Commission
http://www.eeoc.gov

Equal employment opportunity, employment discrimination, enforcement and litigation facts and figures are provided here.

UNIT 2: Meeting Human Resource Requirements

America's Job Bank
http://www.ajb.dni.us

You can find employers or job seekers and lots of job market information at this site. Employers can register their job openings, update them, and request employment service recruitment help.

International Association for Human Resource Information Management (IHRIM)
http://www.ihrim.org

IHRIM is a central network for its members to gain access and in-depth knowledge about HR information management and systems issues, trends, and technology.

Internet References

Sympatico Careers
http://www.sympatico.workopolis.com

A Canadian site that provides a network with an outlet for finding solutions to everyday work problems.

Voice of the Shuttle: Postindustrial Business Theory Page
http://www.vos.scsb.edu/bfrowse.asp?=2727

Many subjects are included in this Web site, including: restructuring, downsizing, flattening, outsourcing, human resources, labor relations, learning organizations, and diversity.

UNIT 3: Creating a Productive Work Environment

American Society for Training and Development (ASTD)
http://www.astd.org

One of the largest organizations in the area of human resources. Publisher of *Training and Development* with local chapters all over the United States.

Commission on the Future of Worker-Management Relations
http://www.dol.gov/_sec/media/reports/dunlop/dunlop.htm

The report of the U.S. Federal Commission on the Future of Worker-Management Relations, which covers many issues, including enhancement of workplace productivity, changes in collective bargaining practices, and intervention in workplace problems by government agencies, may be found here.

The Downsizing of America
http://www.nytimes.com/specials/downsize/glance.html

The complete 7-week series on downsizing in America is printed on the Web by the *New York Times,* in which it appeared.

Employee Incentives and Career Development
http://www.snc.edu/socsci/chair/336/group1.htm

This site states that effective employee compensation and career development is an important tool in obtaining, maintaining, and retaining a productive workforce. There are links to Pay-for-Knowledge, Incentive Systems, Career Development, Wage and Salary Compensation, and more.

UNIT 4: Developing Effective Human Resources

Center for Organization and Human Resource Effectiveness
http://www.iir.berkeley.edu./cohre/cohre.html

The center for Organization and Human Resource Effectiveness Web page will allow you to navigate to policy papers, research in progress, as well as a virtual library. The center's mission is "Anticipating and creating new responses to a continuously changing business environment."

Discrimination and Diversity
http://www.domz.org/society/work/worplace.discriminatiorydiversity

A listing of sites to explore on workplace discrimination.

Employment Interviews
http://www.snc.edu/socsci/chair/336/group3.htm

The importance of proper interview techniques to the building of a workforce is discussed here. The page has links to related sites and refers to a book by Alder and Elmhorst, *Communicating at Work: Principles and Practices for Business and the Professionals.*

Feminist Majority Foundation
http://www.feminist.org

This site houses the Feminist Career Center, an Affirmative Action page, and information of interest to women.

UNIT 5: Implementing Compensation, Benefits, and Workplace Safety

BenefitsLink: The National Employee Benefits Web Site
http://www.benefitslink.com/index.php

This link offers facts and services for employers who are sponsoring employee benefit plans and for participating workers.

Equal Compensation, and Employee Ownership
http://www.fed.org

Sponsored by the Foundation for Enterprise Development, this site includes strategies for making critical decisions to help companies improve their profitability. There are interactive resources and cases.

Equal Pay Act and Pay Inequity
http://www.infoplease.com/spot/equalpayact1.html

Related links are included in this presentation of the Equal Pay Act and the history of pay inequity.

Executive Pay Watch
http://www.aflcio.org/corporateamerica/paywatch/

While keeping an eye on the issue of executive salaries, bonuses, and perks in CEO compensation packages, this labor union site offers suggestions to working families on what can be done to curb exorbitant pay schemes.

Job Stress
http://www.workhealth.org/news/nwprahn98.html

Research on job stress is available on this site.

Social Security Administration
http://www.ssa.gov

Here is the official Web site of the Social Security Administration.

WorkPlace Injury and Illness Statistics
http://www.osha.gov/oshstats/work.html

The Bureau of Labor Statistics Web site presents links to many issues of occupational injury and illness and offers a great deal of statistical information.

UNIT 6: Fostering Employee/Management Relationships

Management, Leadership and Supervision
http://humanresources.about.com/od/managementandleadership/

This site offers input as well as links on how to improve your management and leadership skills.

Internet References

UNIT 7: International Human Resource Management

Cultural Globalization
http://www.inst.at/studies/collab/breidenb.htm

This paper by Joana Breidenbach and Ina Zukrigl discusses the dynamics and myths of cultural globalization.

Globalization and Human Resource Management
http://www.cic.sfu.ca/forum/adler.html

Dr. Nancy J. Adler, a faculty member at McGill University, discusses strategic international human resource development in this thorough summary for the Internet.

India Finance and Investment
http://www.finance.indiamart.com

A guide to investing in India. It addresses taxation, organization, capital market investment as well as other topics.

International Business Resources on the Web
http://www.globaledge.msu.edu/ibrd/ibrd.asp

The Center for International Business Education and Research at Michigan State University permits a key word search and has a great deal of trade information, government resources, and periodicals. It also has country and regional information.

International Labour Organization
http://www.ilo.org

The International Labour Organization's Web page leads to links that discuss the objectives of the organization and summarize international labor standards and human rights. The official United Nations Web site locator will point to many other resources.

Labor Relations and the National Labor Relations Board
http://www.snc.edu/socsci/chair/336/group2.htm

From this site you can explore labor relations in today's international marketplace.

UNIT 1

Human Resource Management in Perspective

Unit Selections

Key Points to Consider

- What are some of the possible changes you see occurring in the workforce in the next several generations? Do you think Human Resources can play a bigger and more important role in organizations?

- What are some of the ways that firms can better utilize the skills and talents of their employees?

- Do you think that the leadership of the HR function is best provided by professionals from HR or from other parts of the organization?

- What were the most important changes for the American worker during the twentieth century, and what changes do you see as likely in the next 20 years?

- In the past 30 years, the government has taken a more active role in the struggle of minorities and other groups in the workforce. How has the ADA changed the workplace?

- Sexual harassment is a very important area of concern for most organizations. What do you think organizations can and should do about it?

- How do you think the events of September 11 will affect organizations and their relations with their employees? Do you think that things will change significantly? Do you think soldiers returning from Iraq or Afghanistan should be receiving the same kind of benefits as the soldiers who returned from World War II received?

Student Web Site
www.mhcls.com

Internet References

Corporate Social Responsibility
http://www.aplink.net/~mikegree/career/social.htm

Employment and Labor Law
http://www.lectlaw.com/temp.html

Institute of Industrial Relations
http://www.iir.berkeley.edu

Law at Work
http://www.lawatwork.com

School of Labor and Industrial Relations Hot Links
http://www.lir.msu.edu/hotlinks

United States Equal Employment Opportunity Commission
http://www.eeoc.gov

The only constant is change. Industrial society is dynamic, a great engine that has brought about many of the most significant changes in the history of the human race. Since the start of the Industrial Revolution in England, a little over 230 years ago, industrialized society has transformed Western civilization in a multitude of ways. Many great inventions of the last 200 years have significantly altered the way people live and the way they see the world.

At the time of the Declaration of Independence, the 13 colonies were an overwhelmingly agricultural society that clung to the Atlantic coast of North America. At the beginning of the twenty-first century, the United States is a continental nation with the world's largest industrial base and perhaps the smallest percentage of farmers of any major industrialized country. These changes did not happen overnight, but were both the result and the cause of the technological innovations of the Industrial Revolution. The technological marvels of today, such as television, radio, computers, airplanes, and automobiles did not exist until after the Industrial Revolution, and a disproportionate number of them did not exist until after 1900.

Along with technological changes have come changes in the ways people earn their living. When Thomas Jefferson authored the Declaration of Independence in 1776, he envisioned a nation of small, independent farmers, but that is not what developed later. Factories, mass production, and economies of scale have been the watchwords of industrial development. Industrial development changed not only the economy, but also society. Most Americans are no longer independent farmers, but are for the most part, wage earners, who make their living by working for someone else.

Changes in the American labor force include the increase in women and minorities working next to white males. The nature of most jobs has changed from those directly associated with production to those providing services in the white-collar economy. Many other changes are developing in the economy and society that will be reflected in the workforce. For the first time since the early days of the republic, international trade represents a significant part of the American economy, having increased greatly in the past 30 years. The economic reality is that the GM autoworker competes not only with Ford and Chrysler, but also with Toyota and Volkswagen.

The society, the economy, and the workforce have changed. Americans today live in a much different world than they did 200 years ago. It is a highly diverse, heterogeneous world, full of paradox. When people think of American industry, they tend to think of giant-sized companies like IBM and General Electric, but in fact, most people work for small firms. The relative importance of the Fortune 500 companies in terms of employment in the economy has been declining both in real and percentage terms. Today, economic growth is with small organizations.

© PhotoLink/Getty Images

Change has brought about not only a different society, but a more complex one. Numerous rules and regulations must be followed that did not exist 200 years ago. The human element in any organization has been critical to its success, and knowing what the human resource needs of the organization are going to be 1, 5, or even 10 years into the future is a key element for continuing success as seen in "Spotlight on HR management."

Individual decisions have also changed. In the first part of the twentieth century, it was common for a worker to spend his or her entire life with one organization, doing one particular job. Now the worker can expect to do many different jobs, probably with a number of different organizations in different industries. Mergers, technological change, and economic fluctuations all put a premium on individual adaptability in a changing work environment for individual economic survival.

The changes in industrial society often come at a faster rate than most people are willing to either accept or adapt to. Many old customs and prejudices have been retained from prior times, and while progress has been made with regard to certain groups—no American employer today would dare to end an employment notice with the letters "NINA" (No Irish Need Apply), as was common at one time—for other groups, the progress has been slow at best. Women represent about half of American workers but they are paid only about 70% of what men earn, and sexual harassment still represents a problem, as discussed in "Implementing sexual harassment training in the workplace."

African Americans, and other minorities, have been discriminated against for centuries in American society, to the point where the federal government has been forced to step in and legislate equal opportunity, both on and off the job. People with disabilities have also sought protection as seen in "The Best 4 Ways to Recruit Employees with Disabilities," "Making Reasonable Accommodations for Employees with Mental Illness under the ADA," and "The Disability Advantage."

The clash of differing cultures seems ever more pronounced in our society. America has traditionally viewed itself as a melting pot, but it is clear that certain groups have historically "melted" more easily than others, a situation that is reflected in the workplace.

Human resource management plays an important role in industrial America. Business leaders recognize the value of their employees to the future of their organizations. Increasingly, competition in world markets is becoming based on the skills and abilities of people, not machines. Indeed, among major competitors, virtually everyone has essentially the same equipment. The difference is often what the people in the organization do with the equipment.

Of special consideration, are the recent events of 9/11. For the first time since the War of 1812, the United States was forcefully attacked on its' home soil with a greater loss of life than at Pearl Harbor. These events will mean changes in the way the economy operates and the way organizations will treat their employees. HR professionals must address these issues as seen in British Prime Minister Tony Blair's "Fighting for Values." An additional concern will be how the returning soldiers will be treated when they return from combat. The current GI bill falls far short of the old GI Bill of World War II, which is discussed in "A Learning Disability."

Society, the workplace, and the way they are viewed have all undergone major changes. Frederick W. Taylor and Elton Mayo, early writers in management, held certain views about industry at the beginning of the twentieth century, while Peter Drucker, W. Edwards Deming, and others have different ideas now, at the beginning of the twenty-first century. The American society and economy, as well as the very life of the average American worker, are different from what they were 200 or even 100 years ago, and both the workers and the organizations that employ them must respond to those changes.

Spotlight on Human Resource Management

JAMES C. WIMBUSH

1. Turnover

Employee turnover continues to be an issue of importance and study among researchers. Recent studies have examined turnover from a unit-level perspective to determine how units are affected, as well as the effect of turnover on interpersonal relationships. A study by Kacmar, Andrews, Van Rooy, Steilberg, and Cerrone (2006) was interested in determining whether turnover affects unit-level performance, and if so, whether there are any mediating mechanisms. The researchers were also interested in the value of a stable workforce. Data from a large "fast" food restaurant chain revealed that turnover does, in fact, affect unit-level performance, and that a stable workforce contributes significantly to efficiency, which in turn enhances performance. The researchers reasoned that the theoretical basis for their findings rests in social exchange, knowledge-based, and strategic choice theories. Testimonies from practitioners confirmed the value of having a stable, well-trained workforce and validated its contribution to performance. The researchers also explored the impact of turnover among crews as compared to managers and found a difference: crew turnover affected food waste, but management turnover affected how long customers waited for service. This finding led the researchers to suggest that, in organizations where fast service is important, a key role played by managers may be to create an environment for quickness.

Similar to the analysis of Kacmar et al. (2006), a study of a small ($n = 38$) chain of restaurants examined the impact on unit performance of losses of individuals in key network positions (Shaw, Duffy, Johnson, & Lockhart, 2005). The researchers found a negative relationship between turnover and store performance such that store performance was low across the board when turnover was high. The study also showed that a loss of key social capital was significantly related to lower performance. The researchers believe the results speak to the importance of understanding that turnover affects both efficiency and important interpersonal relationships.

The effect of turnover on relationships was also examined in a study of health care employees in a public medical center. Mossholder, Settoon, and Henagan (2005) found that network centrality and interpersonal citizenship behavior were predictors of turnover. The study demonstrated that employees who develop strong bonds with their co-workers are more likely to stay with the organization; similarly, employees who engage in helping behaviors where reciprocity is the norm are also more likely to stay. A withdrawal of citizenship behaviors, however, may signal a potential exit. If an employee is contemplating leaving, it is believed that he or she will likely not expend helping behaviors, knowing that his or her co-workers will not have an opportunity to later reciprocate.

2. Teams

Organizations continue to recognize the importance of, and rely upon, teams for conducting work. Accordingly, researchers persist in examining different aspects of team selection and composition, team environment and its effect on important organizational variables, and team training.

A group of researchers (Morgeson, Reider, & Campion, 2005) were curious as to whether traditional selection techniques (structured interviews, personality tests, and situational judgment tests) used to select individuals would also work for selecting team members. With the increasing prevalence of team-oriented work environments, the scholars noticed a paucity of research regarding team member selection. A study employing the three commonly used selection techniques was conducted in a highly team-oriented manufacturing environment to examine relationships between social skills, personality, situational judgment, and contextual performance. It was found that a relationship did, in fact, exist among the variables, and that most of the variables predicted contextual performance. The researchers concluded that the findings provide legitimacy to applying the commonly used selection techniques for team member selection.

Several studies have examined the effect of different types of diversity or team composition on outcomes. One study examined the influence of educational and national diversity on information used by the team (Dahlin, Weingart, & Hinds, 2005). Small MBA teams were comprised of students from different disciplines (i.e., educational diversity) and national backgrounds (i.e., national diversity). Interestingly, the results found that the difference in the type of diversity influenced the team's use of information in different ways. It was found that among the educationally diverse teams, the diversity was both a help and hindrance such that broader ranges and depths of information were used as the diversity increased, but only up to a point. Too much diversity resulted in teams resorting to lesser use of information that was similar to teams with little educational diversity. The finding regarding educational diversity was what the researchers predicted; however, the finding with national diversity was not as predicted. National diversity was shown to result in uses of narrower ranges of information as the diversity increased from low to moderate levels. However, the ranges of information increased as the diversity increased from moderate to high levels, but the depth and integration of information lessened. The researchers pointed out the complexity of the relationship between diversity and use of information, and attribute the complexity to the nature of team processes.

Boone, van Olffen, and van Witteloostuijn (2005) considered the effect of locus of control among team members and how the variable affects leadership structure, information acquisition, and financial performance. What is most interesting about the findings is that the results underscore the importance of going beyond the simple main effects of team composition variables and analyzing basic moderator variables. Based on the results, the researchers go as far as to suggest that lack of significance in many previous studies and mixed findings among some studies may have been due to a failure to examine important moderators.

In terms of locus of control, the study shows that internals process information better than externals at the group level. The findings lead the researchers to suggest that internals are more likely to engage in superior performance without a leader, whereas groups comprised of externals are more productive with a designated leader to guide and direct them.

Gender diversity in teams continues to be an area of research interest. Hirschfeld, Jordan, Feild, Giles, and Armenakis (2005) examined the representation of females in male dominated teams. The study found that a high representation of women did not adversely affect the team's perceived potency, social cohesion, or assessments of the team's work. Additionally, the research was consistent with previous studies that reported greater problem solving and slightly poorer performance on physically demanding tasks with the increased representation of women. The researchers stress that an expected tradeoff of greater problem solving for lesser social—psychological factors, based on previous studies, is not necessarily a given. They suggest that contextual factors, such as cultures and policies promoting inclusion, may play a significant role.

An issue related to gender diversity in teams is sexual harassment. Raver and Gelfand (2005) conducted a study that provided data which shows that sexual harassment may affect team performance. While previous studies focused on individual outcomes, this study linked sexual harassment to team processes and team financial performance. It was found that, at the team level, ambient sexual harassment was positively related to relationship conflict and task conflict, and negatively related to team cohesion and team financial performance. The findings make clear the importance of examining the effects of sexual harassment on team-level outcomes, as well as the need for additional research and theory to better understand the phenomenon.

Many organizations have the need for action teams that are designed to handle a variety of complex, time sensitive, intensive tasks. Examples of action teams include surgical teams and military teams, which must be adaptable and able to handle a wide variety of situations (expected and unexpected) with speed and competence. It has been shown, however, that although team members might have a high level of functional expertise, their teamwork skills and knowledge are often lacking. This, in turn, may lead to unsuccessful outcomes. Ellis, Bell, Ployhart, Hollenbeck, and Ilgen (2005) examined whether providing generic teamwork skills training would boost action team effectiveness. The results of the study showed that team-generic training is beneficial for action team performance. There was evidence that declarative knowledge increases and gains were made in the team's ability to plan, coordinate tasks, collaboratively problem solve, and communicate. The researchers suggest that their results also give some indication as to how the training has its effects.

3. Diversity

Diversity continues to be an area of significant interest among researchers, practitioners, and legislators at all levels of government. While many types of diversity are often examined, racial diversity is still a matter of concern that researchers have designed studies to explore. These studies range from an understanding of how racial conflicts in communities influence work relationships, to the continued examination of the impact of affirmative action policies.

Working from the perspective of realistic group conflict theory, two studies were conducted by a group of researchers (Brief et al., 2005) to determine whether racial conflict within one's community affected racial relationships at work. Realistic group conflict theory holds that hostility may exist when groups compete for limited resources. Consequently, group members will cling to and favor their own groups rather than associate with the competing group. Out of this situation is borne factionalism, resentment, and conflict.

The first of the two aforementioned studies determined whether proximity of whites to blacks in communities would negatively affect hostility among groups in work settings. Results show that the relationship between the quality of work relationships and organizational diversity was moderated by the proximity of whites to blacks where they lived. The relationship became more negative as proximity increased. In the second study, the researchers assessed community intergroup conflict between whites and Latinos, and asked whites to indicate their attractiveness to an employer with a low or high representation of Latino employees. The results showed that increased perceptions of community conflict between the groups led to decreased attractiveness to ethnically diverse organizations. Altogether, the studies provide evidence that conflicts in racially diverse communities may lead to racial tensions in work settings. The researchers offer implications for practice that may be useful for organizations grappling with issues related to racial diversity.

There is a considerable body of literature asserting that supportive relationships among co-workers reap performance benefits for individuals and organizations. Bacharach, Bamberger, and Vashdi (2005) set out to explore the antecedents of supportive relationships among racially dissimilar (black and white) co-workers. The results of the study revealed, interestingly, that individuals tend to look to their own racial group members for support when in work groups with employees who are racially dissimilar to themselves. The study did show, however, that this phenomenon existed until a representational balance of both groups was reached. Accordingly, as a practical implication of this finding, the researchers proffer that managers should strive for racially balanced work groups, as opposed to placing ethnic "tokens" in work groups.

Affirmative action has existed for over 40 years and continues to be controversial. Aquino, Stewart, and Reed (2005) conducted two experiments to examine judgments subjects made regarding an African American employee who was said to be or not be a beneficiary of affirmative action. The scholars wanted to determine whether social dominance orientation (SDO), beliefs favoring group-based inequality, was a predictor of how job performance and career success is evaluated for African American beneficiaries of affirmative action. The research found that high SDO individuals had more predictive evaluative judgments of a beneficiary of affirmative action compared to subjects with low SDO. The research provides additional evidence that SDO is a useful predictor of negative evaluations toward minority groups, and that its effect may be strengthened by social cues (e.g., affirmative action policy). As a practical implication, the researchers suggest that managers may be able to counter negative perceptions of high SDO employees by proactively promoting the competence and sociability of the affirmative action hire.

As part of the same study, the scholars also wanted to explore whether the type of job held by the employee influenced the evaluation. Their findings suggest that minorities in higher level positions were not stigmatized by affirmative action, even if an affirmative action policy was in place. For upper level positions, it is believed that role-based rather than race-based stereotypes affected perceptions about the employee.

4. Summary

As illustrated by this brief review of last year's research findings, human resource management continues to be an area of great interest. Based on the wealth of research generated during the past 12 months, next year's Spotlight will most likely have just as much (or more) to report regarding new insights in the field.

References

Aquino, K., Stewart, M., & Reed, M. (2005). How social dominance orientation and job status influence perceptions of African—American affirmative action beneficiaries. *Personnel Psychology, 58*(3), 703–744.

Bacharach, S. B., Bamberger, P.A., & Vashdi, D. (2005). Diversity and homophily at work: Supportive relations among white and African—American peers. *Academy of Management Journal, 48*(4), 619–644.

Boone, C., van Olffen, W., & van Witteloostuijn, A. (2005). Team locus-of-control composition, leadership structure, information acquisition, and financial performance: A business simulation study. *Academy of Management Journal, 48*(5), 889–909.

Brief, A. P., Umphress, E. E., Dietz, J., Burrows, J. W., Butz, R. M., & Scholten, L. (2005). Community matters: Realistic group conflict theory and the impact of diversity. *Academy of Management Journal, 48*(5), 830–844.

Dahlin, K. B., Weingart, L. R., & Hinds, P. J. (2005). Team diversity and information use. *Academy of Management Journal, 48*(6), 1107–1123.

Ellis, A. P. J., Bell, B. S., Ployhart, R. E., Hollenbeck, J. R., & ilgen, D. R. (2005). An evaluation of generic teamwork skills training with action teams: Effects on cognitive and skill-based outcomes. *Personnel Psychology, 58*(3), 641–672.

Hirschfeld, R. R., Jordan, M. H., Feild, H. S., Giles, W. F., & Armenakis, A. A. (2005). Teams' female representation and perceived potency as inputs to team outcomes in a predominantly male field setting. *Personnel Psychology, 58*(4), 893–924.

Kacmar, K. M., Andrews, M. C., Van Rooy, D. L., Steilberg, R. C., & Cerrone, S. (2006). Sure everyone can be replaced . . . but at what cost? Turnover as a predictor of unit-level performance. *Academy of Management Journal, 49*(1), 133–144.

Morgeson, F. P., Reider, M. H., & Campion, M. A. (2005). Selecting individuals in team settings: The importance of social skills, personality characteristics, and teamwork knowledge. *Personnel Psychology, 58*(3), 583–611.

Mossholder, K. W., Settoon, R. P., & Henagan, S. C. (2005). A relational perspective on turnover: Examining structural, attitudinal, and behavioral predictors. *Academy of Management Journal, 48*(4), 607–618.

Raver, J. L., & Gelfand, M. J. (2005). Beyond the individual victim: Linking sexual harassment, team processes, and team performance. *Academy of Management Journal, 48*(3), 387–400.

Shaw, J. D., Duffy, M. K., Johnson, J. L., & Lockhart, D. E. (2005). Turnover, social capital losses, and performance. *Academy of Management Journal, 48*(4), 594–606.

HR Jobs Remain Secure

Demand for HR professionals will remain strong as companies scramble to replace retiring workers, control high health benefit costs and meet new regulatory requirements.

FAY HANSEN

U nstable labor markets generate new jobs for human resources professionals. The U.S. Bureau of Labor Statistics predicts that job growth in HR will continue to rise at above-average rates as more workers reach retirement age and have to be processed out while their replacements are processed in. With health insurance premiums still rising at an annual rate of 8 percent, more benefit specialists will be needed. The new round of labor-related federal and state regulation on the horizon will also create higher demand for HR professionals to monitor compliance.

More than 820,000 employees work in HR jobs, with 80 percent of these in the private sector, according to the BLS. Demand may be particularly strong for certain specialists. For example, employers are expected to devote greater resources to job-specific training programs over the next decade in response to the increasing complexity of many jobs, the aging of the workforce and technological advances that can leave employees with obsolete skills. This should result in strong demand for training and development specialists. Tighter labor markets for skilled workers will create demand for recruiters and placement specialists.

As the trend toward outsourcing HR continues, more jobs will move out of corporate HR departments and into consulting, staffing and recruiting companies and other vendor firms that handle HR tasks. Demand should also increase in companies that develop and administer benefits and compensation packages. Although higher demand for HR professionals has pushed HR salaries up in recent years, total compensation still lags behind other business occupations. College graduates with degrees in HR or labor relations can be had for $37,000 a year—a full $10,000 below starting salaries for new finance and accounting graduates and more than $5,000 below salaries for other business graduates.

HR Salaries

Salaries for HR professionals still hinge on industry practices, company size and occupational specialization. In the knowledge-based IT industry, salaries for training specialists and recruiters run well above the all-industry averages for these positions.

Total target cash compensation for U.S. HR professionals by level, technology and life sciences companies, 2007.

	Level 1 (1.5 to 3 yrs.)	Level 2 (4 to 5 yrs.)	Senior (6 to 9 yrs.)
Benefits/comp administrator	$45,900	$57,500	$68,600
Benefits administrator	46,100	57,700	69,100
Benefits analyst	48,800	58,100	71,300
HR generalist	47,500	61,600	72,900
Benefits/comp analyst	52,700	64,300	80,100
Comp analyst	54,100	65,000	80,900
Recruiter	58,500	66,300	83,200
Internal training/ development specialist	61,400	67,500	85,300

Note: Based on data from 5,300 HR professionals.
Source: Culpepper (www.culpepper.com).

Labor Markets

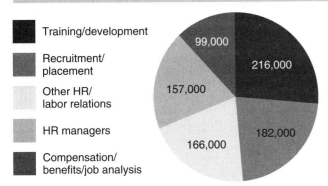

- Training/development
- Recruitment/placement
- Other HR/labor relations
- HR managers
- Compensation/benefits/job analysis

HR Jobs   Distribution of HR jobs by occupational specialty.

Source: Bureau of Labor Statistics (www.bls.gov).

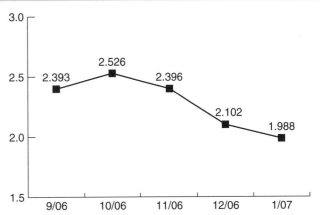

Online Help-Wanted   Number of new ads in millions, September 2006–January 2007.

Source: The Conference Board (www.conference-board.org/economics/helpwanted.cfm).

	9/06	10/06	11/06	12/06
Boston	4.7%	4.0%	4.3%	4.4%
Dallas	4.6	4.5	4.5	4.0
Miami	3.8	3.5	3.4	3.1
Phoenix	3.3	3.4	3.3	3.3
St. Louis	4.8	4.9	4.8	4.6
San Francisco	4.0	3.7	4.0	3.8
Seattle	4.6	4.0	4.6	4.3
Washington	3.0	2.9	3.0	2.9

Unemployment Rates in Major Markets

Source: U.S. Bureau of Labor Statistics (www.bls.gov/sae/home.htm).

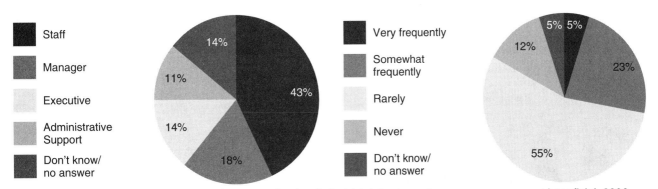

- Staff
- Manager
- Executive
- Administrative Support
- Don't know/no answer

- Very frequently
- Somewhat frequently
- Rarely
- Never
- Don't know/no answer

Telecommuting   Percentage of executives reporting level at which telecommuting programs are most beneficial, 2006. Percentage of executivies reporting frequency with which executives telecommute, 2006.

Note: Survey of 150 senior executives at the nation's 1,000 largest companies.
Source: Office Team (www.officeteam.com).

Economic Context

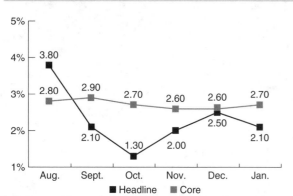

Inflation   12-month percent change in headline and core CPI-U.

Source: U.S. Bureau of Labor Statistics (www.bis.gov/cpi).

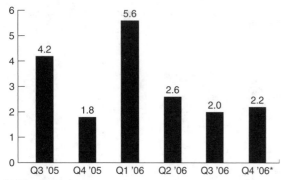

GDP   Percent change, annual rates.
*preliminary estimate
Source: U.S. Bureau of Economic Analysis (www.bea.gov/bea/dn1.htm).

	Productivity	Real Compensation	Unit Labor Cost
Business	2.0%	2.8%	2.8%
Nonfarm business	2.1	3.0	2.8
Manufacturing	3.9	2.3	0.3
Durable	5.3	3.7	0.3
Nondurable	2.3	−0.2	−0.6

Productivity and Costs   Percent change from same quarter a year ago, preliminary Q4 2006.
Source: U.S. Bureau of Labor Statistics (www.bls.gov).

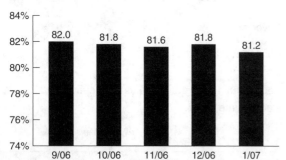

Capacity Utilization   Percentage of total production capacity currently in use.
Note: Economists generally agree that a rate of 82% or above is necessary for new job growth.
Source: Federal Reserve (www.federalreserve.gov/releases/G17).

Salaries & Wages

9/06	10/06	11/06	12/06	1/07
1.0	1.3	0	0.2	−0.3

Real Weekly Earnings   Percent change in average weekly earnings from previous month, adjusted for hours and inflation.
Source: U.S. Bureau of Labor Statistics (www.bls.gov/ces/home.htm).

	25th Percentile	Median	75th Percentile
Salary	$120,668	$137,613	$165,392
Total cash	134,659	164,018	211,153

HR Salaries   Salary and total cash compensation for autonomous HR director, 2007.
Source: Salary.com (www.Salary.com)

	2005	2006
IT management	$104,504	$108,578
Project manager	93,009	96,475
Database administrator	81,301	85,441
Software engineer	78,807	83,524
MIS manager	82,824	82,510
Business analyst	77,158	82,288
Developer, database	73,768	79,911
Security analyst	74,874	79,412
Developer, systems	72,732	78,476
Developer, applications	73,636	78,037
Developer, client/server	75,941	74,602
Technical writer	68,126	73,095
Programmer analyst	65,174	69,757
Quality assurance tester	64,486	68,280
Network engineer	65,122	67,202
Web developer/programmer	61,261	65,327
Systems administrator	63,698	64,917
Network manager	58,434	62,225
Technical support	47,259	49,347
Desktop support specialist	42,204	44,909
Help desk	37,397	39,430

IT Salaries   Average IT salaries by job title, 2005 and 2006.
Note: Survey of 19,182 technology professionals.
Source: Dice (www.dice.com).

Benefits

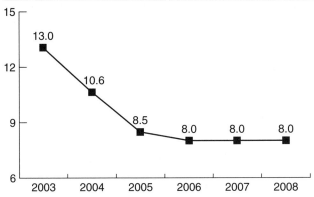

Health Cost Increases. Annual median health care cost increases, 2003–2006 and 2007–2008 projected.

Note: Survey of 573 large employers.
Source: Watson Wyatt Worldwide (www.watsonwyatt.com).

Annual Worker-Contribution %	Take-up Rate
0%	89%
0.1–7.7	88
7.8–11.4	87
11.5–15.2	84
15.3–18.4	84
18.5–20.8	82
20.9–24.4	78
24.5–28.5	76
28.6–36.9	78
37+	68

Take-up Rates Health care plan take-up rates by employee contribution level, single coverage, 2006.

Source: Kaiser Family Foundation (www.kff.org).

	2005	2006
All workers	5%	6%
Worker characteristics		
White-collar	7	9
Blue-collar	3	4
Service occupations	1	2
Full-time	5	7
Part-time	2	2
Union	2	2
Nonunion	5	7
Avg. wage <$15 hr.	3	5
Avg. wage $15 hr. or higher	7	8
Establishment characteristics		
Goods-producing	4	5
Service-producing	5	6
1 to 99 workers	3	3
100 workers or more	7	9

HSAs Percentage of private-industry workers with access to health savings accounts by selected characteristics, 2005 and 2006.

Source: U.S. Bureau of Labor Statistics (www.bls.gov).

Accommodation/food service	72%
Computer/electronics manufacturing	93
Durable manufacturing	99
Finance/insurace	97
Government	127
Health care	94
High tech	94
Media/publishing	90
Nondurable manufacturing	98
Pharmaceuticals	101
Professional/technical services	84
Retail	75
Transportation	98
Utilities	114
Wholesale trade	88

Benefits by Industry Benefit value comparisons by industry as a percentage of market median of 100%, 2007.

Source: Mercer Resource Consulting (www.mercerhr.com).

Why We Hate HR

In a knowledge economy, companies with the best talent win. And finding, nurturing, and developing that talent should be one of the most important tasks in a corporation. So why does human resources do such a bad job—and how can we fix it?

KEITH H. HAMMONDS

Well, here's a rockin' party: a gathering of several hundred midlevel human-resources executives in Las Vegas. (Yo, Wayne Newton! How's the 401(k)?) They are here, ensconced for two days at faux-glam Caesars Palace, to confer on "strategic HR leadership," a conceit that sounds, to the lay observer, at once frightening and self-contradictory. If not plain laughable.

Because let's face it: After close to 20 years of hopeful rhetoric about becoming "strategic partners" with a "seat at the table" where the business decisions that matter are made, most human-resources professionals aren't nearly there. They have no seat, and the table is locked inside a conference room to which they have no key. HR people are, for most practical purposes, neither strategic nor leaders.

I don't care for Las Vegas. And if it's not clear already, I don't like HR, either, which is why I'm here. The human-resources trade long ago proved itself, at best, a necessary evil—and at worst, a dark bureaucratic force that blindly enforces nonsensical rules, resists creativity, and impedes constructive change. HR is the corporate function with the greatest potential—the key driver, in theory, of business performance—and also the one that most consistently underdelivers. And I am here to find out why.

Why are annual performance appraisals so time-consuming—and so routinely useless? Why is HR so often a henchman for the chief financial officer, finding ever-more ingenious ways to cut benefits and hack at payroll? Why do its communications—when we can understand them at all—so often flout reality? Why are so many people processes duplicative and wasteful, creating a forest of paperwork for every minor transaction? And why does HR insist on sameness as a proxy for equity?

It's no wonder that we hate HR. In a 2005 survey by consultancy Hay Group, just 40% of employees commended their companies for retaining high-quality workers, just 41% agreed that performance evaluations were fair. Only 58% rated their

job training as favorable. Most said they had few opportunities for advancement—and that they didn't know, in any case, what was required to move up. Most telling, only about half of workers below the manager level believed their companies took a genuine interest in their well-being.

None of this is explained immediately in Vegas. These HR folks, from employers across the nation, are neither evil courtiers nor thoughtless automatons. They are mostly smart, engaging people who seem genuinely interested in doing their jobs better. They speak convincingly about employee development and cultural transformation. And, over drinks, they spin some pretty funny yarns of employee weirdness. (Like the one about the guy who threatened to sue his wife's company for "enabling" her affair with a coworker. Then there was the mentally disabled worker and the hooker—well, no, never mind. . . .)

But then the facade cracks. It happens at an afternoon presentation called "From Technicians to Consultants: How to Transform Your HR Staff into Strategic Business Partners." The speaker, Julie Muckler, is senior vice president of human resources at Wells Fargo Home Mortgage. She is an enthusiastic woman with a broad smile and 20 years of experience at companies such as Johnson & Johnson and General Tire. She has degrees in consumer economics and human resources and organizational development.

And I have no idea what she's talking about. There is mention of "internal action learning" and "being more planful in my approach." PowerPoint slides outline Wells Fargo Home Mortgage's initiatives in performance management, organization design, and horizontal-solutions teams. Muckler describes leveraging internal resources and involving external resources—and she leaves her audience dazed. That evening, even the human-resources pros confide they didn't understand much of it, either.

This, friends, is the trouble with HR. In a knowledge economy, companies that have the best talent win. We all know that.

Human resources execs should be making the most of our, well, human resources—finding the best hires, nurturing the stars, fostering a productive work environment—just as IT runs the computers and finance minds the capital. HR should be joined to business strategy at the hip.

Instead, most HR organizations have ghettoized themselves literally to the brink of obsolescence. They are competent at the administrivia of pay, benefits, and retirement, but companies increasingly are farming those functions out to contractors who can handle such routine tasks at lower expense. What's left is the more important strategic role of raising the reputational and intellectual capital of the company—but HR is, it turns out, uniquely unsuited for that.

Here's why.

1. HR people aren't the sharpest tacks in the box.
We'll be blunt: If you are an ambitious young thing newly graduated from a top college or B-school with your eye on a rewarding career in business, your first instinct is not to join the human-resources dance. (At the University of Michigan's Ross School of Business, which arguably boasts the nation's top faculty for organizational issues, just 1.2% of 2004 grads did so.) Says a management professor at one leading school: "The best and the brightest don't go into HR."

Who does? Intelligent people, sometimes—but not businesspeople. "HR doesn't tend to hire a lot of independent thinkers or people who stand up as moral compasses," says Garold L. Markle, a longtime human-resources executive at Exxon and Shell Offshore who now runs his own consultancy. Some are exiles from the corporate mainstream: They've fared poorly in meatier roles—but not poorly enough to be fired. For them, and for their employers, HR represents a relatively low-risk parking spot.

Others enter the field by choice and with the best of intentions, but for the wrong reasons. They like working with people, and they want to be helpful—noble motives that thoroughly tick off some HR thinkers. "When people have come to me and said, 'I want to work with people,' I say, 'Good, go be a social worker,'" says Arnold Kanarick, who has headed human resources at the Limited and, until recently, at Bear Stearns. "HR isn't about being a do-gooder. It's about how do you get the best and brightest people and raise the value of the firm."

The really scary news is that the gulf between capabilities and job requirements appears to be widening. As business and legal demands on the function intensify, staffers' educational qualifications haven't kept pace. In fact, according to a survey by the Society for Human Resource Management (SHRM), a considerably smaller proportion of HR professionals today have some education beyond a bachelor's degree than in 1990.

And here's one more slice of telling SHRM data: When HR professionals were asked about the worth of various academic courses toward a "successful career in HR," 83% said that classes in interpersonal communications skills had "extremely high value." Employment law and business ethics followed, at 71% and 66%, respectively. Where was change management? At 35%. Strategic management? 32%. Finance? Um, that was just 2%.

The truth? Most human-resources managers aren't particularly interested in, or equipped for, doing business. And in a business, that's sort of a problem. As guardians of a company's talent, HR has to understand–how people serve corporate objectives. Instead, "business acumen is the single biggest factor that HR professionals in the U.S. lack today," says Anthony J. Rucci, executive vice president at Cardinal Health Inc., a big healthcare supply distributor.

Rucci is consistently mentioned by academics, consultants, and other HR leaders as an executive who actually does know business. At Baxter International, he ran both HR and corporate strategy. Before that, at Sears, he led a study of results at 800 stores over five years to assess the connection between employee commitment, customer loyalty, and profitability.

As far as Rucci is concerned, there are three questions that any decent HR person in the world should be able to answer. First, who is your company's core customer? "Have you talked to one lately? Do you know what challenges they face?" Second, who is the competition? "What do they do well and not well?" And most important, who are we? "What is a realistic assessment of what we do well and not so well vis à vis the customer and the competition?"

Does your HR pro know the answers?

2. HR pursues efficiency in lieu of value.
Why? Because it's easier–and easier to measure. Dave Ulrich, a professor at the University of Michigan, recalls meeting with the chairman and top HR people from a big bank. "The training person said that 80% of employees have done at least 40 hours in classes. The chairman said, 'Congratulations.' I said, 'You're talking about the activities you're doing. The question is, What are you delivering?'"

That sort of stuff drives Ulrich nuts. Over 20 years, he has become the HR trade's best-known guru and a leading proponent of the push to take on more-strategic roles within corporations. But human-resources managers, he acknowledges, typically undermine that effort by investing more importance in activities than in outcomes. "You're only effective if you add value," Ulrich says. "That means you're not measured by what you do but by what you deliver." By that, he refers not just to the value delivered to employees and line managers, but the benefits that accrue to investors and customers, as well.

So here's a true story: A talented young marketing exec accepts a job offer with Time Warner out of business school. She interviews for openings in several departments—then is told by HR that only one is interested in her. In fact, she learns later, they all had been. She had been railroaded into the job, under the supervision of a widely reviled manager, because no one inside the company would take it.

You make the call: Did HR do its job? On the one hand, it filled the empty slot. "It did what was organizationally expedient," says the woman now. "Getting someone who wouldn't kick and scream about this role probably made sense to them. But I just felt angry." She left Time Warner after just a year. (A Time Warner spokesperson declined to comment on the incident.)

Stupid HR Tricks

Can Your Highly Trained Human-Resources Professional Do This? Or Has He Already?

In 2003, **FedEx** for the first time asked employees to make $10 copayments for doctors' visits. But Dave Haynes, a FedEx sales rep and author of *The Peon Book* (Berrett-Koehler, 2004), notes that "in order to ensure that all employees understood the policy and its impact, HR sent us three separate glossy four-color brochures and went to the expense of creating a Web site." Says a FedEx spokeswoman, "We do send four-color brochures to get the attention of employees and their families."

An editor at Disney Press, the **Walt Disney Co.**'s publisher of children's books, was worried about his relationship with his increasingly erratic supervisor. One morning, he arrived at work to find a voice mail from the boss that threatened physical violence. He played the voice mail to a human-resources manager, who told him, "Well, I think it's time for you to start looking for another job." "I said, 'You're kidding, right?'" the editor says now. "She said, 'That's my best solution.' I couldn't believe it." Disney declined to comment.

Regina Blus was managing a large software project across several departments at **Sun Microsystems**. In one department, a new manager, widely disliked, consistently berated and harassed the workers, Blus says, even while engaging one in an affair. Blus approached the local HR manager. "He said, 'Well, I certainly don't think it's appropriate to get involved in these witch hunts. And anyway, it's none of your business.'" The incident was never investigated. Sun says there is no record of Blus's complaint, that any such report would have sparked an investigation, and that it takes such issues seriously.

Part of the problem is that Time Warner's metrics likely will never catch the real cost of its HR department's action. Human resources can readily provide the number of people it hired, the percentage of performance evaluations completed, and the extent to which employees are satisfied or not with their benefits. But only rarely does it link any of those metrics to business performance.

John W. Boudreau, a professor at the University of Southern California's Center for Effective Organizations, likens the failing to shortcomings of the finance function before DuPont figured out how to calculate return on investment in 1912. In HR, he says, "we don't have anywhere near that kind of logical sophistication in the way of people or talent. So the decisions that get made about that resource are far less sophisticated, reliable, and consistent."

Cardinal Health's Rucci is trying to fix that. Cardinal regularly asks its employees 12 questions designed to measure engagement. Among them: Do they understand the company's strategy? Do they see the connection between that and their jobs? Are they proud to tell people where they work? Rucci correlates the results to those of a survey of 2,000 customers, as well as monthly sales data and brand-awareness scores.

"So I don't know if our HR processes are having an impact" per se, Rucci says. "But I know absolutely that employee-engagement scores have an impact on our business," accounting for between 1% and 10% of earnings, depending on the business and the employee's role. "Cardinal may not anytime soon get invited by the Conference Board to explain our world-class best practices in any area of HR—and I couldn't care less. The real question is, Is the business effective and successful?"

3. HR isn't working for you. Want to know why you go through that asinine performance appraisal every year, really? Markle, who admits to having administered countless numbers of them over the years, is pleased to confirm your suspicions. Companies, he says "are doing it to protect themselves against their own employees," he says. "They put a piece of paper between you and employees, so if you ever have a confrontation, you can go to the file and say, 'Here, I've documented this problem.'"

There's a good reason for this defensive stance, of course. In the last two generations, government has created an immense thicket of labor regulations. Equal Employment Opportunity; Fair Labor Standards; Occupational Safety and Health; Family and Medical Leave; and the ever-popular ERISA. These are complex, serious issues requiring technical expertise, and HR has to apply reasonable caution.

But "it's easy to get sucked down into that," says Mark Royal, a senior consultant with Hay Group. "There's a tension created by HR's role as protector of corporate assets—making sure it doesn't run afoul of the rules. That puts you in the position of saying no a lot, of playing the bad cop. You have to step out of that, see the broad possibilities, and take a more open-minded approach. You need to understand where the exceptions to broad policies can be made."

Typically, HR people can't, or won't. Instead, they pursue standardization and uniformity in the face of a workforce that is heterogeneous and complex. A manager at a large capital leasing company complains that corporate HR is trying to eliminate most vice-president titles there—even though veeps are a dime a dozen in the finance industry. Why? Because in the company's commercial business, vice president is a rank reserved for the top officers. In its drive for bureaucratic "fairness," HR is actually threatening the reputation, and so the effectiveness, of the company's finance professionals.

The urge for one-size-fits-all, says one professor who studies the field, "is partly about compliance, but mostly because it's just easier." Bureaucrats everywhere abhor exceptions—not just because they open up the company to charges of bias but because they require more than rote solutions. They're time-consuming and expensive to manage. Make one exception, HR fears, and the floodgates will open.

There's a contradiction here, of course: Making exceptions should be exactly what human resources does, all the time—not because it's nice for employees, but because it drives the

How to Do HR Right

Say the Right Thing

At the grand level, what HR tells employees has to match what the company actually believes; empty rhetoric only breeds discontent. And when it comes to the details of pay and benefits, explain clearly what's being done and why. For example, asks consultant Dennis Ackley, "When you have a big deductible, do employees understand you're focusing on big costs? Or do they just think HR is being annoying?"

Measure the Right Thing

Human resources isn't taken seriously by top management because it can't demonstrate its impact on the business. Statistics on hiring, turnover, and training measure activity but not value. So devise measurements that consider impact: When you trained people, did they learn anything that made them better workers? And connect that data to business-performance indicators—such as customer loyalty, quality, employee-replacement costs, and, ultimately, profitability.

Get Rid of the "Social Workers"

After Libby Sartain arrived as chief people officer at Yahoo, she moved several HR staffers out—some because they didn't have the right functional skills, but mostly because "they were stuck in the old-school way of doing things." Human resources shouldn't be about cutting costs, but it is all about business. The people who work there need to be both technically competent and sophisticated about the company's strategy, competitors, and customers.

Serve the Business

Human-resources staffers walk a fine line: Employees see them as stooges for management, and management views them as annoying do-gooders representing employees. But "the best employee advocates are the ones who are concerned with advancing organizational and individual performance," says Anthony Rucci of Cardinal Health. Represent management with integrity and honesty—and back employees in the name of improving the company's capability.

Make Value, Not Activity

University of Michigan professor Dave Ulrich, coauthor of *The HR Value Proposition* (Harvard Business School Press, 2005), says HR folks must create value for four groups: They need to foster competence and commitment among employees, develop the capabilities that allow managers to execute on strategy, help build relationships with customers, and create confidence among investors in the future value of the firm.

business. Employers keep their best people by acknowledging and rewarding their distinctive performance, not by treating them the same as everyone else. "If I'm running a business, I can tell you who's really helping to drive the business forward," says Dennis Ackley, an employee communication consultant. "HR should have the same view. We should send the message that we value our high-performing employees and we're focused on rewarding and retaining them."

Instead, human-resources departments benchmark salaries, function by function and job by job, against industry standards, keeping pay—even that of the stars—within a narrow band determined by competitors. They bounce performance appraisals back to managers who rate their employees too highly, unwilling to acknowledge accomplishments that would merit much more than the 4% companywide increase.

Human resources, in other words, forfeits long-term value for short-term cost efficiency. A simple test: Who does your company's vice president of human resources report to? If it's the CFO—and chances are good it is—then HR is headed in the wrong direction. "That's a model that cannot work," says one top HR exec who has been there. "A financial person is concerned with taking money out of the organization. HR should be concerned with putting investments in."

4. The corner office doesn't get HR (and vice versa). I'm at another rockin' party: a few dozen midlevel human-resources managers at a hotel restaurant in Mahwah, New Jersey. It is not glam in any way. (I've got to get a better travel agent.) But it is telling, in a hopeful way. Hunter Douglas, a $2.1 billion manufacturer of window coverings, has brought its HR staff here from across the United States to celebrate their accomplishments.

The company's top brass is on hand. Marvin B. Hopkins, president and CEO of North American operations, lays on the praise: "I feel fantastic about your achievements," he says. "Our business is about people. Hiring, training, and empathizing with employees is extremely important. When someone is fired or leaves, we've failed in some way. People have to feel they have a place at the company, a sense of ownership."

So, yeah, it's corporate-speak in a drab exurban office park. But you know what? The human-resources managers from Tupelo and Dallas are totally pumped up. They've been flown into headquarters, they've had their picture taken with the boss, and they're seeing *Mamma Mia* on Broadway that afternoon on the company's dime.

Can your HR department say it has the ear of top management? Probably not. "Sometimes," says Ulrich, "line managers just have this legacy of HR in their minds, and they can't get rid of it. I felt really badly for one HR guy. The chairman wanted someone to plan company picnics and manage the union, and every time this guy tried to be strategic, he got shot down."

Say what? Execs don't think HR matters? What about all that happy talk about employees being their most important asset? Well, that turns out to have been a small misunderstanding. In the 1990s, a group of British academics examined the relationship between what companies (among them, the UK units of Hewlett-Packard and Citibank) said about their human assets and how they actually behaved. The results were, perhaps, inevitable.

In their rhetoric, human-resources organizations embraced the language of a "soft" approach, speaking of training, development, and commitment. But "the underlying principle was invariably restricted to the improvements of bottom-line performance," the authors wrote in the resulting book, *Strategic Human Resource Management* (Oxford University Press, 1999). "Even if the rhetoric of HRM is soft, the reality is almost always 'hard,' with the interests of the organization prevailing over those of the individual."

In the best of worlds, says London Business School professor Lynda Gratton, one of the study's authors, "the reality should be some combination of hard and soft." That's what's going on at Hunter Douglas. Human resources can address the needs of employees because it has proven its business mettle—and vice versa. Betty Lou Smith, the company's vice president of corporate HR, began investigating the connection between employee turnover and product quality. Divisions with the highest turnover rates, she found, were also those with damaged-goods rates of 5% or higher. And extraordinarily, 70% of employees were leaving the company within six months of being hired.

Smith's staffers learned that new employees were leaving for a variety of reasons: They didn't feel respected, they didn't have input in decisions, but mostly, they felt a lack of connection when they were first hired. "We gave them a 10-minute orientation, then they were out on the floor," Smith says. She addressed the weakness by creating a mentoring program that matched new hires with experienced workers. The latter were suspicious at first, but eventually, the mentor positions (with spiffy shirts and caps) came to be seen as prestigious. The six-month turnover rate dropped dramatically, to 16%. Attendance and productivity—and the damaged-goods rate—improved.

"We don't wait to hear from top management," Smith says. "You can't just sit in the corner and look at benefits. We have to know what the issues in our business are. HR has to step up and assume responsibility, not wait for management to knock on our door."

But most HR people do.

Hunter Douglas gives us a glimmer of hope—of the possibility that HR can be done right. And surely, even within ineffective human-resources organizations, there are great individual HR managers—trustworthy, caring people with their ears to the ground, who are sensitive to cultural nuance yet also understand the business and how people fit in. Professionals who move voluntarily into HR from line positions can prove especially adroit, bringing a profit-and-loss sensibility and strong management skills.

At Yahoo, Libby Sartain, chief people officer, is building a group that may prove to be the truly effective human-resources department that employees and executives imagine. In this, Sartain enjoys two advantages. First, she arrived with a reputation as a creative maverick, won in her 13 years running HR at Southwest Airlines. And second, she had license from the top to do whatever it took to create a world-class organization.

Sartain doesn't just have a "seat at the table" at Yahoo; she actually helped build the table, instituting a weekly operations meeting that she coordinates with COO Dan Rosensweig. Talent is always at the top of the agenda—and at the end of each meeting, the executive team mulls individual development decisions on key staffers.

That meeting, Sartain says, "sends a strong message to everyone at Yahoo that we can't do anything without HR." It also signals to HR staffers that they're responsible for more than shuffling papers and getting in the way. "We view human resources as the caretaker of the largest investment of the company," Sartain says. "If you're not nurturing that investment and watching it grow, you're not doing your job."

Yahoo, say some experts and peers at other organizations, is among a few companies—among them Cardinal Health, Procter & Gamble, Pitney Bowes, Goldman Sachs, and General Electric—that truly are bringing human resources into the realm of business strategy. But they are indeed the few. USC professor Edward E. Lawler III says that last year HR professionals reported spending 23% of their time "being a strategic business partner"—no more than they reported in 1995. And line managers, he found, said HR is far less involved in strategy than HR thinks it is. "Despite great huffing and puffing about strategy," Lawler says, "there's still a long way to go." (Indeed. When I asked one midlevel HR person exactly how she was involved in business strategy for her division, she excitedly described organizing a monthly lunch for her vice president with employees.)

What's driving the strategy disconnect? London Business School's Gratton spends a lot of time training human-resources professionals to create more impact. She sees two problems: Many HR people, she says, bring strong technical expertise to the party but no "point of view about the future and how organizations are going to change." And second, "it's very difficult to align HR strategy to business strategy, because business strategy changes very fast, and it's hard to fiddle around with a compensation strategy or benefits to keep up." More than simply understanding strategy, Gratton says, truly effective executives "need to be operating out of a set of principles and personal values." And few actually do.

In the meantime, economic natural selection is, in a way, taking care of the problem for us. Some 94% of large employers surveyed this year by Hewitt Associates reported they were outsourcing at least one human-resources activity. By 2008, according to the survey, many plan to expand outsourcing to include activities such as learning and development, payroll, recruiting, health and welfare, and global mobility.

Which is to say, they will farm out pretty much everything HR does. The happy rhetoric from the HR world says this is all for the best: Outsourcing the administrative minutiae, after all, would allow human-resources professionals to focus on more important stuff that's central to the business. You know, being strategic partners.

The problem, if you're an HR person, is this: The tasks companies are outsourcing—the administrivia—tend to be what you're good at. And what's left isn't exactly your strong suit. Human resources is crippled by what Jay Jamrog, executive director of the Human Resource Institute, calls "educated incapacity: You're smart, and you know the way you're working today isn't going to hold 10 years from now. But you can't move to that level. You're stuck."

That's where human resources is today. Stuck. "This is a unique organization in the company," says USC's Boudreau.

"It discovers things about the business through the lens of people and talent. That's an opportunity for competitive advantage." In most companies, that opportunity is utterly wasted.

And that's why I don't like HR.

KEITH H. HAMMONDS is *Fast Company's* deputy editor.

Strange Bedfellows
Could HR Be Marketing's New Best Friend?

JEFF SMITH AND KRISTIANE BLOMQVIST

I n most companies, brands get limited traction outside of the marketing department. Historically, marketing has meant external communications and customer insights, so it generally has limited internal influence on employees' day-to-day activities. However, the world of brands and marketing is realizing that, to truly create a successful external brand, an organization's employees must be included. Marketing must shift its thinking about the brand and, perhaps most important, the internal partners with which it must collaborate.

The divide between marketing and the human resources (HR) department has developed under the banner of "we have different audiences and different objectives." The tension has grown by comparing ownership of initiatives like corporate vision and values vs. brand vision and brand values; internal communications vs. external communications; employee development vs. business development, and so on. Today, marketing and HR are realizing that, in creating sustainable change inside and outside the organization, the two functional areas need each other to survive. It is no longer one or the other; it is now "we are stronger together."

A truly collaborative partnership between the two departments can create a new kind of company with a culture and related behaviors that are on-brand, on-strategy, and ultimately more effective at delivering bottom-line results for the business. The notion of marketing and HR becoming bedfellows is not so strange when you consider the symbiotic requirements they both share and the tremendous benefits they deliver to an organization and its customers.

HR Supports Marketing

In fact, there are compelling reasons for marketing to team up with HR. These include HR's ability to "attach" the brand message to departmental areas where it may not previously have had a presence, and to provide marketing and brand access to employees in departments that may not have been recognized as needing that information in the past.

HR's primary constituents are the company's internal employees. With that audience, its work is truly cross-functional and company-wide. Therefore, in realizing that a brand's strength lies in its delivery and not just its communication, HR can be an effective conduit for influencing employees through recruiting, new employee orientation, training and development, performance evaluation, and compensation. By infusing the content of the brand into the programs, a brand-based culture starts to emerge.

One company we worked with makes a concerted effort to present a united front during new hire orientation, giving new employees a full day of introduction to the firm that includes basics about the facilities, the history of the company, the vision and key objectives for the future, and the strategies to achieve the stated vision. This is a most opportune time to involve the new employee in what the firm's customers want and what the firm is doing to satisfy them. Imagine a one hour discussion where a video is played of customers speaking about their key needs and wants. This video is then followed up by how the firm is planning to address these needs. External communications can then be shown, viewed in the context of solving these important issues. The combination creates a powerful story, enabling new employees to understand the customer and business better, understand they must behave in a certain way, and see the promises being made to customers by the firm. HR and marketing are completely intertwined in the story, and the result is a new group of brand ambassadors.

We also saw this collaboration in action at a global technology firm that used an interesting contest to create deeper appreciation and understanding for the new brand they were developing. HR and marketing teamed to develop a series of CD-ROM trading cards that had questions about how people would act if they were the brand. Once five questions were answered correctly, the card was traded for another. The first people to collect all six cards won a prize. This created an international network based on the ideals of the brand. Cards went back and forth to all corners of the globe. The more people got into it, the more distribution the cards received. The end result was an incredibly effective internal communications program.

As illustrated, HR can play a key role in helping marketing develop internal communications that demonstrate how employees "live" the brand. David Aaker, author of the new book, *Brand Portfolio Management* (The Free Press, 2004), asserts that the concept of internal role models is one of the most effective ways to enlist a broader population of employees.

Traditionally, in change-management initiatives, these people a recalled "change agents." They are people that embody and live the ideals of the brand and are individuals respected by many people in the organization. By identifying these individuals and aligning their messages and behaviors, a very powerful force of internal role models is created for employees to emulate. No other function is more capable of identifying and encouraging these employees to participate than HR.

EXECUTIVE briefing
Companies are increasingly realizing that, for brand and business strategies to be aligned, the brand can no longer be driven solely by the activities of the marketing department. Delivering against the promises of a company's brand strategy requires every level of the organization to live the brand. Employees must not only accept these strategies, but actually change their behaviors and "walk the talk." However, integrating the brand into all facets of an organization does have its challenges.

Marketing Supports HR

The HR department also benefits from close collaboration with its marketing colleagues. By making its target audiences, positioning promises, and marketing strategies available to HR, marketing can bolster HR's ability to attract and retain employees that believe in and will support the company's brand and business strategies.

HR is increasingly discovering how marketing can help it attract and retain employees, which is critical in the ongoing competitive war for talent. Research has shown that a variety of factors play into what attracts the best candidates to a career opportunity, many of which rank equal to or higher than financial compensation. Sought-after candidates want to work for a company that reflects their own ideals and aspirations and maintains a strong customer focus.

A global services company recently conducted research on its recruiting efforts and found that there has been an evolution in how potential employees look at career opportunities. For example, it's no longer good enough to offer a long career; recruits today are seeking companies that clearly help them build their own market profiles. Candidates are seeking companies they can place on their resume that will build their overall market value, which suggests that marketing and the brand play an ever-increasing role in attracting the best talent. The brand is becoming a primary decision tool for recruits when considering a new career opportunity.

It's important not to forget that employees are often also your customers. They are learning about the organization from the

outside world as well through their exposure to the company's external communications. Many HR departments have realized the potential here: IBM (when it launched e-business), JPMorgan (with the "I am JPMorgan" campaign), and Southwest Airlines all spoke to their employees through their external advertising initiatives. These efforts built a great internal sense of pride in the companies and clearly communicated what the organization hoped its employees would deliver to customers. It also communicated a promise that included the employees.

This has elevated the importance of branding and increased HR's reliance on the marketing department to provide it with processes for developing internal and external communications that support the brand promises the company is making in the marketplace. The marketing group's in-depth understanding of the customer and its ability to develop communications targeted at this group can help HR determine what tools and messages will help current and potential employees deliver against the brand promises.

HR can accomplish this by leveraging the credibility marketing has acquired as a result of its focus on the customer. Generally, the marketing department "owns" market and customer research and thus has the greatest insight into the needs of the market. Whether employees believe in the concept of brand or not, they will always listen when being told what their customers want and how best to deliver against these needs. Providing them the sort of actionable data that's a specialty of marketing will help turn employee attention to other areas that support the needs and goals of the business, in turn making them ambassadors of the brand.

Brand Ambassadors

But creating such sweeping attitudinal change can be problematic. Changing behaviors is not a simple task, and many impediments block a successful implementation. These impediments include compensation systems that are not aligned with brand building, lack of senior management commitment, desire for immediate results, and management vs. leadership of an initiative.

Imagine if you worked in a call center for an insurance company. Typically, you would be compensated based on the number of calls you handle, not the depth and length of the calls. Now imagine the insurance company came out with a brand strategy where the company would understand customer needs better than anyone else. The compensation structure for the call center representative is actually prohibiting the desired experience from taking place. There is virtually no way customers are going to perceive that they are well-understood if they are handled according to the current measurement system. While this example is somewhat simplistic, it's illustrative of a problem faced by organizations of all sizes. How do you align the motivating factors of compensation with the promises the company must keep with customers?

Not only do HR and marketing need to know how the brand translates into specific employee competencies, but they also need to assess how these competencies deliver convincing customer experiences through distinct employee actions.

One company we worked with established a small task force with representatives from both HR and marketing to identify what competencies the target employee should have from the brand, business, and HR perspective. It was a rather lengthy but important process, as those competencies would become the foundation for the company's compensation and recruitment processes and therefore establish a behavioral role model. After primary and secondary research among employees and customers and multiple global workshops and teleconferences, a new target employee emerged. The target came complete with competencies, associated actions, and professional experience requirements by level.

How many "living the brand" initiatives have failed because they were nothing more than communications and a new mouse pad?

Having gone through the process together, marketing and HR had full clarity concerning what competencies this employee possessed and how these competencies were manifested in specific actions. HR could then easily proceed to align the compensation models so the right behaviors would be nurtured and rewarded. Marketing could start to think about the training programs, messages, and reward schemes that would further build the behaviors that supported the brand most strongly. This is the type of teamwork that creates strong customer experiences at Goldman Sachs Group Inc., Hertz Corp., and the Walt Disney Co.

Obviously the aligned compensation system isn't the answer to all problems, although its importance should not be underestimated. How many "living the brand" initiatives have failed because they were nothing more than communications and a new mouse pad? The surest way to end a great internal or external initiative is with a lack of senior management support. Senior managers of HR often hold on closely to their silo because that's how they believe they offer value to the organization. The marketing group often does the same. If an organization is unable to convince both groups to work together, the initiatives will forever be separate and will only confuse employees rather than motivate them. At many firms, the HR group owns the internal values of the organization, while the marketing group owns the values the company wants customers to experience. Each fights to keep its set of values and neither actually achieves its objectives. Each of these sets of values should be virtually the same. Since both departments are hoping to affect the behavior of employees, the message needs to be consistent.

Another impediment to making employees brand ambassadors is the rush to achieve immediate results—a great temptation when it comes to organizational change and brand development. With all of the work that goes into developing a strategy, many companies hope they will see immediate results. But it just doesn't happen when you're asking an organization to think and act differently. Short-term results are quicker to achieve but rarely sustainable and are usually a result of specific instructions

from management. Sustainable change, like enabling employees to see why they must think differently, comes from true leadership—managers demonstrating that changing the way employees think contributes to their personal commitment to the initiative ideals. Combining HR and marketing initiatives into a single program or initiative affords leaders greater clarity and focus and ultimately leads to more effective business results.

Sought-after candidates want to work for a company that reflects their own ideals and maintains a strong customer focus.

One such initiative was implemented at a global financial services company to determine the most effective way to attract the most valuable talent. A cross-functional, cross-geography, cross-business team that included marketing and HR was used to create a strategy. The outcome was a project that was single-minded, that enables the organization to hire the kinds of people who are able to deliver the brand promises, and is completely aligned with the external messages being communicated.

Collaboration Partnership

Truly reaping the benefits of collaboration between marketing and HR requires a solid partnership that strengthens the company's efforts to bring its brand to life internally. At Goldman Sachs, for example, the brand is at the very core of the company's culture. Each employee lives the Goldman Sachs brand—a result of a conscious effort to integrate the efforts of marketing and HR from strategy development to implementation. This sets the company apart and receives partial credit for the company's industry leadership. Internally, marketing employees talk about cultural practices, not branding programs. Recasting branding programs in this light is a far more effective way of engaging employees. Externally, marketing highlights the elements of the Goldman Sachs culture that are most important to its targeted customer segments. HR and marketing work together to ensure brand and business alignment during the intense new-hire training program. Among other things, the program explains how Goldman Sachs' culture and values relate to the client experience. Continuous employee research, including internal surveys, focus groups, and roundtables with senior management, are conducted to ensure that company initiatives always meet employee and customer expectations.

The biggest challenge that companies face in replicating the Goldman Sachs model is that integration isn't natural. Companies typically view vision, culture, and brand as distinct elements to be handled separately by different departments. Often, the company's vision resides with the management committee, its culture within HR, and its brand within marketing. This not only puts the company at risk of a strategic misalignment, but is also a source of tremendous internal and external confusion.

Bridge the Gap

So how can companies bridge the gap between marketing and HR, brand and culture, and inside and outside in order to better assimilate the brand internally?

Strategic alignment of company objectives, marketing and employee objectives, and ultimately communications to all constituents is the most critical pre requisite for success. It's not enough that marketing requests HR's assistance in implementing brand values across the firm or that HR requests marketing's help in adapting tools for HR purposes. If the goal is to deliver greater business value, the two departments need to work together seamlessly. The first step in forging this relationship is for each department to develop respect for the other's expertise. A mutual understanding can be achieved by slating a meeting of the minds where strategies can be exchanged, synergies can be discussed, and overlaps in responsibilities can be resolved. The alignment is best developed around the business objectives, not the departmental objectives. It's not about raising awareness with customers, nor is it about diversity. It's about delivering more profits to the bottom line.

Once marketing and HR are philosophically aligned, specific strategies for attracting and retaining employees and for the integration of the brand throughout the organization need to be discussed and agreed on. The two groups must proceed with a shared objective and a willingness to work together for a common purpose.

A shared objective, for example, might be to turn the company into a technology leader. On the HR side, supporting this objective would involve evaluating employee characteristics, rewards and compensation, management systems, and cultural values. Marketing's task is to specify the traits that are critical from a brand perspective (e.g., employees need to be creative and constantly pushing the envelope), then work with HR to define how these are translated into behaviors that are embedded into processes and systems. That's because the proof lies in the execution, not just in the promise. Another example of a shared objective might be generating employee excitement about recent company achievements or changes in strategic direction. Often, internal campaigns or employee contests are held where marketing leverages its work in external communications, or maybe sponsorship relationships, to bring additional flavor or interest to HR's employee activities.

After the two groups have developed their strategies, it comes down to implementation. The first step in this phase is to assess what needs to be done collectively and as individual functions. This is the time to see if things like rewards and compensation systems, training curriculums, and brand and recruitment communications are aligned with HR and marketing strategies. If not, this is the time to see that it's done. Once the tasks to align marketing and HR are outlined, a plan should be created that details how the brand is reflected across all key initiatives and the scheduled rollout for each initiative, complete with a summary of the roles and responsibilities of all those involved, sample brand actions, and/or language to be used.

Executing the plans becomes the responsibility of the functions themselves. However, there should be some joint management structure that enables frequent assessment of progress and required course corrections. This can be a steering committee made up of senior representatives from the two departments or it can be more of a joint working group that rolls up its sleeves and meets frequently to hammer out progress details and enable each others' programs.

Brand Alignment

The brand's alignment is critical for the implementation phase to be effective. A key step is for marketing to stop talking about the "brand." The reality is that "brand" is merely a buzzword to many in the organization, and discussions a round it often generate indifference. A better way to infuse brand into business practices is to relate it directly to employee benefits using language like: "If you act in this way, you will achieve these results." For example, telling a business machine salesperson that they have to treat their clients with kid gloves may not get the same response as if you said that their clients are looking to place business with someone that really takes care of their requirements.

It's also essential for marketing to be proactive in sharing the promises they intend to communicate internally with employees before the external market actually hears them. BMW Group, for example, has had great success cultivating enthusiasm and motivating employees by sharing its advertising campaigns with employees before they hit the general market. At Southwest Airlines, HR and marketing developed a list of eight employee "freedoms" to summarize the employment experience at Southwest, thereby creating an internal side to the external brand story. The brand identity of "freedom" internally has become: "At Southwest Airlines, freedom begins with me." As a result, employees know exactly what kind of experience they are to create. Successful brand alignment, as such examples illustrate, will help employees and the company as a whole to naturally act on-brand with an on-brand customer experience to follow.

The monitoring and management of the collaborative efforts is ongoing, and marketing and HR should provide updates on progress and relevant information regularly—at a minimum once per quarter. Measuring results can be done in a variety of ways, but conducting quantitative surveys and holding focus groups are two of the most effective. And while HR should continue to monitor the pulse of employees, marketing must stay focused on how best to deliver against the needs of the company's stakeholders. The combined results of internal understanding of the brand, quality of delivery at critical touch points, and customer awareness/loyalty to the brand should be reported back to the leadership team to ensure they have the necessary information to keep brand and business strategy in alignment.

Just how important a story HR and marketing can tell when the two work in tandem is illustrated by the results of HSBC's (Hong Kong Shanghai Banking Corporation) *Global International Brand Survey*. This survey is conducted periodically to test how well all 300,000 employees understand and live the brand as reflected by how they answer 10 statements. Results from the study are compared with a customer metrics system. In an interview with Peter Stringham, group general manager and head of marketing for HSBC, we learned that results correlate strongly. Branches that score high on "living the brand" have a tendency to score higher on both customer satisfaction and brand purchase consideration.

HR and marketing might not be natural bedfellows, but experience shows that, when they do cooperate and work together, an increase in successful recruiting, overall employee understanding, and support of the brand (and thus the work of the marketing group) follows. With a simple formula of communications and coordination, companies can create a strong foundation on which to build a compelling brand and strong culture and drive significant business impact.

About the Authors—Both of the authors work at Prophet, a management consultancy specializing in integrating business, brand, and marketing strategies. JEFF SMITH is an associate partner in the Zurich office and may be reached at jsmith@prophet.com. KRISTIANE BLOMQVIST is a senior associate in the London office and may be reached at kblomqvist@prophet.com.

From *Marketing Management,* January/February 2005, pp. 39–43. Copyright © 2005 by American Marketing Association. Reprinted by permission.

Not the Usual Suspects

A quarter of the *Fortune* 1,000 have selected their HR chiefs from outside divisions, such as legal and finance, reflecting the increasing need for more business-savvy leaders. And for these execs, the job could serve as a springboard to CEO.

Jessica Marquez

Sandy Hofmann cried when she was offered the chief people officer position at her company.

As of 2001, Hofmann had spent most of her career in operations—14 years at IBM and most recently as the head of the Boston business division at Mapics, an Atlanta-based provider of software to manufacturers. In this role, she supervised 150 employees and was the first woman on the company's executive team.

"HR had been seen as a barrier to the business. It was not a respected function within the company," says Hofmann, who recently left Mapics to become COO of a Georgia-based interior storage and design firm. "Quite frankly, for a woman who had worked hard to achieve a role within the senior ranks of the organization, it felt like they were offering me this soft and cushy job that they felt women were supposed to do."

So when Mapics CEO Dick Cook asked Hofmann to take on the role of chief information officer and chief people officer, she felt like she was being demoted.

But Hofmann was wrong. Cook, like an increasing number of CEOs, wanted a business-savvy executive to take on the HR role, which until that point had been shared among various midlevel managers throughout the organization. Mapics was going through tough times in the wake of the dot-com bust and needed someone who could apply business metrics to HR.

Today, 25 percent of *Fortune* 1,000 companies have tapped executives from other divisions—particularly operations, legal and finance—to take on the top HR role, according to the Center for Effective Organizations, a research center in the Marshall School of Business at the University of Southern California.

In some cases, companies are using HR as a steppingstone to the CEO spot, experts say. "HR can be a great development opportunity for line managers," says Claudia Lacy Kelly, global practice leader for the HR practice at Spencer Stuart, a worldwide executive search firm.

However, many companies are tapping business execs to take on HR because they simply can't find business-savvy HR executives.

> **"Even though everyone talks the talk of being business partners, those HR executives who are actually anticipating the future needs of the business from a strategic and operational point of view are few and far between."**
>
> —Wendy Murphy, managing partner, Heidrick & Struggles

"Even though everyone talks the talk of being business partners, those HR executives who are actually anticipating the future needs of the business from a strategic and operational point of view are few and far between," says Wendy Murphy, managing partner at Heidrick & Struggles.

As more companies outsource the administrative HR functions within their organizations, while at the same time find it more difficult to recruit and retain talent, the need for business-savvy HR executives is only going to increase, experts say.

"If HR doesn't step up its game and really focus on the business, more organizations are going to look elsewhere to fill these positions," Murphy says.

Born of Necessity

At many companies, like Mapics, it takes a crisis to expose the need for a business-minded HR executive.

In 2001, Mapics, which had 1,200 employees, was trying to reinvent itself. Hofmann had seen her division cut from

150 to 65 employees. Rather than make deeper cuts, Mapics decided to let employees work from home—a novel concept six years ago.

The initiative would require Mapics to think differently about managing its workforce, and the need for a chief people officer was clear, Hofmann says.

"We were going to have to be more agile and more open with how we shared information with employees since they couldn't just pick up information at the water cooler anymore," she says. "Since I was the one who complained the most about how we were going to support our people in this changing world, I got the chief people officer job."

Three years ago, Roy Vallee, CEO of Avnet, a Phoenix-based worldwide distributor of manufacturing technology products and services, was also targeting an atypical candidate for the top HR spot. Vallee had been struggling with getting HR to focus more on organizational development issues, such as succession planning and performance management, but couldn't seem to find the right person to fill the position.

He thought he found the perfect fit with Steve Church, president of Avnet's electronics marketing division. Church understood Avnet's business and was passionate about workforce management issues, Vallee says. Unfortunately for Vallee, Church didn't want the job.

"I just felt that there had to be someone better out there for the job," Church says. "After all, I had no formal HR training."

Vallee put Church in charge of coming up with a job description and finding the right HR executive. As part of his due diligence, Church spent weeks visiting heads of HR at other companies to ascertain their main challenges, and how they were addressed.

"I met with about 20 of my counterparts at companies like Texas Instruments and General Mills," he says. "And what I realized in those meetings was that I knew more about HR issues than I thought I did."

After eight months of searching for an outside HR executive, Church changed his mind and took the position.

Growing Pains

Not surprisingly, non-HR executives who come into the top HR job often are met with significant challenges, not the least of which is raised eyebrows from their colleagues.

"There was lot of skepticism inside our own organization, particularly among the board of directors, about why we weren't bringing on an HR expert," Vallee says.

To address this, Vallee took time with the board, as well as members of the HR team, to get their support.

"I explained the risks of bringing someone in from the outside and talked about how Steve understood our business," he says.

Humility helps a lot in these kinds of situations, Church says.

"I remember the first meeting I had with my HR team. They knew and I knew that I didn't know anything about HR," he says. "Rather than hide behind it I just said, 'Everyone in this room knows more about HR than I do, so let's get that off the table.'"

In the first several months, Church often went to his team with questions. "There was a lot of me saying, 'I don't know the answer to that, but I will go find out,'" he says.

> **It is essential for those outside of human resources who go into an HR role to have a good team. "If you don't have those individual pockets of strength, it's not going to work, because HR is quite technical."**
>
> —claudia Lacy Kelly, global practice leader, Spencer Stuart

That's why it's essential for outsiders who go into the HR role to have a good team, says Spencer Stuart's Lacy Kelly. "If you don't have those individual pockets of strength, it's not going to work, because HR is quite technical."

Also, executives new to the HR role often become disheartened by the inherent amount of bureaucracy.

Hofmann's key challenge was making the HR team feel like an important part of the organization and focusing them on the company's business objectives.

"At the time, HR felt like a bunch of chumps because everyone was always irritated with them all the time and then they had to lay off a lot of people. But they didn't even know about the layoffs until the day before they happened," she says.

Under Hofmann's leadership, Mapics' HR team started using business metrics to gauge success. They met with line managers periodically to make sure their activities supported the business goals, she says. Those who could not make the transition were asked to leave.

Julie Fasone Holder, corporate vice president of marketing and sales, human resources and public affairs at Dow Chemical, says that one of the biggest challenges she faced when she took over HR two years ago was realizing how different heading up HR is from supervising any other business division.

> **"You are running a function, which is very different than running a business. "You have to take more of a back seat and keep in mind how what you are doing is enabling business success, rather than driving change."**
>
> —Julie Fasone Holder, VP of marketing and sales, HR and public affairs, Dow Chemical

"You are running a function, which is very different than running a business," she says. "You have to take more of a back seat and keep in mind how what you are doing is enabling business success, rather than driving change."

Outside Experts Crunch Numbers for Luxottica HR

While many companies are tapping legal and finance professionals to take over HR, Luxottica Retail has taken a different approach.

Rather than supplant HR managers, the Mason, Ohio-based manufacturer of glasses and sunglasses has created a division of legal and finance experts to provide analytics to its HR team.

Luxottica Retail, which oversees well-known names like LensCrafters, Pearle and Sunglass Hut, has a distinct business challenge as a retailer of high-end glasses and sunglasses, says Robin Wilson, senior director of HR technology and analytics.

The average buying cycle for a pair of prescription glasses is once every two or three years. That means that store associates need to do everything they can to encourage customers to buy a few pairs of glasses during that one visit.

"But before we can impact customer behavior, we need to impact associate behavior," Wilson says.

Luxottica agreed in 2006 to have Wilson, who is an attorney and has some financial analysis experience, head up a new HR analytics team. Wilson previously worked as senior counsel and senior director of associate relations at Luxottica, but also has experience working as a financial analyst at General Electric and has a bachelor's degree in business administration.

Wilson's job is to analyze how HR affects the company's various business initiatives. Through extensive analysis of workforce data, Wilson and her four-person HR technology and analytics team arm HR with the knowledge it needs to refine all of the initiatives, she says.

"Instead of just telling people that turnover is up, we can say turnover is costing you $4.1 million a year," she says. "We always had this kind of data, but we weren't bringing it together."

For example, one of the first things Wilson and her team did was to provide productivity rankings for 5,000 of the company's frontline store associates.

Each associate was given a ranking from a low of 1 to a high of 5, based on sales productivity.

"It was a big 'Aha!' moment for a lot of managers because so many people got 1s and 2s, but they had 3s and 4s on their performance reviews," Wilson says. "Someone could be a great leader, but not a great seller. But this is a sales culture, and we need to be better at selling."

Wilson's team now can run predictive modeling as a result of the rankings to see how hiring associates with better sales skills would affect the bottom line, she says. And the company has conducted various types of analysis on HR initiatives using sales productivity as a correlating factor.

"When you can speak in numbers, it gets people's attention," Wilson says.

The challenge with having strong analytics, however, is communicating them in a way that the HR team can understand.

"Typically, HR executives are familiar enough with the financials to talk about budgets and for forecasting purposes, but when you start talking about different types of analytical tests, correlation of data sets or predictive modeling, people start fuzzing up," she says.

For that reason, Wilson and her team need to make sure that they present the data in a clear and concise manner.

The learning curve is shortening, she says, particularly as more HR professional organizations talk about the importance of analytics in understanding and managing a workforce.

"When I go to HR events, this is what people are talking about," she says. "This is the buzz and where HR is going."

—J.M.

And unlike marketing or sales, which Fasone Holder had overseen for years, everyone thinks they are an expert in HR, she says.

"Everyone is an employee and most people are leaders, so everyone has an opinion," she says. "It can be hard to forge consensus on people issues."

Bringing Business Expertise to HR

Despite these challenges, executives agree that the key to non-HR leaders being successful in the field is in trusting their business instincts.

"When I first started, someone said to me, 'Remember, you got here because you are a great leader, not because you are a subject-matter expert,'" Fasone Holder says.

Her marketing and sales expertise has been integral in her approach to improving Dow's corporate reputation, both internally and externally, to better recruit and retain employees.

For example, Dow serves its employees just like a company would its customer base—through customization and target marketing. Dow has segmented its organization into corporate, "people leaders"—the 2,500 managers at Dow—and employees.

"We needed to look at who we served and how we served them," Fasone Holder says. The company realized that while it had focused on corporate communications, it hadn't done much to communicate with and respond to the needs of its employees and leaders.

"Often HR is in the position where expectations are high but they don't have the budget or technology to deliver on those expectations. This can be a rude awakening for an executive who is used to getting whatever resources they need to get the job done."

—Tom Darrow, principal, Talent Connections

To address this, the company created leadership development curricula for its leaders. It also unveiled an intranet site where employees could access all of their HR tools and customize them according to their needs.

Fasone Holder's marketing approach also has helped Dow refine its recruiting strategy through more succinct messaging. Today on college campuses, Dow recruiters talk about the company's emphasis on sustainability, a buzzword among environmentally conscious college students.

As a result, Dow has been able to keep up with its hiring needs. This year it will hire 4,000 to 5,000 employees, compared with 4,000 last year and up from fewer than 1,000 in previous years.

Just like Fasone Holder used her marketing experience to revamp HR at Dow, Steve Church was able to use his operational skills to instill standards across Avnet's HR organization.

When Church took over HR at Avnet in July 2005, the company didn't have an HR information system outside of North America. "So if you called on an HR manager and asked how many employees we had worldwide, it would take two or three days to get an answer," he says.

Church and his team worked to implement standards and metrics for all HR processes, including compensation, performance management, training and development, and succession planning.

While all of these processes happened on an ad hoc basis four years ago, Church put the operational vigor behind it so HR managers were held accountable for meeting metrics like managers in any other part of the company.

> **"Today I measure everything. I measure overall turnover, turnover of top performers, turnover of new hires, for example.
> I measure HR expenses as a percentage of gross profit as well as HR expenses as a percentage of operating profits."**
> —Steve Church, Avnet

"Today I measure everything," he says. "I measure overall turnover, turnover of top performers, turnover of new hires, for example," he says. "I measure HR expenses as a percentage of gross profit as well as HR expenses as a percentage of operating profits."

Church's eye on metrics and accountability seems to be paying off. Gross profits per employee have jumped from $148,000 in 2005 to $181,000 in 2007.

JESSICA MARQUEZ is New York bureau chief for Workforce Management. To comment e-mail editors@workforce.com.

Employers Prepare to Keep, Not Lose, Baby Boomers

Diane Cadrain

In 2005, one in four workers was over age 50. By 2012, it will be nearly one in three, according to the U.S. Bureau of Labor Statistics. In fact, between 2002 and 2012, the fastest-growing group in the nation's workforce will be the one made up of people between ages 55 and 64, noted Kathleen Rapp, manager of AARP's State Workforce Program.

"There are skills shortages already among health professionals, teachers and public administrators," Rapp said. "The average age of an RN [registered nurse] is now 47. And there are upcoming shortages among scientists, engineers and manufacturing employees."

Employers are beginning to take more notice of—and more action about—the impending drain on talent and loss of knowledge, according to findings of a Society for Human Resource Management Weekly Online Survey of 483 HR professionals in March/April 2007, titled Future of the U.S. Labor Pool.

More HR professionals indicated that they were beginning to examine their internal policies and management practices in 2007 (45 percent) than in 2005 (39 percent). And, in 2007 more HR professionals (33 percent) responded that their organization had made some change in recruiting, retention and management policy or practice because of retiring baby boomers than in 2005 (26 percent).

Older employees want health care and retirement benefits, Rapp said. In addition, they want nonmonetary rewards such as flexible work arrangements, worker-friendly environments, the opportunity to learn something new and a good work/life balance.

Rapp acknowledged that health care premiums for workers ages 50 and over might be marginally more expensive. But, she said, workers in that age group have a lower rate of dependent coverage, are less likely to take sick time and show more motivation as they grow older.

Rapp detailed some best practices for recruiting and retaining workers ages 50 and over:

Recruitment. Atlanta-based Home Depot and the CVS drugstore chain, based in Woonsocket, R.I., offer programs to bring retirees back to the workforce. "Both have created a 50-plus employee brand," Rapp said. "CVS has 'Talent is Ageless,' and Home Depot's is 'Passion Never Retires.'"

Employers Preparing for Baby Boomer Retirements

Activity	2005	2007
Beginning to examine internal policies and management practices	39%	45%
Just becoming aware of the issue	38	36
Have proposed specific policy and management practice changes	7	9
Have implemented specific policies and management practices	11	8
Have agreed internally on a plan to change policies and management practices	5	3

Note: Percentages may not total 100 due to rounding.
Source: Society for Human Resource Management's Weekly Online Survey on the future of the U.S labor pool, March/April 2007.

Both companies feature pictures of older workers on their web sites and have made their hiring and screening practices age-neutral.

Flexibility. Some employers, such as Stanley Consultants of Muscatine, Iowa, have formal phased retirement programs that allow employees to move into retirement gradually by reducing their work schedules and permitting them to continue to receive a portion of their salaries as well as benefits such as health care and pension funds. Carondelet Health Network of Tucson, Ariz., has a seasonal worker program where older employees work under three-, six- or nine-month contracts. Borders, of Ann Arbor, Mich., and CVS have "snowbird" programs aimed at retirees who split their time between homes in different climates.

Benefits. Home Depot offers benefits and tuition reimbursement for anyone who works more than 10 hours a week. The company provides annual wellness visits to identify and prevent chronic health conditions.

Did You Know?

Hispanics in 2005 represented 14 percent of the nation's population—but 22% of workers. If things continue on their present course, Hispanics in 2050 will represent 32 percent of the nation's population, but 55 percent of workers.

Source: *HR and the New Hispanic Workforce* (SHRM and Davies-Black Publishing, 2007).

Work environment. Baptist Health of South Florida has raised the level of its hospital beds to ease back strain on employees caring for patients. Pinnacol Assurance of Denver has implemented an ergonomics program that has reduced its workers' compensation costs by 38 percent.

Training and growth. Hoffman LaRoche of Nutley, N.J., has established an on-site temporary agency that allows experienced employees to deploy their talents in different places in the organization. Acuity of Sheboygan, Wis., offers leadership training for senior-level employees.

Rapp recommended using the AARP Assessment Tool, available through the Employer Resource Center on AARP's web site. The tool has a series of questions to help test-takers diagnose their situations, and can help company officials analyze their business plans, understand their critical talent needs, and address the coming skills and labor shortages.

DIANE CADRAIN, a frequent contributor to *SHRM Online* and *HR Magazine,* is a West Hartford, Conn., Attorney who has been covering workplace legal issues for 20 years.

The Best 4 Ways to Recruit Employees with Disabilities

Yoji Cole

Kathy Martinez, who is blind, was shocked to be asked questions such as "How will you find the restroom?" and "What should we do about employees who wonder if they'll have to pick up your slack?" at the end of a job interview. She felt she had proved she was well suited for the job, but those questions told her that the interviewer only saw her disability. Fortunately, she had the opportunity to choose another company.

"Now I'm managing a $2.1-million company," says Martinez, executive director of the Oakland, Calif.–based World Institute on Disability (WID).

Her experience is not unique. People with disabilities face stigmas and stereotypes daily, especially when they enter the corporate world, which is why those who are able to hide their disabilities often choose to do so. And that, Martinez believes, is a tragedy for companies, employers and potential employees.

Fear of the unknown is the main reason so many in corporate America struggle to recruit and retain its employees with disabilities. "As a person with a disability, you have a different perspective because thinking outside the box happens for someone with a disability every day," says Alan Muir, executive director of the group Career Opportunities for Students with Disabilities (COSD). "People with learning disabilities figure out how to do things differently every day, and companies want people who think outside the box and who think creatively."

However, even among the most active companies that recruit for people with disabilities, networks are relatively new. General knowledge about where to find recruits with disabilities is just beginning.

To learn how to best recruit people with disabilities, DiversityInc interviewed companies from the DiversityInc Top 10 Companies for People With Disabilities list. The companies included Merrill Lynch (No. 1), SSM Healthcare (No. 3), Eastman Kodak (No. 5) and Citigroup (No. 7).

1. Partnerships

Merrill Lynch partners with the Eden Institute, which provides services for people with autism. The firm also partners with the Special Olympics and with groups for students with disabilities for recruiting purposes on college campuses.

SSM Healthcare has found success partnering with ParaQuad, an organization designed to highlight the capabilities of people who are paraplegic or quadriplegic.

Citigroup partners with the National Business & Disability Council and the American Association of People with Disabilities. The company works as a corporate sponsor for both organizations and participates at their events.

"We've partnered with the National Business & Disability Council to bring in students and professionals from the metro area [of New York]; we tap into them to recruit and to find mentors for people with disabilities and to educate our human-resources community," says Ana Duarte-McCarthy, chief diversity officer for Citigroup.

Meanwhile, Eastman Kodak has partnered as a sponsor and employer of choice for the past three years with the National Technical Institute for the Deaf, which is associated with the Rochester Institute of Technology.

"These efforts put you in touch with folks you wouldn't otherwise meet," says Duarte-McCarthy.

Relationships with organizations are built through networking, calling disability organizations to tell them the company is interested in recruiting people with disabilities.

"We're trying to normalize disabilities," says Chris Fossel, national leader for Merrill Lynch's Disability Awareness Professional Network, adding, "Through work-ing with the Special Olympics and having volunteers go there, it's helped employees understand disability."

> **"This is a community where you could be born with disabilities, you could become disabled, your spouse, partner or child could become disabled and everyone knows someone with a disability."**
>
> —Ana Duarte-McCarthy, Citigroup

Finding qualified recruits with disabilities is so important to Merrill Lynch that the firm is creating a list of core suppliers

Helping Companies Find Students with Disabilities

There are more than 2.6 million reasons why organizations such as Career Opportunities for Students with Disabilities (COSD) and Entry Point! are necessary.

Recent census data shows that there are 2.6 million people with disabilities between the ages of 5 and 15. Organizations such as COSD and Entry Point! are working to make sure that by the time these children enter college and then the work force, corporations will be ready for them and—more importantly—know how to find them.

While 78 percent of The 2006 DiversityInc Top 50 Companies for Diversity® have active programs to recruit people with disabilities, most Fortune 500 companies don't—and even those that do report difficulty finding "qualified" candidates. This is because they don't know where to look and they don't actively start a pipeline for future employees.

"We know students with disabilities are an untapped talent pool . . . Businesses have to understand that being disabled does not mean your intelligence is disabled," says Virginia Stern, the director of the American Association for the Advancement of Science's (AAAS) Entry Point! internship program.

Students with disabilities often learn about organizations and programs such as Entry Point! and COSD through career-services offices or disability student centers, according to Laureen Summers, an Entry Point! program associate.

Entry Point!, which started in 1996, matches students with disabilities who have demonstrated high motivation and achievement in STEM (science, technology, engineering and mathematics) fields in internships in research and development throughout the United States. Students are paired up with mentors who provide guidance for future undergraduate coursework, plans for graduate study, and often potential employment opportunities.

"The reason employers may say they do not know where to find them is because of the law (the ADA). Students with disabilities are attending just about every higher-education institution in United States," says Stern. "Employers can't go to one place as they could by going to an HBCU or a predominantly Latino campus and just find 1,000 students with disabilities who meet their skills or needs. Our focus is on the skill needs of the employers. We don't generalize about hiring people with disabilities just because they are disabled. This is not a social program. This is a program to find talent among graduate and undergraduate students who have skills."

Entry Point! places students in internships with organizations such as Merck & Co. (No. 34 on The 2006 DiversityInc Top 50 Companies for Diversity® list, and No. 4 in the Top 10 Companies for People With Disabilities), IBM, Google, the National Aeronautic and Space Administration and the National Oceanic and Atmospheric Administration. To be eligible for the 10-week program, students first have to apply and submit their transcripts and two letters of recommendation from professors. Students considered also must have a 3.0 average or better.

"Our goal is to bring the best and brightest and we recognize that there are multiple sources to find them. Entry Point! is definitely one of those resources," says Regina Flynn, the director of university relations at Merck, which has had partnerships with Entry Point! and COSD for several years.

"It took a bit, but I would do this again in a heartbeat," says Chad Cheetham, a recent graduate of the University of California at Riverside who wrapped up his first internship through Entry Point! at Merck's Rahway, N.J., research laboratory in the department of metabolic disorders of obesity. Cheetham, who is partially blind, will be attending the University of Alabama at Birmingham for his graduate studies.

"The way [Entry Point! selects] students, you know they are already the best. You know you are not getting a student because of a disability, you know you are getting talent that could have been overlooked elsewhere," says Cheetham. "I highly recommend any student out there to do what I did. It has been the best experience."

"Every year we get approximately 600 inquiries and end up with about 120 to 150 students in the pool of possible applicants," says Summers, who adds that approximately 25 percent of students selected return the following year. "We have made [approximately] 500 placements [to the work force] over our 11-year existence, and we know that 74 are currently pursuing graduate degrees, 18 of which are pursuing or have achieved Ph.D.'s. Students begin with internships, but there is a lot more to it."

COSD was started in 2000 by Alan Muir, executive director, and Robert Greenberg, the former director of career services (he has since retired), because the two realized that students with disabilities were simply not receiving necessary career-planning services and job-placement assistance. There was a gap in communication between the disability-services and career-services offices, limiting exposure for people with disabilities to recruiters visiting their campuses. COSD educates career counselors in colleges and universities around the United States on the various internships, fellowships and career-training programs available for students with disabilities. It also makes companies and their recruiters aware of this talent pool. "Before COSD, career services and recruiters did not focus on this student population," Muir says.

"Our students are really outstanding, and that's what the companies want. It's about the skills, and if you have the skills, the disability is minor," says Stern.

—Brenda Velez

who help candidates find jobs. "Centralizing this list and leveraging it to increase our ability to source talent will be a key focus for the remainder of 2006 and 2007," says Fossel.

2. Human-Resources Training

Sensitizing employees to the capabilities of people with disabilities and the issues they face is critical.

SSM Healthcare's Mission Awareness Team educated employees who do not have disabilities to the lives of employees with disabilities by putting them in situations that made them feel disabled for a period of time. The Mission Awareness Team put SSM Healthcare employees in wheelchairs, plugged their ears with wax and covered their eyes for up to two hours. Following the exercise, employees talked about their frustration and ways they had to think outside the box to accomplish tasks.

Training at Citigroup occurs on a local basis: "In the businesses, we do offer training, some in class, some online, and some training that occurs at the point of hire," says Duarte-McCarthy. "Citigroup is focusing on integrating disability awareness in its leadership training.

"We've always talked about the idea that anyone can be a member of this community at any time," says Duarte-McCarthy. "This is a community where you could be born with disabilities, you could become disabled, your spouse, partner or child could become disabled, and everyone knows someone with a disability."

Cingular features a disability task-force team that focuses on policies, practices, training and accommodating the needs of employees with disabilities, says Bob Reed, vice president of diversity for Cingular.

"All of our diversity training incorporates creating an inclusive work environment, which includes people with disabilities," says Reed. "We train all hiring managers in Targeted Selection, which covers EEO/AAP—appropriate questions in this area, and others."

3. Use Employee-Resource Groups

"If people [with disabilities] get a sense they're welcomed in a company, they will apply," says Martinez.

An employee group for employees with disabilities can help a company provide amenities to make recruits with disabilities feel welcome. Kodak's chief technology officer, Bill Lloyd, is the champion of its employee group for employees with disabilities. The group—along with Lloyd—meets with CEO and Chairman Antonio Perez at least once a year to update him on the various issues they face in the workplace.

At Cingular, the employee-resource group, ENABLE, helps the company keep its pulse on the community, says Reed.

"ENABLE helped us ensure the on-boarding experience and work environment are welcoming," says Reed. ENABLE made Cingular aware that providing accessibility for employees with disabilities, such as computers screens for people who have vision impairments, attracts recruits.

At Merrill Lynch, during a discussion with his network's sponsor, Fossel recently asked what he would do in the following scenario: If two applicants, both suitable for the position, came across his desk and one of the applicants happened to be a college student with a disability while the other was not, who would he choose for the position?

"He said the one with the disability because that showed they could go through issues and deal with their disability—that shows creativity, persistence," says Fossel, whose Disability Awareness Professional Network at Merrill Lynch works with the Princeton University Development Institute for People with Autism, talking to students with disabilities about the career opportunities offered at Merrill Lynch.

4. Use Government Organizations/Job Boards

The Department of Labor's Vocational Rehabilitation and Employment Service group is geared toward helping veterans with disabilities. It is used by SSM Healthcare and Cingular.

"We publish our job openings at local military-transition offices," says Yvonne Tisdel, corporate vice president of human resources and system diversity at SSM Healthcare. Tisdel suffered a back injury while in the military.

"It is likely that people coming out of the military have a technical background," she adds.

Reed serves on the Department of Labor's Corporate Executive Advisory Council's Circle of Champions and also serves on the board of the Georgia Council for Employing People with Disabilities. Cingular, on a state-by-state basis, also taps into the databases of Employment Security Career Centers and State Workforce Commissions and the Department of Blind Services.

Companies utilize diversity-related Internet job boards, such as DiversityInc.com, where they know their job posting will be seen not only by people of color, women and GLBTs but also by people with disabilities. Besides DiversityInc.com, Diversity-Workings.com and Project EARN's online job board are used by companies on the Top 10.

"Folks with disabilities like to integrate into the work force," says Muir. "To call themselves out as different and say they need this and this, unless they have a strong advocacy sense, that could be difficult . . . It all comes down to the supervising managers and how enlightened they may be."

Making Reasonable Accommodations for Employees with Mental Illness under the ADA

Jonathan Hafen

Title I of the Americans with Disabilities Act (ADA) is an elaborate set of regulations designed to provide protection for "qualified" employees in the workplace. Although the ADA restricts qualifying a disability to "a physical or mental impairment that substantially limits one or more of the major life activities of such individual," its reference to "neurological systems, mental or psychological disorders," has paved the way for employees to bring lawsuits against employers in an attempt to prove various mental conditions should be eligible for accommodations under the Act.

Moreover, as the stigma of mental illness diminishes in this society, employees may find less reason to conceal such illnesses on the job. In fact, some may try to exploit coverage under the ADA as a way to change their jobs or work environments into something more preferable for themselves.

Fortunately for employers, various jurisdictions as well as the Supreme Court have acted to narrow the scope of impairment and limit the protection Title I provides employees with disabilities. Even with this guidance, understanding ADA coverage for mental illness as well as compliance obligations for accommodations can pose challenges for employers.

Does the Employee's Mental Disorder Warrant ADA Protection?

Broadly speaking, the ADA only protects employees who have severe mental disabilities meeting ADA standards yet who are nevertheless able to perform the essential functions of the jobs they hold or for which they could be considered. The first issue, therefore, is to determine whether the employee actually has a qualifying mental illness. While this may seem an obvious place to start, most ADA litigation focuses on whether an impairment "substantially limits . . . a major life activity," not whether an individual actually has an impairment.

In case after case, plaintiff employees have tried to benefit from the ADA by claiming behavioral difficulties such as not getting along with co-workers or supervisors, poor concentration, being depressed, and poor judgment are conditions that deserve

ADA protection. The good news for vigilant employers is that the courts have been fairly clear on distinguishing between qualifying mental illness and non-qualifying employee personality or behavior problems. For example, in one case, an employee claimed to have a qualifying mental illness which made it hard to get along with co-workers. The court rejected the claim, ruling that "paranoid, disgruntled, oppositional, difficult to interact with, unusual, suspicious, threatening, and distrustful" were behavioral characteristics, not qualifying mental impairments. Many other court rulings also have supported the premise the ADA was never intended to categorize people with common personality traits as disabled.

Assuming a mental illness exists, employees have two more hurdles to overcome before establishing a right to a "reasonable accommodation." Employees must demonstrate that the mental illness causes a substantial limitation to a major life activity and, despite this disability, can perform functions essential to their job.

As discussed below, employers should require proof of a qualifying mental illness and an ability to perform essential job functions before making a commitment to provide workplace accommodations.

Does the employee actually have a qualifying mental illness? Employers often do not spend enough time determining whether an employee requesting accommodation has a qualifying disability. In general, short-term conditions are not covered by the ADA, while permanent or long-term impairments may be eligible. Confusion still exists within the courts regarding the cross-over point from short to long-term and, unfortunately, there is no definite answer.

Some courts have concluded that disorders such as ADHD and depression are not qualifying disabilities, if the conditions can be effectively treated with medication. On the other hand, depression with an indefinite duration could be considered a disability. Episodic disorders also may be covered by the ADA, provided employees can prove the underlying reasons for the episodes are long-term conditions and are not rare occurrences.

When possible, it is advisable to have the employee obtain and provide a medical diagnosis from a qualified professional, though this is not always supported by the courts. In some cases, the courts have stated that a medical diagnosis is not always needed to support an individual's claim of impairment.

Is there a "substantial limitation" to a "major life activity?" A majority of litigation centers on whether an alleged disability substantially limits an employee's ability to perform a job and whether the limitation impacts a major life activity. This area continues to be controversial as there is a fair amount of disagreement over what constitutes a major life activity and, furthermore, whether there need be a strong connection between the limitation, life activity and the workplace. There have been cases where courts have maintained an employee is eligible for ADA protection even though the major life activity did not impact the employee's ability to perform in the workplace. For the most part, though, courts have employed common sense when it comes to ADA eligibility and the impact a disability has in the workplace.

The US Supreme Court defined "substantially limits" as "considerable" or "to a large extent" and a major life activity as something of central importance to daily life. Under this definition an employee seeking ADA protection must have a disability preventing or severely restricting the individual from doing activities of central importance to most people's lives. The EEOC's description of this analysis suggest that an individual must be unable to perform a major life activity the average person in the general population can perform and is significantly restricted compared with the manner or duration the average person could perform the activity. In one Third Circuit court case, the court found that an employee's ADHD did not substantially limit her ability to think, learn, remember, or concentrate and that "many people who are not suffering from ADHD/ADD must regularly cope with" such limitations.

As for major life activities, the EEOC lists caring for oneself, performing manual tasks, walking, seeing, hearing, speaking, breathing, learning, and working. Due to the broad nature of the activities described by the EEOC, many cases have tried to create more precise direction on what constitutes a disability. For instance, bipolar disorder is a disability, but the resulting inability to sit and think is not a major life activity. Often the criteria which employees use to establish that an impairment impacts a major life activity miss the mark and are dismissed by the courts.

On the topic of whether the major life activity must have a connection to the workplace, most courts have agreed it does not, sometimes making the direct impact of the disability on the job an irrelevant issue.

Is the employee "qualified?" The ADA defines the term "qualified" as having the requisite education, skills, experience, licenses, or certifications for the job and the ability to perform the essential functions of the job, with or without reasonable accommodation. Therefore, employees claiming mental disorders must nevertheless be able to perform the essential functions of the job with or without an accommodation.

Courts have made it clear the burden of proof as to whether an employee is qualified for a job rests with the individual. According to a case in the Sixth Circuit court, the employee must also prove how they remain qualified with a reasonable accommodation. The employer's burden is to prove which aspects of an employee's job are essential functions.

It stands to reason that an employee without the appropriate background may not qualify for a particular job. If an employee is not qualified for the job due solely to a disability, however, the employer may find itself in a position to defend the requirements, standards or prerequisites of a job. Licenses or certifications necessary to perform a job allow straightforward explanations. Other job requirements may not be as easy to support, but the consistency and uniformity with which an employer enforces the essential job requirements among like kinds of employees strengthens the legitimate need for the functions.

What are the essential functions of the job? Not only must an employer be prepared to address what the essential functions of a job are, they must also address why the functions are essential. When essential function is the issue, courts often have relied on an employer's judgment of what is necessary to perform a particular job and written job descriptions prepared in advance of advertising for or interviewing candidates. While an employer's judgment is never conclusive, it does carry a lot of weight with the court provided there is consistent application of the requirement among similar employees. Carefully crafted job descriptions detailing essential job functions can provide compelling evidence against ADA claims where specific aspects of the job are in dispute. As a word of caution, incomplete or inaccurate job descriptions can work against employers just as effectively.

It is advisable to include all functions deemed essential to the effective execution of a job in a written description prior to the interview process. It is also critical to understand the difference between whether a specific task is an essential function or whether it is a way of performing the function. The EEOC states a task becomes essential when the position exists to perform the function. Additionally, justification for a function can include the degree of specialization required, the amount of time devoted to the task, terms of a collective bargaining agreement, the consequences of not performing the function, as well as the experience of those who have performed or are currently performing the same job. All of these factors should be considered when drafting job descriptions.

A Cautionary Note: The "Regarded as Disabled" Employee. Any employee who has been "regarded as" having a mental (or physical) disability, whether it impacts a major life activity or not, is covered under the ADA. In situations where employers base their actions on perceptions of an employee's condition rather than fact, the employer may open itself to a discrimination case under the ADA. Regarding an employee as disabled can come in many forms such as a notation in an employee file, passing the employee up for a job because of the perceived limitation, moving an employee to a new position based on the disability perception, or restricting job responsibilities. On the flip side, the courts have generally agreed with the EEOC in stating that employers that make requested changes to a job to help an employee with a medical condition have not necessarily regarded the employee as disabled. In an ADHD case, the court concluded an employer did not regard the employee as disabled simply because modifications such as installing a partition and allowing a radio to block noises were made.

The ADA does not try to discourage employers from assisting employees, but doing so may set precedents and inadvertently open the door to litigation should "regarded as" employees decide they have a case for a "better" accommodation under the regulations. Fortunately, courts seem to fairly consider these types of cases and are often reluctant to punish the employer for showing goodwill towards employees.

Process for Investigating "Reasonable" Accommodation

Once it is determined an employee is qualified for the job and has a qualifying disability that substantially limits a major life activity, employers are obligated to make reasonable accommodations so the employee can continue to experience the same workplace opportunities that those without disabilities would automatically enjoy.

The basic steps recommended for investigating accommodations include:

1. *Requiring written requests for accommodations.* Employers are under no obligation to provide accommodations for employees if they are unaware a disability exists. In cases involving mental disorders, courts have ruled that an employee cannot remain silent about limitations caused by a disability and expect the employer to bear the burden of identifying the need and finding appropriate accommodations. Employers may have a policy requiring employees to submit written requests which include a description of the disability, the major life activity being substantially limited, and suggestions for accommodations. The courts have been favorable to employers when requests were ambiguous and did not adequately describe the accommodation being sought.

   Employers cannot, however, require employees to use specific or magic language when requesting an accommodation. The requests should be reviewed with a fair and open mind, provided the fundamental criteria for accommodation are met. Further, if an employer is aware of both the qualifying disability and need for accommodation, it may be obligated to begin an investigation into finding a suitable solution even if an employee request was not made.

2. *Engaging in an interactive process.* When a request has been made or a need discovered, the employer should engage in a productive interaction with the employee regarding accommodation possibilities. On appeal, some courts have suggested that an interactive process may be mandatory. During this part of the process, the employer should analyze which job functions are essential. The interaction should always be conducted in good faith and involve direct contact with the employee to identify the nature of the limitations, the barriers to successfully performing the essential job tasks and discussion about potential accommodations.

Courts have held that employees must participate in the interactive process or risk having their claims denied. They must be willing to discuss and try accommodations suggested by the employer as well as provide requested documentation on the disability and the nature and extent of the limitation. Courts generally agree with the EEOC's position allowing employers to ask for documentation, particularly for non-obvious disabilities. Additionally, the employer may require cooperation from the employee in future investigations regarding the ongoing need for the accommodation.

3. *Offering an accommodation.* An employer's obligation is to find an effective accommodation for the employee-one that allows the employee to successfully complete essential job functions without causing an undue hardship to the employer. Selecting an appropriate accommodation is the employer's choice and no pressure need be felt in accepting the employee's preference for modification.

   Should an employee refuse the offered, effective accommodation, the employer has no further obligation under the ADA. It has met its obligation to offer reasonable accommodation. The employee is free to dispute the nature of the accommodation, particularly if the accommodation could be considered ineffective. If there is a dispute over the offered accommodation, the employer must be able to explain and support its effectiveness.

4. *Telling other employees.* Employers hands are often tied in discussing why one employee receives seemingly preferential treatment. Revealing why an employee has been given an accommodation can violate federal laws restricting the disclosure of medical information. Nonetheless, the employer is sometimes put in a position of needing to provide an explanation. To avoid violating ADA and HIPAA laws, it is advisable to work with legal counsel to draft a statement indicating the accommodation was made to comply with federal law, but other federal laws prohibit additional disclosure. For supervisors, especially if the employee is being reassigned, disclosure should inform the supervisor that the employee has a disability and the ADA requires the reassignment, assuming the employee is qualified.

Considerations for Reasonable Accommodation

An accommodation is reasonable if the costs and benefits of providing it are properly weighted. Employers are not required to make accommodations which create an undue hardship, but proving a hardship in court can be difficult. Accommodations can include physical barriers, procedures, or rules. Employers cannot, however, demand employees take medication as an accommodation. Medication and other treatments are deemed personal choices. Should an employee wish to take medication or get treatment, a reasonable accommodation could be made allowing the individual time to do so.

Other reasonable accommodations can include, but are not limited to:

- A leave of absence;
- A job reassignment;
- A shift change;
- Job restructuring;
- A modified work schedule;
- Working at home;
- Modifying equipment or the work environment; and
- Changing or modifying policies, procedures or standards.

If an employee cannot fulfill the essential tasks of a job even with an accommodation, they are not qualified for the job. The employer can seek other alternatives, but is not obligated to create a new position, reallocate essential functions, promote the employee, put the employee in a job for which they are not qualified or reassign another employee to create a vacancy.

A frequently asked question is whether the employer must continue to pay the original salary and benefits if the job changes or the employee is reassigned. There is broad agreement that the employer need only pay salary and benefits commensurate with the new duties.

The complexity of the ADA and nuances from state to state make it advisable to seek legal counsel when developing and implementing policies for handling ADA claims as well as when investigating requests for accommodations by employees.

JONATHAN HAFEN, a shareholder with Parr Waddoups Brown Gee & Loveless in Salt Lake City, has extensive experience in federal and state courts with employment law issues and has published and lectured widely on a variety of topics including legal ethics, litigation strategy, and employment. He can be reached at joh@pwlaw.com.

The Wonder of Work

A grumbling and disenchanted workforce can learn a lot about gratitude from those who treasure any job they can get—individuals with mental retardation and other severe developmental disabilities.

TERI S. ARNOLD

Is your place of business driving you crazy? Do your co-workers get on your nerves? There is no question that being on the job can test your patience by lifting you up, tearing you down, or sometimes completely ignoring your contributions. It can be a place of passion and drive or a place of frustrated and burnt out clock-watchers. Yet, there are many, many people with mental retardation and other severe disabilities who have a refreshingly honest point of view about work and how attitudes on the job can greatly affect happiness and job satisfaction. We all can learn a lot from how they choose to see the world.

Be grateful that you have a job to go to every morning. Some 20,300,000 people with severe developmental disabilities are unemployed in this country, and consequently often suffer mentally and physically, while digressing developmentally. Those who have a job, however, come into work with big smiles on their faces. They want to come to work on the weekends, holidays, and even during inclement weather because they know how it dramatically affects theft lives for the better. Regardless of who you are, having a job and a purpose in life is essential to self-esteem, independence, and overall well-being. It might be difficult to drag yourself out of bed on Monday morning, but without a job to go to, your quality of life would suffer immensely.

Each and every job—no matter how small it may appear—is important. Whether you have difficulty communicating, moving, hearing, seeing, or comprehending, every job for a person with a severe disability is important. To someone without a disability, putting a cable into a bag can seem monotonous and boring. It may appear to be just a very minute part of a larger contractual obligation with an outside company but, to the individuals performing the task, it is their one chance to be like everyone else. When they are on the job, they are not people with mental retardation; they are coworkers and an essential part of a team with goals and objectives. Status and titles have no meaning here because everyone is a vital cog in the company's success.

Greet your coworkers with a kind word or smile when you pass them in the hallway or when they enter your workspace. In a world that increasingly is cut off from people and emotions, simple gestures that display kindness and openness are harder and harder to find. Walking onto the work floor is an instant mood-lifter. Everyone who visits is welcomed with open arms and greeted in a positive manner, regardless of who they are or how much money they make. Everybody wants to know how your day is going, shake your hand, and tell you how excited they are to be on the job. Think of how differently your day would go if you treated your coworkers in that manner.

Look for ways to encourage your coworkers to perform better and everyone will reap the rewards. It is not uncommon to see people on the work floor assisting others with their daily tasks or giving an encouraging word. No one is viewed as competition or as somebody to fear, but rather as individuals who all are in the same boat, trying to make the best of some very challenging situations. When someone accomplishes a personal or professional goal, his or her achievements are championed by all. There is a deeper understanding that, when one person wins, everyone wins.

Take breaks and have fun, even if for just a few minutes. Understand the value of balance in your life. Due to physical, mental, and emotional limitations, breaks throughout the day are mandatory for our clients. Because of the unique circumstances, becoming stressed and overwhelmed not only affects one person, but quickly can permeate the entire workforce and wreak havoc for everyone concerned. Knowing when to stop, to give your mind and body a respite, is essential to maintaining a happy and healthy work environment for people with and without disabilities.

Take pride in what you do, regardless of the pay or recognition. We all want to be known for being the best at what we do. It is human nature to crave recognition and monetary compensation for hard work and dedication. Many of the jobs here are assembly-line, labor intensive, or entry level positions that most people would dread. However, every single person is proud of the work he or she does and is eager to tell everyone they know about it. The work is not glamorous, or that creative or dynamic—and it probably never will be seen as something deserving of high wages or praise. Yet, it serves a very important function in our society. These are jobs that give incredible meaning and value to countless lives.

Life is too short to gossip, back-stab, or criticize. People who have the most compelling reasons to complain about difficult life circumstances choose not to. Life is challenging for everyone. We all deal with the daily frustrations of having to work with people who are not like us. Some individuals communicate differently; some are slower or faster than us; and some do not share our enthusiasm, but we all are required to work together. Conflicts arise on the work floor, but they never last long or become spiteful, catty, or mean. Being focused and grateful on the job leaves little time or energy for negative interactions with coworkers. Positive attitudes give way to positive interactions.

Focus on what you have, instead of what you do not. It is easy to get caught up in keeping up with the Jones'. In a society where it is all about the nicest car, clothes, and house, we miss out on enjoying what we have in the constant search for something bigger and better. Many of the clients with mental retardation, autism, and other severe disabilities have very little in life. Almost all cannot drive, do not own a home, and wear the same clothes year after year. However, that does not change how happy and fulfilled they are. The one thing they want is to feel normal in the here and now. Working gives them that—and as long as they are provided the opportunity, they feel like millionaires.

Enjoy the little things in life. Some of the clients get paid two dollars every two weeks but, to them, it is like getting $2,000. It is not about the monetary value of the check, but the paycheck alone that gives them pride in themselves and what they do. While most people take it for granted, for them, going to the mall and buying something with their own hard-earned money is an indescribable joy. The next time you buy something for yourself, remember how hard you worked to get it. It will make your purchase even more rewarding.

Get excited about going to work. Even if it is raining outside or you are stuck in traffic or are running late, you were hired because of your unique abilities and talents. You specifically were chosen because someone was impressed by what only you can bring to the table. Someone had faith in you and believed in you. Celebrate and enjoy that fact. So many people with severe developmental disabilities never even are considered for employment. All too often they are perceived as not being useful to society, much less on the job. Imagine how it would feel knowing you have a lot to contribute to the world, but no one will give you a chance. As a result, you spend your entire life hoping that someone will come along who will see you for who you really are and give you that opportunity to shine.

People with mental retardation and other severe disabilities are elated to be at work. They often are the first to arrive and most days dread having to leave. Their work ethic is something beyond compare because they know how it feels to be isolated and segregated away from normal life. They appreciate the opportunities they are given and show their gratitude by excelling on the job.

Our motto is: "It's not about the work they produce, but what the work produces in them." That is true for all people in all work environments. In many ways, your work defines who you are and brings to the surface your core values and character. It can make your life enjoyable or completely miserable. It is all in how you choose look at it and how you choose to let it affect you. Take some time to see life from someone else's perspective and learn the important lessons that they are trying to teach you. It often is in the most unexpected places where we find the greatest gifts.

TERI S. ARNOLD is director of public relations, Chesapeake (Va.) Service Systems, a nonprofit organization that provides meaningful work opportunities to people with mental retardation and other severe disabilities.

The Disability Advantage

Even as the number of workers with disabilities grows because of factors like the Iraq war, fewer of them are finding jobs. Here's one employer that bucks the trend.

ALISON STEIN WELLNER

On a recent morning, Connie Presnell pulled into the parking lot of Habitat International, a carpet, turf, and contract manufacturing company in Chattanooga. She drove past towering lawn ornaments (one's a metal giraffe), and then parked near the building, where she manages the factory floor. As the company's 30 employees punched in, Presnell received word that Habitat had to ship 13,000 boxes to a Tropicana cannery overnight. She assigned a dozen of her fastest workers to the task and, as the sound system cranked up rock music, they got down to work. As usual, the order was delivered on time.

What makes this story remarkable is that Presnell's A-team was made up entirely of people with cerebral palsy, Down syndrome, schizophrenia, and other disabilities. At Habitat, in fact, nearly every employee (including some managers) has a physical or mental disability or both. And yet, Habitat excels by many measures. Its quality-control statistics are especially enviable. During peak season, from January to June, the factory turns out up to 15,000 rugs a day, five or six days a week. Yet the plant's defect rate is less than one-half of 1%. Only about 10 rugs have been cut incorrectly in the company's history. "We've never had a back order" boasts David Morris, Habitat's owner and CEO. "If we fall behind one day, we'll all work hard to catch up."

Morris credits his workers—who are paid regionally competitive wages for factory work—with the company's impressive financial performance. Profits have risen every year for the past decade, against a steady $14 million in sales. And to think, Morris says, shaking his head, that at first, giving these workers a chance "had to be forced down my throat."

More Disabled, but Fewer Are Employed

It's been 15 years since the first President Bush signed into law the Americans With Disabilities Act, which prohibits discrimination against people with disabilities in all parts of society, including the workplace. Nearly 50 million Americans—a segment of the population larger than the number of either Hispanics or African Americans—are covered by the ADA.

But while the ADA improved the treatment of people with disabilities in many tangible ways—think curb cuts and wheelchair ramps—its legacy with respect to employment has been mixed. In fact, since the ADA went into effect, employment among people with disabilities has declined. Between 1990 and 2004, employment rates dropped by 30% for people with disabilities, according to

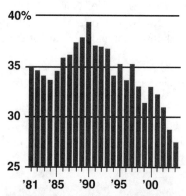

DECLINING JOB PROSPECTS. Employment among people with disabilities peaked in 1990.

Source: Andrew J. Houtenville/Cornell.

Hiring Employees with Disabilities

Three in four firms have no ADA workers. Rookie employers should:

1. Temper Their Enthusiasm

Go slow at first. "Don't hire 20 people with disabilities if you've never been around someone with a disability," says Nancy Henderson Wurst, author of *Able!,* a new book about Habitat International.

2. Find Expertise

Make sure at least one manager really understands how to work with people with disabilities. A person who has had a family member with a disability is probably a good candidate, says Wurst.

3. Do Adequate Screening

Interview prospective workers' caregivers because their commitment is crucial. "The biggest failures are with the family or the caregivers, not the employees," says David Morris, Habitat's CEO.

4. Team up with a School

Habitat has an internship program with the special ed department of a nearby school. The school is only too happy to share information and help with training.

research conducted by Andrew J. Houtenville, a researcher at Cornell University (see chart). "And this in a time frame when employment rates for other people increased" notes Pamela Loprest, of the Urban Institute.

Economists and policy experts argue over why this is so. Some think specific language in the ADA scares employers, others contend that Social Security's disability insurance program compels people not to work. Whatever the cause, one thing is clear: People with disabilities constitute a growing share of the available work force—their ranks swelling because of medical advancements, the aging population, and importantly, the war in Iraq. More than 15,000 troops are likely to be wounded this year, and the rate of amputation, in part because of the prevalence of roadside bombings, is twice that of any previous war. Meanwhile, Social Security and Medicaid are in the midst of reforms aimed at encouraging employment among people with disabilities, says Houtenville. One proposal would move people into training programs more quickly following an injury. Another would allow people to keep federally funded benefits while they get back on the job, he says. But who will hire these workers?

Managers' Concerns, Real and Imagined

Managers who employ people with disabilities often say that many of the perceived concerns are exaggerated. Hidden costs are rare, for example. Researchers at Rutgers University found that 73% of companies employing people with disabilities spent nothing on accommodations, while those that did spent $500 on average. What's more, federal and state tax credits are available to defray the costs. Fears that disabled workers are injury-prone also seem to be overblown.

Still, managing workers with disabilities does require sensitivity and stamina. At Habitat, workers have had seizures on the factory floor. Every couple of weeks, an employee loses bowel or bladder control. To cope, Morris installed showers in the factory. Employees clock out, clean up, and change into a fresh set of clothes that they keep on hand. Then there are workers who have chronic behavioral issues. "I have one employee who has temper tantrums a couple of times a week" says Presnell. "He hits himself, and jumps up and down and screams."

The outbursts can happen without warning, although they are sometimes triggered when Presnell assigns a new task to the worker, who has autism and doesn't always adapt well to change. At first, Presnell was frightened by these episodes. Now she calmly tells the employee to punch out, then sends him to the break room for 15 minutes. "This is a very bad punishment for him" she says, "because he knows he's not making money."

Forfeiting a Million-Dollar Account

Some employers rely on a middleman—either a sponsoring public agency or a nonprofit group—to take responsibility for their workers. Though many companies stand by this model, Habitat's Morris thinks it's bad to have a buffer. Early on, he worked with a nonprofit whose mission was to offer "clients" as many work experiences as possible. As a result, the nonprofit rotated workers from company to company, which meant a good staffer might disappear the day before a shipment deadline. When Habitat couldn't persuade the agency to change this policy, Morris ended the relationship.

Today Habitat eschews sponsors and applies for no government funds because these programs sometimes cap workers' salaries, which drives Morris crazy. "I hate red tape," he says.

He also hates an inescapable fact of human nature, which is that some people treat people with disabilities poorly. Nine years ago, Morris worked with a group of independent sales representatives to gain distribution to a large West Coast chain. On a visit to Chattanooga, two of the reps made derogatory comments about Habitat's workers.

Though none of his employees heard the comments, Morris was furious. But he couldn't ignore the $1 million the account was worth. The head of the rep firm called to apologize, and that settled matters, but only for a while. Subsequently, some of the reps said still more hurtful things, and so Morris dropped the firm. It took Habitat two years to get revenue back to where it had been before, but it's a tradeoff he's happy that he made.

Just as some people display prejudice, he says, others give Habitat their business specifically because of the company's work force. And while he faces challenges that other business owners do not, Morris prefers them to the challenges he'd face if he ran a typical factory. He doesn't have to worry about turnover or absenteeism. During the winter, his employees often try to sleep at the plant so they can be sure to get in the next day if it snows. "A lot of companies have token ADA employees," Morris says; the difference at Habitat, he explains, is that "we're run by them."

ALISON STEIN WELLNER can be reached at Alison@wellner.biz.

Implementing Sexual Harassment Training in the Workplace

Dave Gottwals

As sexual harassment becomes more prevalent in the workplace, states are incorporating requirements in addition to the federal harassment laws that protect businesses and employees. These laws are established to prevent potential lawsuits and to teach companies to be proactive by training their employees about how to avoid sexual harassment. The laws may seem burdensome, but businesses will benefit in the long run from the requirements.

Sexual harassment training is more than a good idea in California, it is now the law. Along with only four other states (Connecticut, New Jersey, Massachusetts, and Maine) that have their own sexual harassment laws, California joined the list with its recently passed AB 1825.

California was not the first state to add a requirement to the federal law. In fact, California's law is modeled after Connecticut's existing statute. The new requirement calls for companies to implement sexual harassment training for all supervisory employees.

Converting to any new corporate process can be a consuming and costly matter. The burden of initiating a new training program along with the proper documentation practices can place a strain particularly on a company's human resource department.

National Harassment Requirements

Title VII of the Civil Rights Act of 1964, which outlaws discrimination in the workplace based on protected classes, is overseen by the Equal Employment Opportunity Commission. Harassment training is highly recommended, but there are no specific requirements for it. Companies are not obligated by federal law to provide sexual harassment training. However, it is strongly recommended and considered to be an excellent idea. Besides encouraging employees to treat each other with respect and professionalism in hopes of creating a positive and productive work environment, harassment training can reduce your company's liability, should a suit be brought at the state and federal levels.

California's AB 1825 Requirements

The requirements and definitions of AB 1825 are more comprehensive than most people realize. Effective January 1, 2006, all supervisory employees will be required to receive at least two hours of harassment training every two years. In addition, all supervisory employees who have been employed as of July 1, 2005, must have completed their two hours of training by the end of December 2005.

Supervisory employees that are hired or promoted after July 1, 2005, must complete their initial two hours of sexual harassment training within the first six months of their hire or promotion date. This basic requirement triggers several follow up questions with respect to who needs to comply, how do you count employees, how is a supervisor defined, and what is included in the training?

Companies Required to Comply

AB 1825 directly affects all businesses that have 50 or more employees regardless of where the 50 employees are located. All 50 do not have to be located in California. For example, a company with 100 employees, with 80 employees outside of California and 20 employees in California, must comply. Furthermore, whether the supervisory employee for the 20 California employees is located in California or not, that supervisory employee must be trained in compliance with AB 1825.

Counting 50 Employees

AB 1825 requires anyone that is "regularly employed" or "regularly providing services" to count toward the 50 employees. Therefore, employers must count temp-agency staff, independent contractors, and consultants, along with their regular employees. It does not matter if workers are part time or full time, they all count.

Defining Supervisory Employees

This is another part of AB 1825 that can be overlooked accidentally. Though AB 1825 does not have a specific definition of supervisory employee, the Fair Employee and Housing Act (FEHA) does. And since AB 1825 is a new section of FEHA, it is considered prudent to review supervisory employee in other parts of FEHA.

Besides the usual and obvious language of "any individual having the authority to . . . hire, transfer, lay off, promote, . . .", it also includes "the ability to direct other employees," as a criteria for a supervisor as defined by the law.

Therefore, any employee having the ability to direct other employees may be considered a supervisory employee and must be trained in compliance with AB 1825. The employee does not need "supervisor" or "manager" in their title.

For example, in many instances in the high tech industry, engineering leads frequently are responsible for directing engineers on specific assignments within projects. Therefore, it would meets FEHA's definition of supervisory employee.

Although, it is mandatory for only supervisory employees to undergo harassment training, it is good practice to inform and train all employees on this issue. Harassment training is a form of risk management and it allows a company to manage and limit future liability.

Requirements of the Training Content

The training time of two hours is a minimum and it should not discourage a company from additional training time as needed. Although the words "Sexual Harassment" are frequently used for AB 1825, the law requires additional topics be covered in the training session for it to be considered compliant. The training must cover:

- State and federal level laws prohibiting all forms of harassment (not just sexual harassment);
- Discrimination and the protected classes;
- Prevention techniques;
- Correction of harassment;
- Remedies available to harassment victims; and
- Practical examples to help supervisory employees prevent harassment, discrimination, and retaliation.

Additionally, the employer is required to provide at least two hours of "classroom or other effective interactive training." This can be tricky. Usually "effective interactive training" means participants should be able to ask questions and get answers from trainer to trainee and from trainee to trainer.

If your company cannot feasibly provide classroom training to all its employees, compliance can be met with effective online training. Just understand the interactive requirement before setting up a training program.

Penalties and Liability

Although the penalty for noncompliance of AB 1825 itself is minimal (FEHA issues an order to provide the training), the liability for noncompliance in a harassment lawsuit can bring a company to its knees. This includes noncompliant training programs as well as those companies that have neglected to complete the harassment training within the training timelines.

Companies that are confronted by the court of law face heavy disciplinary action if they have not taken all "reasonable measures" to prevent harassment and have not kept good records (documentation). In these instances, the judge will view the company as having bad practices or being negligent about the issue. This obviously can contribute to a verdict against the company and awarding the plaintiff with punitive damages. Historically, courts tend not to be lenient since most of the jury's are comprised of employees, not employers.

HR and Harassment Training

Many companies throughout the United States are unaware or have little understanding of the sexual harassment laws in California. Of the employers who are aware of the requirements, many do not have the time and resources to examine AB 1825 in great detail.

We have found that many human resource departments are aware that the training is a good defense mechanism, yet they do not have a compliant sexual harassment training program in place. This is often because there is no person in the company who is equipped with the expertise needed to lead the training.

It is often helpful to bring in a third-party consultant, who is an expert in AB 1825, to deliver effective sexual harassment training. Also, bringing in a third-party consultant may be beneficial as they can discuss scenarios with your employees and deliver what can be an awkward message about what behaviors are acceptable for your company.

Companies that do not have an internal employee or lawyer that concentrates in employee benefits and human resource practices can refer to outside sources that specialize in consulting for human resource departments in its legal practices and risk management.

Additional Information Liberty Benefit Insurance Services Provides during a Training Session

Listed below are a sampling of items reviewed by your consultant that provides sexual harassment training that will enhance the required contents of harassment training.

A clear explanation of what the government mandates: supervisory employees are required to participate in harassment training and that is a necessary starting point for the training.

Sexual harassment training participants are handed a pretest upon the entry of the training session. The pretest encompasses basic harassment concerns in the workplace and assesses what employees know about sexual harassment prior to the training. Most employees are aware of the concerns; however, the pretest helps to show them some things they are not aware of. The test is reviewed at the end of the training session and corrected.

In the training, employees learn about two forms of sexual harassment—*quid pro quo,* when something is given or received for something else, and *hostile work environment,* unwelcome conduct of a sexual nature that inhibits the employee's ability to work.

Trainers inform the employees of harassment statistics, share multiple examples and discuss cases that have gone to court and their outcomes. One such case that proves that even large established companies can make mistakes is that of, Agilent Technologies, formerly of Hewlett Packard. It lost a court case in March of 2005, which cost the company $438,000 in punitive damages.

Participants will also learn which forms of sexual harassment are on the rise and which are most common in the workplace.

Trainers will then explain discrimination and the protected classes.

Participants will learn that harassment is not about the intent—it's about the perception by the individual who feels that they were harassed. Participants will be made aware of the "reasonable woman" test that the state of California applies to each case to determine if it was harassment or not.

Participants will learn about the need for a formal investigation process. Sexual harassment complaints must be taken seriously and handled with a rapid response. Action should be taken within 24 to 48 hours upon receiving the complaint. This action should include the company delegating trained personnel to initiate an investigation. An alternate person should be on standby to handle the investigation if the delegated employee is not available. Any delay in action may lead to a penalty.

Trainers also review techniques for conducting interviews while doing the investigations, as well as who should be interviewed. And after the investigation has been conducted, the company then needs to determine what its response will be.

Participants will learn that if by chance they have a claim that goes to court, the court will review the entire process a company implements. This includes the training process, as in which employees were trained and when, the harassment policy, the required posters, communications, the response time to a complaint, the investigation process, the interviews, the remedy, the follow-up after the remedy, and of course, all the supporting documentation.

Participants will learn that prevention techniques work to help a company avoid liability. Supervisory employees become knowledgeable about company policy in a training session, and discuss how to make sure their staff knows the company policy.

In the training they should learn how to maintain a neutral attitude and create a climate of respect among their employees. The supervisory employees need to be trained to be cognitive of the office environment and of how not to allow offensive behavior to persist. They should reflect neutral behavior towards gender, race, and all the protected classes. Supervisory employees should learn how to be "model citizens," setting an example for their employees to follow.

Participants will learn that even though the harasser is the one to blame, the company can be held liable for his or her actions. The employer can be determined responsible if it has not provided adequate training, made efforts to prevent harassment, or does not have its efforts documented. And, more alarming, the individuals who are a supervisory employee may be held liable in certain circumstances.

Trainers will also discuss the fact that associates other than employees of your company can be the harasser. Your company may be liable for their actions as it would an employee. For example, vendors, suppliers, and customers of a company can initiate harassment and a company may be held liable if it is aware and did not take appropriate actions.

Trainers may also present a video with several vignettes that display situations of harassment in the workplace.

Each vignette shows how a common situation can easily lead to comments or jokes that can be considered as harassment.

Third-Party Consultants and Risk Management

A good third-party human resource consultant can not only provide a sexual harassment trainer but it can help manage the company's risk, compliance issues, benefit costs, turnover, morale, and overall have a positive impact on the company's bottom line and growth. They focus on finances, legal compliance, and performance issues—not just insurance renewals.

Compliance Check is a strategic risk management tool from Liberty that has 18 modules, including sexual harassment. This risk management tool allows it to review and audit the company from a human resource perspective, identifying the noncompliant components and suggesting fixes to be compliant and reduce risk. Both companies work together strategically to create remedies for these issues. Some examples of the 18 modules include the review of the Employee Handbook, COBRA practices, FMLA practices, FLSA practices, HIPAA practices, and ADA practices. By keeping these practices up to code, companies are able to manage their liability.

What Should Human Resource Departments Do Next?

The best next step for human resource departments is to hire an experienced consultant to handle their sexual harassment training. Select a consultant who will become a strategic partner with its clients to help the human resource department contribute to the reduction of the company's bottom line. Instead of hiring a company for a fee of $2,000 to $3,000, or more, it should partner with a firm that offers sexual harassment training as part of its services. It has four qualified members with extensive industry service to provide the harassment training.

DAVE GOTTWALS is a Benefit Consultant for Liberty Benefit Insurance Services, Inc., a nationwide, full service benefit and human resource consulting firm based in San Jose, CA. He is certified as a Compliance Check auditor helping companies manage their risk.

Fighting for Values

The struggle against Islamic extremism is not a clash between civilizations, the British prime minister argues. It is a clash *about* civilization.

TONY BLAIR

O ver the past nine years, Britain has pursued a markedly different foreign policy, justifying our actions at least as much by reference to values as to interests. The defining characteristic of today's world is its interdependence. Whereas the economics of globalization are well matured, the politics of globalization are not. Unless we articulate a common global policy based on common values, we risk chaos threatening our stability, economic and political, through letting extremism, conflict or injustice go unchecked.

The consequence of this thesis is a policy of engagement, not isolation; and one that is active, not reactive.

Confusingly, its proponents and opponents come from all sides of the political spectrum. So it is apparently a "neoconservative" or right wing view to be ardently in favor of spreading democracy around the world. Others on the right take the view that this is dangerous and deluded—the only thing that matters is an immediate view of national interest. Some progressives see intervention as humanitarian and necessary; others take the view that, provided dictators don't threaten our citizens directly, what they do with their own is up to them.

The debate on world trade has thrown all sides into an orgy of political cross-dressing. Protectionist sentiment is rife on the left. On the right, there are calls for "economic patriotism." Meanwhile some voices, left and right, are making the case for free trade not just on grounds of commerce but of justice.

The true division in foreign policy today is between those who want the shop "open" and those who want it "closed;" between those who believe that the long-term interests of a country lie in it being engaged—and those who think the short-term pain of such a policy and its decisions is too great. This division has strong echoes in debates not just over foreign policy and trade but also over immigration.

Progressives are stronger on the challenges of poverty, climate change, and trade justice. It is impossible to gain support for our values unless the demand for justice is as strong as the demand for freedom; and the willingness to work in partnership with others is an avowed preference to going it alone, even if that may sometimes be necessary.

We will not ever get real support for the tough action that may well be essential to safeguard our way of life unless we also attack global poverty and environmental degradation or injustice with equal vigor.

Neither in defending this interventionist policy do I pretend that mistakes have not been made or that major problems do not confront us.

I also acknowledge that the standoff between Israel and Palestine remains a genuine source of anger in the Arab and Muslim world that goes far beyond usual anti-Western feeling. Yet it is in confronting global terrorism today that the sharpest debate and disagreement is found. Nowhere is the supposed "folly" of the interventionist case so loudly trumpeted as in this case. Here, so it is said, as the third anniversary of the Iraq conflict took place, is the wreckage of such a world view. Under Saddam Iraq was "stable." Now its stability is in the balance. Ergo, it should never have been done.

This is the conventional view of foreign policy since the fall of the Berlin Wall. Countries should manage their affairs and relationships according to their narrow national interests. The basic posture represented by this view is not to provoke, to keep all as settled as it can be, and to cause no tectonic plates to move. It has its soft face in dealing with issues like global warming or Africa and reserves its hard face only if directly attacked by another state, which is unlikely. It is a view which sees the world as not without challenge but basically calm, with a few nasty things lurking in deep waters, which it is best to avoid. It believes the storms have been largely self-created.

This is the majority view of a large part of Western opinion, certainly in Europe. According to this opinion, the policy of America since 9/11 has been a gross overreaction; George Bush is as much if not more of a threat to world peace as Osama bin Laden; and what is happening in Iraq, Afghanistan, or anywhere else in the Middle East is an entirely understandable consequence of U.S./U.K. imperialism or worse, of just plain stupidity. Leave it all alone or at least treat it with sensitivity and it would all resolve itself in time; "it" never quite being defined, but just generally felt as anything that causes disruption.

This world view—which I would characterize as a doctrine of benign inactivity—sits in the commentator's seat, almost as a matter of principle. It has imposed a paradigm on world events that is extraordinary in its attraction and its scope. The effect of this paradigm is to see each setback in Iraq or Afghanistan, each revolting terrorist barbarity, each reverse for the forces of democracy or advance for the forces of tyranny as merely an illustration of the foolishness of our ever being there; as a reason why Saddam should have been left in place or the Taliban free to continue their alliance with al Qaeda. Those who still justify the interventions are treated with scorn.

Then, when terrorists strike in the nations like Britain or Spain, who supported such action, there is a groundswell of opinion formers keen to say, in effect, that it's hardly surprising—after all, if we do this to "their" countries, is it any wonder they do it to "ours"?

So the statement that Iraq or Afghanistan or Palestine or indeed Chechnya, Kashmir, or half a dozen other troublespots is seen by extremists as fertile ground for their recruiting—a statement of the obvious—is elided with the notion that we have "caused" such recruitment or made terrorism worse, a notion that, on any sane analysis, has the most profound implications for democracy.

The easiest line for any politician seeking office in the West today is to attack American policy. Earlier this year, as I was addressing young Slovak students, one got up, denouncing U.S./U.K. policy in Iraq, fully bought in to the demonization of the United States, utterly oblivious to the fact that without the U.S. and the liberation of his country, he would have been unable to ask such a question, let alone get an answer to it.

I recall the video footage of Mohammed Sadiq Khan, the man who was the ringleader of the 7/7 bombers in London. There he was, complaining about the suppression of Muslims, the wickedness of America and Britain, calling on all fellow Muslims to fight us. And I thought: here is someone, brought up in this country, free to practice his religion, free to speak out, free to vote, with a good standard of living and every chance to raise a family in a decent way of life, talking about "us," the British, when his whole experience of "us" has been the very opposite of the message he is preaching.

There was something tragic but also ridiculous about such a diatribe. He may have been born here. But his ideology wasn't. And that is why it has to be taken on, everywhere.

This terrorism will not be defeated until its ideas, the poison that warps the minds of its adherents, are confronted, head-on, in their essence, at their core.

This terrorism will not be defeated until its ideas, the poison that warps the minds of its adherents, are confronted, head-on, in their essence, at their core. By this I don't mean telling them terrorism is wrong. I mean telling them their attitude to America is absurd; their concept of governance pre-feudal; their positions on women and other faiths, reactionary and regressive; and then since only by Muslims can this be done: standing up for and supporting those within Islam who will tell them all of this but more, namely that the extremist view of Islam is not just

theologically backward but completely contrary to the spirit and teaching of the Koran.

But in order to do this, we must reject the thought that somehow we are the authors of our own distress; that if only we altered this decision or that, the extremism would fade away. The only way to win is to recognize this phenomenon is a global ideology; to see all areas in which it operates as linked; and to defeat it by values and ideas set in opposition to those of the terrorists.

A reforming book. The roots of global terrorism and extremism are indeed deep. They reach right down through decades of alienation, victimhood, and political oppression in the Arab and Muslim world. Yet this is not and never has been inevitable. The most remarkable thing about reading the Koran is to understand how progressive it is. I speak with great diffidence and humility as a member of another faith. I am not qualified to make any judgments. But as an outsider, the Koran strikes me as a reforming book, trying to return Judaism and Christianity to their origins, rather as reformers attempted with the Christian Church centuries later. It is inclusive. It extols science and knowledge and abhors superstition. It is practical and way ahead of its time in attitudes to marriage, women, and governance.

Under its guidance, the spread of Islam and its dominance over previously Christian or pagan lands was breathtaking. Over centuries it founded an empire, leading the world in discovery, art, and culture. The standard bearers of tolerance in the early Middle Ages were far more likely to be found in Muslim lands than in Christian.

But by the early 20th century, after renaissance, reformation, and enlightenment had swept over the Western world, the Muslim and Arab world was uncertain, insecure, and on the defensive. Muslims began to see the sorry state of Muslim countries as symptomatic of the sorry state of Islam. Political radicals became religious radicals and vice versa. Those in power tried to accommodate the resurgent Islamic radicalism by incorporating some of its leaders and some of its ideology. The result was nearly always disastrous. The religious radicalism was made respectable, the political radicalism suppressed, and so in the minds of many, the cause of the two came together to symbolize the need for change. So many came to believe that the way of restoring the confidence and stability of Islam was the combination of religious extremism and populist politics.

The extremism may have started through religious doctrine and thought. But soon, in offshoots of the Muslim brotherhood, supported by Wahabi extremists and taught in some of the madrassas of the Middle East and Asia, an ideology was born and exported around the world.

The different aspects of this terrorism are linked. The struggle against terrorism in Madrid or London or Paris is the same as the struggle against the terrorist acts of Hezbollah in Lebanon or the PIJ in Palestine, or rejectionist groups in Iraq. The murder of the innocent in Beslan is part of the same ideology that takes innocent lives in Saudi Arabia, Yemen, or Libya. And when Iran gives support to such terrorism, it becomes part of the same battle with the same ideology at its heart.

Clash about civilization. Which brings me to the fundamental point. "We" is not the West. "We" are as much Muslim as Christian or Jew or Hindu. "We" are those who believe in religious tolerance, openness to others, to democracy, liberty, and human rights administered by secular courts.

This is not a clash between civilizations. It is a clash about civilization. It is the age-old battle between progress and reaction, between those who embrace and see opportunity in the modern world and those who reject its existence; between optimism and hope on the one hand, and pessimism and fear on the other. And in the era of globalization where nations depend on each other and where our security is held in common or not at all, the outcome of this clash between extremism and progress is utterly determinative of our future. We can no more opt out of this struggle than we can opt out of the climate changing around us. Inaction, pushing the responsibility on to America, deluding ourselves that this terrorism is an isolated series of individual incidents rather than a global movement and would go away if only we were more sensitive to its pretensions; this too is a policy. It is just that; it is a policy that is profoundly, fundamentally wrong.

And this is why the position of so much opinion on how to defeat this terrorism and on the continuing struggle in Iraq and Afghanistan and the Middle East is, in my judgment, so mistaken.

It ignores the true significance of the elections in Iraq and Afghanistan. The fact is: Given the chance, the people wanted democracy. OK, so they voted on religious or regional lines. That's not surprising, given the history. But there's not much doubt what all the main parties in both countries would prefer, and it is neither theocratic nor secular dictatorship. The people—despite violence, intimidation, inexperience, and often logistical nightmares—voted. Not a few. But in numbers large enough to shame many Western democracies. They want government decided by the people.

And who is trying to stop them? In Iraq, a mixture of foreign jihadists, former Saddamists, and rejectionist insurgents. In Afghanistan, a combination of drug barons, Taliban, and al Qaeda.

In each case, the United States, the U.K., and the forces of many other nations are there to help the indigenous security forces grow, to support the democratic process, and to provide some clear bulwark against the terrorism that threatens it.

Of course, and wholly wrongly, there are abuses of human rights, mistakes made, things done that should not be done.

There always were. But at least this time, someone demands redress; people are free to complain.

So here, in its most pure form, is a struggle between democracy and violence. People look back on the three years since the Iraq conflict; they point to the precarious nature of Iraq today and to those who have died—mainly in terrorist acts—and they say: How can it have been worth it?

But there is a different question to ask: Why is it so important to the forces of reaction and violence to halt Iraq in its democratic tracks and tip it into sectarian war?

The answer is that the reactionary elements know the importance of victory or defeat in Iraq. Right from the beginning, to them it was obvious. For sure, errors were made on our side. It is arguable that de-Baathification went too quickly and was spread too indiscriminately, especially amongst the armed forces. Though in parenthesis, the real worry back in 2003 was a humanitarian crisis, which we avoided; and the pressure was all to de-Baathify faster.

But the basic problem from the murder of the United Nations staff in August 2003 onwards was simple: security. The reactionary elements were trying to derail both reconstruction and democracy by violence. Power and electricity became problems not through the indolence of either Iraqis or the multinational forces but through sabotage.

These were not random acts. They were and are a strategy. When that strategy failed to push the multinational forces out of Iraq prematurely and failed to stop the voting, they turned to sectarian killing and outrage.

They know that if they can succeed either in Iraq or Afghanistan or anywhere else wanting to go the democratic route, then the choice of a modern democratic future for the Arab or Muslim world is dealt a potentially mortal blow. They play our own media with a shrewdness that would be the envy of many a political party. Every act of carnage somehow serves to indicate our responsibility for disorder, rather than the act of wickedness that causes it.

What happens in Iraq or Afghanistan today is not just crucial for the people in those countries. In their salvation lies our own security.

This is a battle of values and progress; and therefore it is one we must win.

Tony Blair is prime minister of Britain. This article is adapted from a speech he gave on March 21.

UNIT 2

Meeting Human Resource Requirements

Unit Selections

Key Points to Consider

- Job requirements and working conditions have changed over the past several years. What new changes do you foresee in the workplace in the next 10 years? How do you see the impact of the 24/7 work schedule on employers and employees? What impact do you think telecommuting will have on the workplace? Do you think you will be working in the same kind of position as your parents? Do you think you will be working from 9 to 5? Do you think workers are as respected as they should be? Why or why not?

- The first step in the process of working is getting hired. The last step is termination, whether for cause, leaving for a new job, retirement, or a "reduction in force." What trends do you see in the workforce concerning individuals and their careers? What do you think the impact of race or diversity in the workforce is? What about globalization? Do you see any changes coming?

- How do you see computerization being applied to human resources, and how will this change human resources? What do you see as some of the issues concerning computerization of employee records?

- What are some of the trends in the workforce? How do you see organizations responding to those trends? What are some of the strategies that organizations are now using and/or could use in the future to hire and develop their workforces?

Student Web Site

www.mhcls.com

Internet References

America's Job Bank
http://www.ajb.dni.us
International Association for Human Resource Information Management (IHRIM)
http://www.ihrim.org
Sympatico Careers
http://www.sympatico.workopolis.com
Voice of the Shuttle: Postindustrial Business Theory Page
http://www.vos.scsb.edu/bfrowse.asp?=2727

Organizations, whether profit or nonprofit, are more than collections of buildings, desks, and telephones. Organizations are made of people—people with their particular traits, habits, and idiosyncrasies that make them unique. Each individual has different needs and wants, and the employer and the worker must seek a reasonable compromise so that at least an adequate match may be found for both.

The importance of human resource planning is greater than ever and will probably be even more important in the future. As Thomas Peters and Robert Waterman have pointed out in their book, *In Search of Excellence:*

> Quality and service, then, were invariable hallmarks of excellent firms. To get them, of course, everyone's cooperation is required, not just the mighty labors of the top 200. The excellent companies require and demand extraordinary performance from the average man. Dana's former chairman, Rene McPherson, says that neither the few destructive laggards nor the handful of brilliant performers are the key. Instead, he urges attention to the care, feeding and unshackling of the average man. We labeled it "productivity through people." All companies pay it lip service. Few deliver.
>
> —Thomas Peters and Robert Waterman, *In Search of Excellence*, New York, Warner Books, 1987

In the future, organizations are going to have to pay more than just lip service to "productivity through people" if they want to survive and prosper. They will have to practice it by demonstrating an understanding of not only their clients' and customers' needs but also those of their employees. The only way they will be able to deliver the goods and services and achieve success is through those same employees. Companies are faced with the difficult task of finding the right people for the right jobs—a task that must be accomplished if the organization is going to have a future.

Organizations are trying to meet the needs of their employees by developing new and different approaches to workers' jobs. This means taking into account how society, the labor force, the family, and the nature of the jobs themselves have changed. Training and development will be key in meeting future human resource requirements. Employers will have to change the way they design their positions if they are to attract and keep good employees. They must consider how society has changed and will change in the future. Learning from experience that there are fewer young people and more middle-aged employees, as well as dual-career couples in the workforce, struggling to raise children, and dealing with aging parents, they will have to consider how the very nature of jobs has changed, especially from predominantly blue-collar to white-collar jobs, from "9 to 5" to "24/7." Meeting these problems will entail new and different approaches to how jobs are structured. Companies will have

© Imagestate Media (John Foxx)/Imagestate

to learn to experience flex-time and other approaches to job design if they are to attract and keep valuable and productive employees.

"Managing in the New Millennium: Ten Keys to Better Hiring," human resource planning, selection, and recruitment are going to be more critical in the future. Companies will have to go to extraordinary lengths to attract and keep new employees. There is no mystery about the reasons for this situation. America is aging, and there are fewer people in their late teens and early twenties to take the entry-level jobs that will be available in the future. Women, who for the past 20 years have been the major source of new employees, now represent almost half the workforce. As a result, new groups must be found, whether they are retirees, high school students, workers moonlighting on a second job, minority group members, people with disabilities, or immigrants. One thing is certain: the workforce is changing and organizations will need to unlock the potential of all their employees. Other means of recruitment will need to be employed in the future, and old ideas and prejudices will have to go by the boards in all post-industrialized societies. Organizations will be faced with the problem of building a better workforce, and some of these strategies are discussed in "Six Ways to Strengthen Staffing." But, this will be no easy task.

Another aspect of human resource planning involves both the selection process and the termination process. The days of working for only one company and then retiring with a gold watch and a pension are over. People are going to change jobs, if not companies, more frequently in the future, and many of the tasks they will be doing in the next 10, 15, or 20 years do not even exist today because of technological change. Midlife and mid-career changes are going to be far more common than they have been in the past, requiring people to change and adapt.

47

Human resource information systems offer important tools in managing human resources. The ability of computers to handle large amounts of data is now being applied to human resource management with very interesting results. These practices, applied to hiring and internal information management, promise much greater automation of human resources in the future as well as reduced costs. There are, however, concerns. Privacy, security, and confidentiality are all key issues for employees who have their employment records encoded in a computer system. These concerns are highlighted in "Balancing HR systems with Employee Privacy."

Meeting the human resource needs of any organization in the future is a difficult task. Assuming that the economy continues to grow at an acceptable rate, the need for workers will continue to increase, but many of the traditional sources of supply for new workers will be either exhausted or in decline. Management must plan for this shortage and consider alternative sources of potential employees. In turn, the individual employee must be ready to adapt quickly and efficiently to a changing environment. Job security is a thing of the past, and workers must remain flexible in order to cope with increased uncertainty.

White Collared

When did our jobs turn into a joke?

JULIE HANUS

Remember *Laverne & Shirley?* Archie Bunker? Louie De Palma on *Taxi?* Norm and Cliff on *Cheers?* As these working-class characters live on in late-night reruns, a very different sort of everyperson is dominating the airwaves: the charmingly disengaged, sometimes bungling, always put-upon white-collar worker.

It's a logical trend. Since 1984, the number of U.S. workers has increased by more than 30 million, and 90 percent of that growth has been in the white-collar and service sectors. More citizens work at non-manual labor than ever before, and as technology, outsourcing, and offshoring continue to eliminate blue-collar jobs, pop culture has turned its attention to the office dweller.

The most popular and pointed TV treatment of this phenomenon is a biting satire more or less hijacked from Britain. In *The Office,* the interactions between big boss Michael Scott, played by comedian Steve Carell, and his underlings at Dunder-Mifflin are governed by a rubric under which each character is reduced to his or her fundamental office identity. Dwight, assistant (to the) regional manager, is the guy guzzling the Kool-Aid. Sales rep Jim is smart, but often slacking. Pam, meekly poised behind the front desk, hopes to become an illustrator someday, because "no little girl ever dreams about becoming a receptionist."

The show's lead characters cleave into two groups: those who "get it" and those who don't. The latter class is represented by the clownish, not-so-lovable nerd Dwight who gullibly fawns over his foolish manager and mercilessly pursues advancement. He and his kind are the show's jesters. The better half, employees in the know, are its heroes.

They immediately spot the stupidity in empty managerial parables, sigh as they play along (for now, of course), and fend off lunacy by playing mostly harmless tricks on their naive officemates. They also demonstrate their superior grasp of the situation by casting incredulous glances at the camera, pained conspiratorial gazes that say: *Can you even believe this? You see that this is all B.S., right?*

For NBC, the formula has proven to be comedic gold. Lurking just below the public's laughter, though, is a grim reminder of what it means to be a modern-day worker bee.

The white-collar workspace hasn't always conjured up visions of monkeylike morons shuffling papers and wasting time on the Internet. When the United States began shifting to a postindustrial society in the aftermath of World War II, writes Nikil Saval in the Winter 2008 issue of the culture journal *n+1,* corporations like General Electric and IBM offered a new breed of white-collar workers highly secure, salaried work, along with decent benefits and abundant vacation time. What's more, working *meant* something.

By the 1980s, however, economic instability had prompted companies to spread resources thin—to cut pay, slash benefits, and eliminate good jobs in favor of low-pay positions—in order to beef up profit margins. Swaths of Generation X watched their boomer parents get dropkicked in return for decades of good, hard work. Perhaps most notably, those who were affected responded by doing very little to protest—and white-collar workers have been rolling over ever since.

"Young technical and professional workers are as bewildered by the 'new economy' as manufacturing workers have been for a generation," labor activist Jim Grossfeld writes in the January 2007 issue of the online political journal the *Democratic Strategist.* However, in "White Collar Perspectives on Workplace Issues," Grossfeld's study for the Center for American Progress, an important difference between the two groups is revealed. Whereas blue-collar laborers organized to protest workplace issues such as unsatisfactory wages and benefits, white-collar workers have gone on the defensive with a disillusioned attitude. Believing instability and declining workplace conditions are "unavoidable in today's economy," and that corporations are too formidable, they've concluded that nothing can be done but to lower expectations and dodge disappointment. Reject loyalty and avoid betrayal.

The standards slid, unchecked. These days, U.S. workers put in longer hours than workers in any other developed country and take the least vacation. If they're actually insured, the benefits are often astronomically expensive. There's no stability, either; white-collar workers hold an average of nine jobs before the age of 35. Instead of getting angry, they turn a scorned cheek to their employers, defiantly laughing along with *The Office* heroes at the absurdity of it all.

Assistant (to the) regional manager Dwight isn't mocked because he's an insufferable suck-up; he's ridiculed because he fails to recognize that it's all a waste of energy.

When the cartoon strip *Dilbert* first appeared in 1989, it depicted employees who knew better than their buzzword-slinging managers. In that two-dimensional universe, the people making things inefficient were the ones who were portrayed as fools; the evolving workplace was problematic, but the work had potential for value. Now the work itself is what's mocked, which, given the fact that most people spend a bulk of their lives at work, can't help but threaten the collective psyche and further damage the domestic workplace.

White-collar workers already report more occupational stress than their blue-collar counterparts and suffer twice as much from severe depression. Job satisfaction is falling, dropping from 60 percent in the mid-'90s to about 50 percent in 2005, according to a report from the Conference Board, a business-research organization. Forty percent of workers feel disconnected from their employers, and a quarter admit to showing up just to collect a check. In other words, some 35 million workers are either content to not care or have bought into the idea that there's no reason to. (Managers know it, too. Why else would they grit their teeth and bring in "fun" consultants who promise to boost sagging employee morale?)

This culturally sanctioned slacking that results from job insecurity is a self-fulfilling prophecy. Over the past few years, technology has made it possible for work once done in U.S. offices to be performed just as easily anywhere in the world. National Public Radio's *Morning Edition* recently likened the current threat to white-collar jobs to steelworkers' complaints of a generation past. "Fewer and fewer jobs are safe," said Ethan Kapstein, a guest expert in international economic relations. "It means that all of us, people like myself as well, have to continually upscale, we have to continually invest in our skills to maintain our productivity levels."

"What [white-collar workers] need is a new model of unionism that focuses on assuring their employability, mobility, and earning power rather than protecting specific jobs or compensation packages," Will Marshall, president of the Progressive Policy Institute, writes in the January 2007 issue of the *Democratic Strategist.* He echoes Kapstein, arguing that if U.S. white-collar workers want to keep their jobs, they'll have to focus on company productivity as much as on their own needs: "Modern labor associations . . . could operate, in short, like a back-to-the-future update on the old craft unions, which were defenders of quality workmanship as well as workers' interests."

To avert crisis, Kapstein and Marshall both call on the redeeming power of doing *good* work, of investing in skills and focusing on craftsmanship—which would require believing in the value of labor and the value of the laborer. Such a shift in mindset could protect white-collar jobs, even transform domestic white-collar work. After all, the same technology that produced an outsourcing threat could just as easily make widespread telecommuting a reality. As Matt Bai writes in a November 2007 issue of the *New York Times,* "Why shouldn't more middle-class workers whose jobs can now be done remotely have the option to structure their own hours and still enjoy the security of a safety net? Why shouldn't . . . anyone who spends his day staring at a terminal in some sterile environment straight out of *Office Space* be able to work in shorts and spend more time around the kids?"

Shedding all those vestiges of cliché office work (the inflexible hours, the fluorescent-lit cubicles, the impossible work-home balance), can't happen if this generation of workers continue to find validation in checking out.

It's a lovely vision, shedding all those vestiges of cliché office work (the inflexible hours, the fluorescent-lit cubicles, the impossible work-home balance), but it can't happen if this generation of workers continue to find validation in checking out, backhandedly assuring themselves that they're better than their disappointing jobs and, in the process, proving to their employers that they're utterly replaceable and entirely outsourceable.

If white-collar workers seized this moment to check in, to believe in the value of their work and in themselves as workers, they might do more than save their jobs or even kick open the door for a reinvention of the workspace. They might remember what it feels like to care about what they do—or find out for the first time.

Managing in the New Millennium
Ten Keys to Better Hiring

Patricia M. Buhler, D.B.A.

With the war for talent in full swing, it is essential that every manager be better prepared to make more effective hiring decisions. The consequences of poor hiring will be exaggerated in the coming years as the worker shortage continues to grow. It will be more difficult and more expensive to replace employees. As a result, those organizations that make more hiring "mistakes" will have a multitude of critical negative financial and productivity consequences to address.

There are specific steps the organization can take to help managers improve their ability to make better hiring decisions. These include training managers in the appropriate skills and addressing hiring on the performance appraisal. There are definite steps that managers can learn to take as well. They may take a more future oriented approach to hiring, learn to read the subtle cues, conduct behavioral interviews, use more creative interview questions, evaluate all the selection tools, and consider the whole package when hiring.

Step One: Train, Train, and Train Some More

The importance of training cannot be stressed enough. To increase the likelihood of making better hiring decisions, organizations must provide training for managers. While the human resource department in larger organizations generally partners with managers and takes the lead in screening many job candidates, the line managers still play a big role in the hiring process and almost always make the final decision.

While the mechanics of the process are important, soft skills development is equally important to improve hiring. These might include general interpersonal skills, communication, etiquette, and even the legal do's and don'ts of interviewing.

The Performance Appraisal— You Get What You Measure

The ability to identify, hire, and retain top talent should be an integral responsibility of every manager. After all, it directly impacts the manager's own success (and ultimately, the organization's as well). It has been said that one is only as good as the people one surrounds oneself with. And of course, the old adage about only being as strong as the weakest link can be appropriately applied to people as well.

The organization must place an emphasis on good hiring. This can be achieved, in part, by including hiring effectiveness on the manager's performance appraisal. With so many responsibilities pulling managers in different directions, those that are included on the performance appraisal are likely to be higher priorities. It communicates to managers that it is an important organizational objective and deserves their attention.

Be Future Oriented

It is essential that managers think more broadly—beyond just the position. True strategic recruiting requires an eye to the future. This is usually a moving target, though, that must be constantly reevaluated to meet changing organizational objectives. It is important to think about the position that is currently open, but it is also necessary to engage in future-oriented strategic human resource planning.

Replacement charts can assist in planning at this stage. This involves thinking through the future needs and anticipating the skills and competencies required going forward. Managers must also consider how the position will evolve over time and the general development of skills needed for the overall organization's growth.

Extraordinary Results with Ordinary People

O'Reilly suggested that in winning the war for talent, organizations no longer have to hire the 10 percent cream of the crop in the workforce, but could actually cultivate and develop the talent within the organization. This philosophy must obviously begin with the hiring process. Applicants demonstrating potential can be hired for future development.

Organizations have the choice to "make" or "buy" their employees. When the decision is made to "make" an employee, he or she is hired without a fully developed skill set recognizing that with training opportunities, the employee can acquire the necessary skills to meet the needs of the organization. Even if the candidates don't currently possess all the skills required, talented individuals may be "made".

The manager can commit a critical mistake if he or she passes on a talented individual just because a few technical skills are missing. The manager, however, must exercise judgment to ensure the "missing" skills are not essential for the effective performance of the current job and can, indeed, be acquired in a reasonable period of time. There is a fine line between hiring a marginal employee and hiring a talented employee with the untapped potential to be a star performer. One can drag the organization down and the other can contribute immensely to the company's successful performance.

Read the Subtle Cues

There are often subtle cues (sometimes provided unconsciously by applicants) that are disregarded or purposely ignored. Interviewers should listen to their instincts (or that "gut feeling") and pay particular attention to these subtle communications. For example, the handshake provides a good opening. It should always be firm with eye contact. Interviewers should also consider if the applicant was dressed appropriately with attention to personal grooming and if the applicant was enthusiastic. If the candidate was not enthusiastic in the interview, chances are things will only go downhill once he or she 'is on the job. When something appears to be questionable, it is best to pursue it rather than relegating it to the backburner or avoiding it altogether.

Managers should not be so impressed with the ends reported by some candidates that they overlook any less than reputable means by which they were accomplished. The manager must live with these mean-spirited characters who often have no people skills and are hard to get along with. They may create havoc and disharmony in the organization. While some may try to hide this tendency in the interview, there are generally telltale signs that are red flags. The "fit" of candidates (and their personalities) must be considered along with their ability to meet the technical requirements of the job. The soft skills should definitely be inventoried.

Conduct Behavioral Interviews

The best indicator of future performance is past performance. To explore more of the applicant's past performance, behavioral (or situational) interviews are a great tool. These questions may be either hypothetical or actual. To gain insight into how an applicant handles tough personnel issues, a hypothetical behavioral question could ask "If you were approached by an employee who reported that a fellow worker was stealing merchandise from your warehouse and selling it out of the trunk of his car at the local mall, what would you do" Or an applicant may be asked to relate how a real situation in the past was actually handled. For example, "Tell me the circumstances under which you last terminated an employee." Responses to

these questions will shed substantial light on applicants and their likely behavior in the future. The key is to look for specific responses not vague generalities.

Break out of the Mold with Interview Questions: Ask the Unexpected

Most job candidates will prepare for the more traditional, expected interview questions. Responses can be canned or well rehearsed and may or may not genuinely reflect the candidate's sincere feelings. The unexpected questions with no "one right answer" can provide additional insight into an applicant. For example, asking "What was the last book that you read" can shed light on the interests of the candidate—and perhaps insight into whether they read books in their field. Even traditional questions can used with a fresh approach. For instance, asking about an applicant's weakness allows the interviewer to see how the applicant overcomes and deals with weaknesses.

Another recommended question is "Why did you choose this company" or "Why do you want to work for this organization" This provides an opportunity for the manager to see if the applicant did his or her homework and learned something specific about the firm. "Tell me about your worst boss" is a loaded question that opens the door to see how the job candidate handles an opportunity to talk negatively about someone. Some more general questions can provide insight into the applicants' ability to think on their feet. For example, "Tell me about something you are truly passionate about". While unexpected and an "out of the box" question, it is the candidate's ability to remain composed, non-flustered, and think quickly that is being evaluated more than the actual topic.

Familiarity with Job Requirements

Before one can consider applicants for a job, it is important that the job description and job specification be clearly understood. Both are critical documents used in the recruitment and selection process. To hire effectively, managers must understand the responsibilities of the job—found in the job description. Equally important is the consideration of the knowledge, skills, and abilities required to successfully perform the job. These are identified in the job specification.

As part of the screening process, managers (in partnership with the human resource department) must review job applicants in light of the job requirements and specifications. It is important that this alignment be identified to avoid wasting either the manager's or the applicant's time.

Weighing Selection Criteria

Successful employees often fit a general profile. This may include some combination of experience, educational level, specific field of study, or even involvement in sports or community service projects. It is important for a manager to know who has been successful in the position (and in the organization) and what they brought to the table. It is more likely (but not an iron-clad guarantee) that a candidate possessing several of these critical success factors will then also be successful.

Some organizations today use weighted application blanks that place more emphasis on those criteria that have been identified in the firm's more successful employees. For example, some companies may weigh the education of the applicant more heavily than the years of experience in the field. All of the selection tools can then be assigned a percentage—reflecting greater importance of some criteria over others.

The Complete Package

A number of selection tools should be utilized when making hiring decisions. Reliance on just one tool is a recipe for disaster. The primary trap most managers fall into is putting an undue emphasis on the interview and their "read" of the applicant. Research has proven repeatedly that the interview is the least reliable of all selection tools used. That is certainly not to say it should not be used, but it should be used as one of several tools upon which the decision is made.

Taking the complete package into consideration also involves rounding out the team and avoiding the "similar to me" bias. While it is human nature to surround oneself with those who are similar, this tendency must be avoided to build a team with complementary skills.

Finally, to create a complete picture it is a great idea in today's digital age to "google" the applicant. Checking for "digital dirt" often reveals unexpected insider information (both positive and negative) about the candidate. This may be information that would not normally be revealed during the interview process.

Organizations today must prepare for the talent shortage. There is less room for error than ever before. This means that an emphasis must be placed on effective hiring—in the first place—since there will be less opportunity to "correct" for those bad hiring decisions in the future workforce shortage.

Six Ways to Strengthen Staffing

**A company's performance hinges on the quality of its people.
And that means your staffing activities need to be in tip-top shape.**

ADRIENNE HEDGER

You know the drill. There's an open job and you need to find an ideal candidate—someone with the perfect mix of talent, knowledge and personality. Someone who will exceed the company's expectations. Oh—and you need to find that person right away.

Make a mistake, and it could cost dearly. Indeed, experts place the cost of losing an employee at somewhere between 30 and 150 percent of the person's yearly salary.

Staffing has never been an easy endeavor—but over the next five years the playing field will become even more interesting and challenging. With a labor shortage, changing work preferences and the rapid evolution of online recruiting, the industry is entering an era unlike any other.

"The next few years will be dynamic," says Mike Lafayette, Director of Product Development for the Staffing business segment at Monster.com.

"There is no status quo," agrees Diane Shelgren, Executive Vice President of Strategy and Client Development at Veritude, which provides a range of strategic human resources services. "Companies that understand the changes will be able to attract the best talent."

What should you consider as you fine-tune your staffing strategies? Here are six areas of focus that leading companies will be addressing over the next year.

1: Get Better at Finding the Needle in the Haystack

Currently there are more than 52 million resumes sitting in the Monster.com database. And roughly 40,000 resumes are added every week. That's more than 280 added every hour, around the clock.

Meanwhile, profiles are constantly being created and updated on networking sites like LinkedIn, Plaxo, Jobster and Spoke.

All this is creating pathways to millions of potential employees—and while this certainly improves the odds of finding the right person, it can also lead to resume overload.

In response, companies are becoming more sophisticated about searching for qualified candidates. The Web site Zoominfo, for instance, extracts information from online sources including Web sites, press releases and electronic news services and bundles it in one report. Services such as W3 Data and Accurint also allow for targeted searches.

Advances in search technology are underway at sites like Monster.com as well. There, the company's SmartFind Resume Search helps employers and staffing companies quickly identify the most qualified applicants, reducing the number of resumes that need to be reviewed.

Meanwhile, companies are also working niche job sites into their recruiting strategies. In fact, media research firm Borrell and Associates predicts a "proliferation of specialized job sites" in 2007.

No matter which strategy-or combination of strategies-a company takes, the ability to conduct a fast, targeted search will be crucial in the years ahead.

2: Knock on New Doors to Find Talent

With a labor shortage inching closer and closer, more companies are investigating alternative talent sources, such as retirees or stay-at-home moms who want part-time work.

In fact, according to one survey by CareerBuilder.com, 20 percent of employers plan to rehire retirees from other companies or provide incentives so their own employees delay retirement.

At The RightThing, Inc., an end-to-end provider of recruitment process outsourcing, the staff knows firsthand that tapping into these talent sources can be good for business.

"We've built a culture that values flexible work schedules," says Jamie Minier, Vice President of The RightThing. "Our company routinely employs retirees and work-at-home moms as part-time staff, and we help our clients recruit from these unique groups as well."

In part because of this strategy The RightThing was named one of the "25 Best Small Companies to Work for in America" by the Great Place to Work Institute.

Similarly, Veritude has tapped into an alternative talent source—this one in India. The team in India searches online for qualified job candidates, then sends the names to the company's recruiters in the United States.

"When our recruiters arrive at work in the morning, they already have a list of people to contact," says Shelgren. "This speeds the entire process."

Alternative talent sources will only become more essential as the pool of available workers begins to drain. "At this point," adds Minier, "if you're not tapping into alternative talent sources or looking globally, you're not ahead of the game."

3: Embrace Flexibility

Tapping into alternative talent sources dovetails with another emerging trend: more flexibility.

Indeed, 19 percent of employers say they are "very" or "extremely" willing to provide more flexible work arrangements for employees, according to a survey by CareerBuilder.com.

Meanwhile, the American Staffing Association reports that people are looking for flexibility in their employment arrangements—and an increasing number of people are deciding to become temporary or contract workers instead of entering traditional employment contracts.

In fact, according to the association's 2006 staffing employee survey, two-thirds of respondents said flexible work time was an important factor in their decision to become a temporary or contract employee. And a recent report by Veritude predicts that independent and contract workers will make up 25 percent of the workforce in the next five years.

This rise in flexible arrangements is inspiring companies to design creative staffing solutions. Shelgren points to one example: "We're seeing an increase in an arrangement known as 'homeshoring,'" she says. "Basically, organizations are establishing technology that allows employees to conduct call center activities from home offices."

4: Get to (Really!) Know Your Candidates

Shelly Wheeler, Human Resources Director at Roche Diagnostics, remembers a recent close call in staffing.

"We had a candidate we thought was perfect for the job," she recalls. "But after he completed our assessment tool, we realized there were some gaps that we couldn't fill. Without the assessment data, we likely would have hired him."

Assessment tools have been around for a long time, but lately there has been an increase in the number of companies using them—and this upward trend is expected to continue.

In fact, according to a 2006 survey by Rocket-Hire, the number of companies using assessment tools to gauge personality measures hit 65 percent in 2006, up from 34 percent in 2005.

And 53 percent were using the tools to measure a candidate's "fit," up from 35 percent in 2005.

"One of the key benefits is that these tools allow you to look ahead," says Gary Schmidt, Ph.D. and President of Saville Consulting. The company provides an online assessment tool called The Wave that is used by Roche Diagnostics and others. "For example, instead of just talking to the candidate about their previous jobs, you can assess whether they have the talent, skills and motivation to do something they've never done before."

The key to finding a good assessment tool: "Look for one that is scientifically validated, customizable, Internet-based and easy to use," says Schmidt. "You also don't want it to be too long—30 to 40 minutes maximum is a good target."

Some assessment tools can even deliver benefits after the candidate is hired. "We continue to rely on The Wave assessment tool to develop and coach our employees," says Jim Messina, Vice President of Sales for Maritz Learning, a division of Maritz Inc. "It's been a great tool for us."

"It doesn't cost much to have that other check in the system," adds Wheeler. "And it can save you from hiring the wrong person."

Another similar trend underway: giving prospective employees a "test drive." From simulated job environments to company tours, companies like Veritude, The RightThing and others are incorporating creative strategies to make sure the employee/employer fit is just right.

"These strategies work," says Shelgren. "We recently used a simulated environment to help reduce turnover at a call center by 50 percent."

5: Think "Temp to Hire"

Assessment tools and trial runs are powerful, but some companies are going a step further and using "temp to hire" scenarios, where an employee starts on a temporary basis through a staffing company, then later gets hired.

One telling statistic: When the American Staffing Association surveyed current and former temporary and contract employees, it found that more than 53 percent of the survey participants who remained in the workforce had moved on to permanent jobs.

"These arrangements seem to be growing in popularity," says Steven Berchem, Vice President of the American Staffing Association. "It's a win for the candidate as well as the customer because it's a great way to determine if there actually is a good fit."

Some professionals see temporary work as a good way to get a foot in the door at highly sought-after companies. Indeed, companies like Veritude and The RightThing routinely place highly skilled workers in industries such as pharmaceuticals, advanced technology, product development and animation.

Still others prefer the flexibility and lifestyle that temporary and contract work provides.

Either way, this growing body of highly skilled and highly educated professionals is rapidly debunking the myth that only low-skilled workers or recent college graduates align themselves with staffing companies.

For their part, businesses are waking up to this fact and increasingly looking to staffing firms as a good source for talent—and potentially permanent employees.

"More businesses are using staffing strategically," confirms Berchem. "They are using temporary and contract workers to fill specific, targeted needs—projects that demand highly skilled workers."

"One way to look at it," says John Hennessy, Senior Vice President of the Staffing business segment at Monster.com, "is that there are roughly 145 million employed people in the U.S.—and 35 million are currently employed or have had a relationship with a staffing company during their career. That's a significant number."

Taking all this into account it makes sense that, according to the Bureau of Labor Statistics, the U.S. staffing industry will grow faster and add more jobs over the next decade than just about any other industry.

6: Consider the Outsourcing Option

As the staffing industry continues to change and evolve, employers will need to rely on new technologies, new strategies and new online tools to stay ahead. Some companies will manage this internally—but for others the answer will be outsourcing.

"We've definitely seen an increase in business over the past 12 months," says Minier at The RightThing. "And we expect this boom to continue over the next 18 to 24 months."

The advantages of outsourcing can be compelling. Many RPO vendors are equipped with the latest technology and have the broad, deep networks required to fill a large number of jobs—even highly specialized jobs—very quickly. Companies also find that an RPO strategy allows them to tap into a more diverse workforce, as well as outsource the labor-intensive work of tracking compliance.

"If a company does decide to outsource recruitment activities, it is essential to find a vendor that understands your culture," says Shelgren. "Ideally, the vendor will assign someone on site, so that person experiences the company the same way any employee would."

"Client expectations are very high in the RPO arena," adds Minier. "Companies want service providers who consistently deliver quality, use robust and unique strategies to find talent, and are highly reliable."

In response, RPO providers are stepping up their offerings to go beyond recruiting and deliver end-to-end talent management. "Our consulting practice at Veritude is growing rapidly," Shelgren notes.

Putting It All Together

A number of trends are reshaping the staffing world, but the industry's ultimate goal remains the same: find great employees as cost effectively and quickly as possible.

The challenge in the year ahead will be to stay on top of emerging trends and adapt staffing strategies in response. The staffing teams who get it right will secure the top talent, and will fuel their company's success.

"Selecting and hiring people is one of the most important skills a manager can have," says Jim Messina of Maritz. "If you pick the right person, that's 99 percent of the battle."

Shelgren agrees, adding, "The thing that ends up differentiating a company is the people. Every day they are a living embodiment of your brand, your values, and your culture. If you get the right ones, it's so powerful."

From *Workforce Management*, January 15, 2007, pp. 25–26, 28, 30–31. Copyright © 2007 by Crain Communications. Reprinted by permission.

Balancing HR Systems with Employee Privacy

Breaches of employee data continue to make headlines and extra work for HR professionals at the organizations that have had problems. The growing reliance on systems for corporate functions including HR is one cause of the heightened risk, despite the many rewards that technology can provide.

How can your organization balance its needs for efficiency and productivity that HR systems can provide with its efforts to protect the privacy and security of employee information? A presentation at the IHRIM conference in Washington, D.C., helped shed light on the effectiveness of a joint approach by HR and HRIT working together. Carolyn Anker of the HR Data Privacy Office and Brenda Striggo, employee privacy architect in the Global Business Integration Project (GBIP; global SAP implementation and integration) at Eli Lilly and Company (Indianapolis), discussed this issue from both the HR and IT points of view.

They acknowledged that there is no perfect solution. "HRIT [HR information technology] versus privacy is a conundrum," Anker said. "HRIT is about accessibility, but privacy should be limited access on a need-to-know basis. How can the HR organization handle this?"

What's Causing the Conflict?

Anker explained some trends that are affecting the security of data, including:

- Multiple states/countries. In the U.S., there is no national law; information privacy is a state issue.
- More telecommuters and distance workers.
- More use of vendors and outsourcing.
- Enterprise resource planning.
- Demand for ease of use via email, downloads, and so forth.

There are privacy realities for all organizations, she said, including a more complex business and regulatory environment. Privacy law is growing and changing throughout the world, while state laws keep changing in the United States.

Eli Lilly has devoted resources to addressing the privacy versus technology challenge, in part because of a consent decree from the Federal Trade Commission in response to an e-mail accidentally sent to a list of Prozac users instead of a "bcc" message, Striggo acknowledged.

The company has been additionally challenged through the need to adapt its centralized SAP installation, which inadvertently set up violations of multinational privacy laws. The system is being adjusted so that it can adhere to local privacy requirements.

Another challenge has been adapting technology so that the company could obtain safe-harbor certification, which enables the use of data from European nations in the U.S.

From the technology side, there have been privacy challenges from the use of test data (personal information in an environment where development work is being conducted) in a production environment, Striggo noted. *A related issue:* A systems life cycle approach that includes the use of production data in test environments violates European laws. These challenges have meant that the Lilly HRIT team has had to address issues such as the effects of scrambling data within SAP.

All of these situations call for a coexistence of HRIT and HR privacy issues, noted Anker. "Practicality must be the reality" in finding a middle ground. Hard copies are risky, but e-records are even riskier if systems pre-date privacy issues (and so aren't designed to protect privacy). As a result, errors are often only "one click away." The solution to this latter problem was developed jointly by the HRIT and HR business team. A tool was used with rules to convert and scramble data, making the people anonymous in the development environment.

This is just one example of how joint efforts by both HR and HRIT personnel help address the conflict between privacy and technology. Eli Lilly has made this an official arrangement through its privacy audits initiative.

Privacy Audits

The company has a dedicated privacy audit team, with a regular schedule approved by its board. The audit looks at system privacy, including HR business process audits, site audits, and vendor audits. This process helps to identify new challenges and enables you to start work toward solving existing challenges. IT people are often "loaned" to the audit teams, since it is crucial to understand IT to perform the privacy audits. Other privacy issues that have to be considered are consumer and medical privacy, such as clinical trials.

HR privacy proves to be especially challenging, Anker noted. "HR privacy is the sleeping giant of HR issues," she said. "Everyone has employees, and employee data is everywhere. People feel a lot freer and looser with HR data since it is inside the company."

Using the U.S. recruiting and staffing as an example, Anker and Striggo explained how the HR business process audit tracks where employee information goes within the system. Most personal information (more than 90%) enters the system through recruiting. The data then may move through manual processes and IT systems to vendors. Each destination for the information must be examined to make sure it is being protected and properly conveyed to the next place in the system.

Any findings that violate Eli Lilly's global privacy policy must be resolved via action plans, to which HR must commit with HRIT agreement on feasibility, budget, and timeline. HRIT can't commit to any actions unless the privacy office signs off.

The issue of privacy protection when information goes out to vendors can be another problem. "Vendors processing data on your behalf is a big risk," Striggo pointed out. "Relationships and communication are very important here." Requiring vendor protections through a certification process developed by the IT department is helping Eli Lilly with this issue.

"It's all about containing risk," Anker concluded. "The more people you can restrain from making a mistake, [the more you can] reduce risk."

Technology Tames Password Overload, Boosts HR Data Security

Bill Leonard

The proliferation of passwords isn't just a headache for employees—it also can compromise security and become a costly burden for businesses.

HR can play an important role in ensuring that employees are educated in safe password maintenance practices that will reduce business risks, security experts say.

The typical employee relies on multiple passwords to handle everyday functions like accessing e-mail, making benefits selections and completing time sheets, according to Martin Carmichael, chief security officer for McAfee Software in Santa Clara, Calif.

"Much of this can be very sensitive personal information, so it's very important to keep it secure," Carmichael said.

"You really need to protect your passwords, put them under some sort of lock and key like an encrypted file and not keep them written on a Post-it Note stuck to your monitor," said Donald Harris, president of New York-based consulting group HR Privacy Solutions. "Employees need to be educated about these good practices."

The importance of safe password maintenance practices has grown with the increasing reliance on mobile technologies such as laptop computers. The theft of a single laptop—particularly one holding HR data—can compromise the personal data of countless workers. Data that are not protected by secure passwords are that much more accessible to a computer thief, hacker or other interloper.

Though employers have long relied on passwords and employee identifiers that include some or all of a worker's Social Security number (SSN), the practice has gone out of favor. In fact, unnecessary use of SSNs, or even parts of SSNs, as passwords is illegal in some states.

A better practice, according to Harris, is to use so-called "strong" passwords.

Online Resources

See www.shrm.org/hrmagazine/07Trendbook for links to:

- The SHRM *Workplace Forecast,* 2006.
- A SHRM webcast on protecting HR data.
- A SHRM article on biometrics.
- Tips from Microsoft on choosing strong passwords.

A strong password is usually six or more characters long and uses a combination of alphanumeric characters. Passwords that use combinations of letters with two or three numbers or even symbols such as a dollar sign or ampersand are safest because they are difficult for an unauthorized user to guess.

However, these passwords can create problems for workers simply because they are harder to remember.

"According to the IT departments of our clients, the No. 1 call they get for help from employees is to recover lost or forgotten passwords," said Sharyle Doherty, vice president of product management for Ultimate Software in Weston, Fla.

Doherty said the increasing number of user names and passwords is further complicated by the necessity to change passwords frequently. Many computer security experts recommend changing passwords at least every 60 days. According to a recent survey by the computer security firm RSA, nearly one-quarter of U.S. businesses require employees to change passwords once a month.

"With all the passwords you need and then changing them every few months, you can see how it can be pretty

Actions Organizations Are Taking or Planning to Take in Response to Science and Technology Trends

	Yes	Plan To	No
Implementing technology usage policies for employees	78%	8%	14%
Implementing an employee privacy policy	65	14	21
Investing in technology and services designed to protect company data in the event of a disaster or cyber attack	64	14	22
Expanding the use of the web for the delivery and use of HR applications	59	20	21

Source: Society for Human Resource Management *Workplace Forecast*, 2006.

confusing, and no wonder people forget which passwords they're using," Doherty said.

To help ease password burden, some companies are turning to so-called "single sign-on" (SSO), a form of software authentication that enables a user to authenticate once and gain access to the resources of multiple software systems.

Among employers, according to Carmichael, "The interest in single sign-on solutions is very high."

Single sign-on allows each employee to log on to a corporate computer system with one user name and one password. Depending on how the network is configured, the SSO might provide a key to various web-based applications such as e-mail, HR self-service, benefits administration, payroll, accounting and expense reporting.

"We have had a single sign-on for several years, and it has worked quite well throughout the organization," said Sidney Simon, director of product strategy for Unum Corp. in Chattanooga, Tenn. "You sign on to the system with one user name and one password, and you have access from your desktop or laptop to all the systems we use. It's very popular with our employees."

"Single sign-ons are definitely a hot item right now, and employers are looking for the best way to develop a single sign-on for their systems," said Doherty. "We are working with a number of clients right now to develop single sign-ons for their systems."

Because of its high cost—as much as $80 per user—SSO technology has traditionally been practical only for large companies. In addition, the technology tends to hog server space.

But those obstacles may soon disappear, some technology experts say.

Many companies are developing single sign-on systems by using Lightweight Directory Access Protocol (LDAP). LDAP allows a computer system to look up and verify encryption certificates and generate a single log-on.

Carmichael said encrypted portable devices are popular alternatives to passwords. These devices are available in various forms, such as smart cards that you swipe through a scanner that reads your passwords and flash drives that connect to a PC's USB port and supply passwords when needed.

Businesses are exploring systems such as 'password vaults' to secure passwords and credential-checking systems that download 'cookies' to ensure users are authorized.

In addition to the "password token" devices, Carmichael said, businesses are exploring the use of systems such as "password vaults" to secure passwords and credential-checking systems that download "cookies" to ensure that someone is authorized to use the systems.

However, Carmichael and Doherty said password-based authorization could be made obsolete by bio-metric technology.

"Fingerprints, retinal scans and voiceprint identification is technology that is currently being used in some businesses that require high levels of security, like government contractors," said Doherty. "But as the technology develops, it will become more available and cost-effective to use."

Microsoft, for example, already offers keyboards that include fingerprint scanners and is marketing the scanners as cost-effective alternatives to password overload. However, the system is still new, and any business executive who might be considering using fingerprint scans should plan to use them in combination with passwords, security experts advise.

Biometric devices have other problems too.

"Studies show that most people don't want to use retinal scans because they don't want to put their eyes up to the device," said Carmichael. "Voiceprints typically won't work if the user has a cold or sore throat, and fingerprint identification isn't exact either. If someone cuts or burns their finger, then the scans may not work properly."

Could DNA scans be the answer?

Perhaps, said Carmichael, although culturally and legally that might be a faint prospect.

"Two years ago, the technology was so new and so expensive that it probably didn't seem possible, but, as we all know, technology changes and [that] improves the cost. There have been some major developments in this technology," he said. "Within 10 years and maybe even as soon as five, we will begin to see a proliferation of this type of technology, which should reshape the way we sign on to use our computers."

BILL LEONARD is senior writer for HR News.

UNIT 3

Creating a Productive Work Environment

Unit Selections

Key Points to Consider

- What are some things you might do to motivate employees, especially young women to stay in an organization? What are some of the things that motivate you?

- In today's environment, do you think people should be viewed more as partners or as workers?

- What strategies could you employ to communicate more effectively with your peers or your instructor? What things can destroy effective communication? What role does correct communication play in projecting a desired image?

- Do you think feedback is important? In conversation? In your career?

- How would you deal with a bully in the workplace?

Student Web Site

www.mhcls.com

Internet References

American Society for Training and Development (ASTD)
   http://www.astd.org
Commission on the Future of Worker-Management Relations
   http://www.dol.gov/_sec/media/reports/dunlop/dunlop.htm
The Downsizing of America
   http://www.nytimes.com/specials/downsize/glance.html
Employee Incentives and Career Development
   http://www.snc.edu/socsci/chair/336/group1.htm

Whenever anything is being accomplished, it is being done, I have learned, by a monomaniac with a mission.
—Peter Drucker

For years, management theorists have indicated that the basic functions of management are to plan, direct, organize, control, and staff organizations. Unfortunately, those five words only tell what the manager is to do. They do not tell the manager how to do it. Being a truly effective manager involves more than just those five tasks. It involves knowing what goals to set for the organization, pursuing those goals with more desire and determination than anyone else in the organization, communicating the goals once they have been established, and having other members of the organization adopt those goals as their own.

Motivation is one of the easiest concepts to understand, yet one of the most difficult to implement. Often the difference between successful and mediocre organizations is that the usual 20% in successful organizations are motivated, and the other 80% are also motivated. They are excited about the company, about what they do for the company, and about the company's products or services. Effective organizations build upon past successes. All of the employees are performing at very high levels. If people feel good about themselves and good about their organization, then they are probably going to do a good job. Whether it is called morale, motivation, or enthusiasm, it still amounts to the same fragile concept—simple to understand, difficult to create and build, and very easy to destroy.

In order to maintain a motivated workforce for any task, it is necessary to establish an effective reward system. A truly motivated worker will respond much more effectively to a carrot than to a stick. Turned-on workers are having their needs met and are responding to the goals and objectives of the organization. They do an outstanding job because they want to, which results in an outstanding company.

Perhaps the single most important skill for any manager, or, for that matter, any human being, is the ability to communicate. People work on this skill throughout their education in courses such as English and speech. They attempt to improve communication through an array of methods and media, which range from the printed word, e-mail, and television, to rumors and simple conversation. Yet managers often do not do a very good job of communicating with their employees or their customers. This is very unfortunate, because ineffective communication can often negate all of the other successes that a firm has enjoyed. "Managing in the New Millennium: Interpersonal Skills," and "Managing Employee Relations," address this issue. This is something that managers must strive for if they want to have people working together for a common goal. Managers,

© Keith Brofsky/Getty Images

and the firms they represent, must honestly communicate their goals, as well as their instructions, to their employees. If the manager does not do so, the employees will be confused and even distrustful, because they will not understand the rationale behind their instructions. If the manager is successful in honestly communicating the company's goals, ideals and culture to the employees, and is able to build the motivation and enthusiasm that are necessary to successfully accomplish those goals, then he or she has become not just a manager, but a leader, and that is, indeed, rare.

Positive work environments are also work environments that are free of fear and intimidation. Bullying is being recognized as a problem in the workplace, just as it is in the society. While some people may scoff at bullying as being a problem, they should be reminded that twenty years ago sexual harassment was also scoffed at as a problem. Many lawsuits and millions if not billions of dollars later, nobody underestimates the importance or potential danger of sexual harassment in the workplace, and "Banishing Bullying," should be a top priority for any organization.

Creating a positive work environment is not easy. Communicating with and motivating people, whether employees, volunteers, citizens, or Boy Scouts, is difficult to do. Managers, however, are faced with the task of doing exactly that.

The 'Brain Drain': How to Get Talented Women to Stay

What happens when you don't get the promotion or title you've consistently been promised and deserved? You stop trying. And maybe you leave.

JENNIFER MILLMAN

Rosie Saez, now senior vice president and Leadership Practices Group director for Wachovia, got burned twice early in her banking career. The first time, it happened after a merger. Saez's manager was impressed with a selection process she helped develop and told her he would submit her name for a vice-president title.

A few months later, he came back to apologize. "We have Gus who's a black man and he's been working on some of this, so we're going to put him in first and we'll put you in next," recalls Saez.

There was another excuse the following quarter, when Saez's manager told her, "There was this white woman who was really upset and felt like she should be promoted."

"I thought, 'Why is it one or the other? Why can't it be both?'" she says. "By the time I got the VP title, it wasn't worth what it was supposed to be."

Saez didn't give up, but many women do. Even the most progressive companies, The 2007 DiversityInc Top 50 Companies for Diversity®, still struggle to promote women at levels equal to their representation in the talent pool. Many companies are paying attention to this, yet too many women in corporate America still feel excluded from important networks, have fewer role models, receive limited experience in line-management positions and face gender stereotypes.

"Women who don't feel like there is much progress in breaking the glass ceiling are more likely [than men] to reduce their aspirations," says Ellen Galinsky, president and cofounder of the Families and Work Institute.

That's not something companies can afford. The talent pool is drying up, and women make up most of it. Women have earned most of the associate's, bachelor's and master's degrees granted each year for the last two decades; by 2014, they will supersede men on the doctorate level, according to the National Center for Education Statistics.

"The women who advanced have had to change jobs. It's not that they weren't talented; they got locked into the perceptions in their former company," says Galinsky. "It's the meeting when a woman says something and nobody responds, and then the man says the same thing a few minutes later and everyone says, 'What a good idea!'"

Here, five talented women tell you in their own words why they've stayed in corporate America, or if they've left, what companies could have done to keep them.

Rosie Saez
Senior Vice President, Director, Leadership Practices Group, Wachovia, No. 11 in the Top 50.

I started out as a strong community activist. The first couple of years in a nonprofit allowed me to begin to understand that you can't change the world overnight, and that it takes patience, skill, learning how to influence, be more strategic.

When I moved into the banking industry, I was the one woman of color in the human-resources organization in a leadership position and all of the people that I supported in a staff function were white men, who led all the big functions.

There were times when I wasn't included. I'd hear things like, "What are you doing here? You don't belong in this meeting." I **could have** been a **victim,** but I just figured out ways to **develop one-on-one relationships** with a lot of them, show the **added value** that I could bring. With time, I didn't have to ask to be included; it was natural for them to say, "We need to make sure Rosie's at the table."

As a woman of color, I experience things and I step back and say, "Wow, did that just happen because I'm a woman of color?" I've learned to say, "Let me meet people where they are, give a little bit of grace, trust that the intent is really a good intent and be patient while people learn to change."

When you're beginning the work, you want things to happen quicker, faster. [Some people wonder] why you can't understand that what I'm trying to get you to do is really the right thing, and three years later you figure it out.

Through predecessor banks, I have spent 19 years here. Because I've performed and I've been willing to take risks, the company has always been willing to take risks with me.

You can lose a job, but you don't lose your skills. I do bring some skill sets that are transferable, so I don't question myself. I trust my gut a lot more than I used to. If I could've given my younger self some counsel, it would've been to learn early on that yes, I want to change the world, but I have to do it in a way where I model it so that as I leave these prints on people's lives, others can actually hear me and see me perform.

Sherry Nolan
Vice President of Diversity and Workplace Development, Pepsi Bottling Group, No. 2 in the Top 50.

I've had seven jobs in seven years. Women need to examine the landscape and take stretch assignments that put them in places where they're less comfortable, because there is a tendency sometimes to excel vertically. I had to put myself out there and say, "If I want to be a [chief people officer], what do I need to know?"

"I don't know that there are a lot of type A executives who aren't also type A mothers."

—Sherry Nolan, Pepsi Bottling Group

I took a cross-country relocation to California. I'm a **single mother.** I don't know that there are a lot of **type A executives** who aren't **also type A mothers.** I don't want to be a fantastic player for Pepsi and a lousy mom, so I try to do both. You have to have a strong sense of your resources at home. When I went to California, that was the most challenged because my network was changing. I had to excel in a new job and make sure my daughter was excelling as well.

Make decisions about career and family that feel like choices, not sacrifices. If you continue to make things feel like sacrifices, it's not sustainable. California was absolutely a choice, but it was a hard choice. I knew that in order for me to lead a function like I'm leading now, I needed to lead a regional business in the field. For me, the sacrifice would more have been not taking it and limiting my career growth.

We own it. Organizations can provide all the right tools like great leaders, clear career expectations, challenging work, autonomy, and those are all the reasons I stay, but you own it. This confidence comes from delivering, getting recognized and being willing to step out into something that's perhaps more challenging than you've had before.

You have to deliver results no matter what. We calculate every day [whether we are] winning or losing. You have to know that you're delivering on the organization's big bets.

May Snowden
Vice President, Operations/Consultant, Creative Wealth Alliance Former Vice President, Global Diversity, Starbucks.

I was raised by a very strong mother who taught me I was valued. She also helped me understand that it is my responsibility not to feel devalued by others, because it's so easy. I had to fight with that constantly in my career because I was often the only black person in the role, and in many cases, the only woman.

I remember when I was promoted to a plant-manager job and then to a district position where I had all of outside telecommunications, which was a 98 percent-male organization. This little voice would just constantly chat at me about "You can't do this, you don't have the experience," and I constantly had to talk to myself and say, "You can do this; that's why they selected you for the job."

"There are some men who depend on women being sexist against women."

—May Snowden, Creative Wealth Alliance

There are some men who depend on women being sexist against women. You think a woman in a position can bring in other women, but they won't. You get a person of color in a position; a person of color could bring more people of color, but they won't. [There's] this concept of **expecting the individual** who is the **minority not** to **bring in others like them.** That's why women come in and they're not promoted; they don't have any support.

You have to have people that are willing to fight for you, to bring up your name when there are opportunities, to ensure that if issues come up, they're on your side.

Women of color sometimes call me in tears because they fear they're not heard and that people are threatened by them, which causes them to be in fear, and nothing positive comes about when there's fear. When women of color can embrace white women and white women can embrace all women of color, we can really be strong. We have so much power; we've got to take it, do something with it and hold people accountable.

Linda Denny
President and CEO, Women's Business Enterprise National Council (WBENC).

I was the fifth woman to be a managing partner for New York Life Insurance (one of DiversityInc's 25 Noteworthy Companies) and I continued up the ranks into the home office. About three years into that, Aetna (also one of the 25 Noteworthy Companies) came along and made me an offer I couldn't refuse. The section of Aetna that I worked for was sold to ING; then ING merged all 14 companies they had and that became a real challenge.

"I just thought, 'I'm killing myself here, and I don't think I want to kill myself.'"

—Linda Denny,
Women's Business Enterprise National Council

I had 45 days when I had hardly slept in my own bed, and they wanted me to move again . . . and I just thought, "I'm killing myself here, and I don't think I want to kill myself."

8 Tips for Advancing Women

1. Change the Mindset around Work/life

"People don't use work/family benefits because we find in our national studies that 39 percent of employees feel there's a penalty," says Galinsky. "If you ask bosses in a company whether there is a penalty, they'll say no; ask employees and they'll say yes, so where is the truth? It's probably somewhere in the middle but closer to the employees."

PricewaterhouseCoopers, No.12 in the Top 50, couldn't get people to take vacations or stop e-mailing, so they have closed offices down and shut off e-mail between Christmas and New Year's; they make time off a value. Deloitte, No. 19 in the Top 50, has a mass career-customization program that enables people to rethink careers as being linear with fixed schedules.

"The problem with the notion of off-ramps and on-ramps is that there is the ideal job and there are others," says Galinsky. "It's the industrial model of success where presence equals productivity. There is the ideal notion of how you do it, and an ideal way."

It's not the only way. "My manager asked me to run the entire region—15 teams in 15 states—and allowed me to do it out of Philadelphia. I had a sister who was dying at the time and my father who was very ill, and she was very conscious of the need for me to have some balance in my life," says Saez.

"She didn't have to worry about if I would get the work done because she knew I would; she didn't need for me to do it between 9 and 5," she adds.

2. Build Strategic Relationships

"In any Fortune 500 company, the alignment process that you have to go to be successful can be five to 20 people depending on who's in the zone," says Nolan. "I made sure I had relationships that would facilitate productivity for me. This notion about growing vertically in organizations can lead to lack of confidence."

"You become comfortable in one particular discipline, and then when you need to cross over, if you're not nimble because you haven't started thinking about those tactical relationships, you're probably not considered for a role because you don't have that dexterity," she explains. "If you don't have that dexterity, another counterpart—either male or female—will be chosen to get that work done."

3. Move Diagonally

"A lot of my jobs were lateral," says Snowden. "After spending 30 years in a company, you'd expect to have had senior-level or officer positions; I did not make officer until I left telecommunications and went to Eastman Kodak."

"I don't think young people will stay as long as I did in one industry without being promoted. The expectation is that if they're career-minded, they would be an officer," she adds. "People have to know when it's time to move, even though

they may be happy and satisfied, because I was content. In being content, you stay wherever you are and leave it up to others to see your worth."

4. Communicate Candidly

"Communication at home is as important as it is at work," says Nolan. "You're driving a car with passengers in the back; you're not alone."

"Everybody needs to be able to put their thoughts aside and see the other person's position, but it's really hard when you're at a standoff because no one wants to give," adds Snowden. "I've been the first one to give, but after I give, the other person can. Then we can come up with a compromise that's going to be better than the [ideas] each of us had on our own."

5. Have a Game Plan

"You have to work right to left; know where you want to go and look for experiences that are going to round you out. If it's a book, does each chapter make sense?" says Nolan. "I've had great leadership. They're tactical about delivering me assignments and feedback that are progressive. I ask for it on a regular basis, but just when you hit the point and you're wondering what's next, something comes because you've been talking about what the next steps are for you."

6. Find a Mentor, Be a Mentor

"Every day that we are in leadership positions, particularly as women of color . . . we are leaving footprints in the lives of people," says Saez. "We've got so many people thinking, "How did she get there? If she can get there, I can get there.""

7. Network Proactively

"You don't want to be a solo person. I've seen that happen to people, where they do good work and that's all they want to do. They go to work, keep their head down and they have no help," says Snowden. "Networking is so important; you just have to do it. Pick and choose what you're going to participate in and know why and network with different individuals."

8. Involve Women in Decision Making

"Have women involved in a visible way in setting goals for women, and then addressing the issues that they face in a visible way where there is real follow-through, not just lip service," says Galinsky. "IBM sets up a group of women to say what stands in the way of their success, what could we do to make it more successful at this company, both in your personal life as well as in your work life. What could we do to also attract people like you as customers or as clients?"

I burned out. I had spent all these years climbing the ladder, and I loved my career, but I was ready for something fresh and different. I took 10 months off and went to work for WBENC. Come April, I will have been here five years. I had thought I would go back to work for another corporation, but after all of my years of travel and having such a level of responsibility, I was just exhausted in every way you could be exhausted—mentally, physically, spiritually. I had to step back, regroup, find myself again, and look at what I wanted to achieve.

I don't mind demands and I don't mind pressure, but I was just ready to make a little more impact and have more control. I can tell you of so many [women who] left corporate careers and started their own business because they reached that point of **burnout** or felt like they were **never going to go where** they felt **they had the ability to go.**

The pipeline is full of women who are going to have the job experience and the capabilities of moving into those senior executive-level positions. When I was coming through, that pipeline just wasn't there. I just got to the point of saying, "I've had enough. I don't want to do this. I want to go have some life."

Louise Liang
Senior Vice President, Quality/Clinical Systems Support, Kaiser Foundation Health Plan and Hospitals, Kaiser Permanente, No. 27 on the Top 50.

One of my executive admins said that she had never had a woman boss and she didn't know whether that was going to work for her. I was startled because it never dawned on me, at least not for women. We worked well together and she realized that was just borne out of her experience of not having a woman boss or observing one. Several men over the years clearly had questions in their mind as my supervisory role began.

There's always a person who's just not going to be able to work that through. I haven't had any of them working for me. Most of the people I've encountered assess on merit. At the end of the day, it's **not about gender or race.** It's about whether you have the **capabilities** and you can develop a working relationship and guide and support people who work for you in a way that gets the work done. Be open-minded and willing to learn about how different systems work and what the levers are. Those can vary from company to company, different kinds of cultures or mechanisms. Having been successful in different places, you're able to identify the elements you can use to create change and drive an agenda.

Right after I completed my clinical training, I was hired by Henry Ford Hospital as the first pediatrician in a brandnew clinic. They made me chief of the department. I had no training to do it. Take the opportunities that present themselves. People either want to have experience or special training, but sometimes you just have to go with it.

That means there will be occasions when you'll stumble, but opportunities don't always come in exactly the size, shape and timing you'd prefer. It's only by trying things out that you find out what you might be really good at.

Managing in the New Millennium: Interpersonal Skills

PATRICIA M. BUHLER

Management is defined as "getting things done through others." Without strong interpersonal skills, then, it is not possible to be a successful manager. Interacting with others is an essential building block of management effectiveness. Unfortunately, few management development courses specifically address how to interact with others. Instead, the majority of these programs focus on the technical skills of management—addressing such skills as how to engage in strategic planning, how to structure organizations, or how to manage a budget. The development of interpersonal skills is often left to the individual.

What were traditionally labeled "soft skills" in the past, have now been identified as the "hard" skills in today's business environment. One of these skills is interpersonal skills. Nearly every aspect of business—and management in particular—requires an ability to interact effectively with others. Organizations themselves are collections of people. Teams are utilized more extensively today than ever before. Without finely developed people skills, then, a manager's performance and ability to be successful is substantially hindered.

A variety of research studies have emphasized the importance of these interpersonal skills. Katz's research on managerial competencies identified three key skills important to success. These are technical, human, and conceptual skills. The technical skills involve performing the actual work of the organization. The human skills are the interpersonal skills and the conceptual skills involve the ability to see the "big picture." While these three skills are important at all management levels, the technical skills become less important as one moves up the organizational hierarchy (and further away from the operations employees). The conceptual skills, in contrast, become more important. And according to Katz, the human skills are identified as equally important throughout the management ranks.

Managers can enhance their interpersonal skills by addressing several key components. They can develop their emotional intelligence, learn to recognize the uniqueness of each employee, acknowledge the impact of the details (and the "small stuff"), learn to listen, empower others, and build trust.

Emotional Intelligence

The business literature in the last decade has focused on the need for emotional intelligence in the workplace—moving beyond the importance of one's general intelligence. Daniel Goleman, founder of Emotional Intelligence Services, has suggested "the people who will become the leaders, the people who will become the star performers, are the ones who have the strength in the key emotional intelligence abilities." Effective relationships can be better built with emotionally intelligent employees. The probability of developing effective relationships increases as individuals are more aware of their own emotions and can read the emotions of others since emotions are not checked at the door as employees go to work.

Emotional intelligence (identified by the acronym EI) requires first mastering capabilities in self-awareness. Recognizing one's own emotions is the foundation for later understanding others. The second component is self-regulation. Once people are aware of their emotions, they must then learn to manage those emotions and the conditions that elicit their emotional responses. Those two components are then used to self-motivate and understand the role of emotions in performing at high levels. The fourth component is empathy. This involves "walking in another's shoes" so to speak and understanding their perspective and their feelings. Finally, these prior components enable individuals to develop effective relationships.

Recognizing the Uniqueness of Each Employee

While it is often easier to take the approach of "one size fits all," when it comes to people it simply does not work in today's diverse workplace. To build more effective relationships, each individual must be treated as the unique individual they are. This requires investing time in getting to know each employee and coworker.

Identifying what drives the behavior of others enables the astute manager to better interact with them. Getting out of the office helps to gain an understanding of others and ultimately how to better interact with them.

Getting to know others involves people at all levels in the organization. While sometimes ignored or overlooked, building effective interpersonal relationships includes managing upward in the organization. It is each manager's responsibility to manage relationships in all three directions—downward, laterally, and upward. Too often, managers assume that the only relationship they need to manage involves their employees.

The Small Stuff Is the Big Stuff

Remembering the details is critical in developing interpersonal skills. A failure to "sweat the small stuff" can actually be a mistake. It is, indeed, the small stuff that can make a big difference to employees. For example, when delivering rewards, the small ideas can often generate the biggest payoff. A simple hand-written thank you note to an employee or a peer can reap big benefits and mean a lot to the recipient.

Too often, managers take the easy way out by using budget constraints to explain why they can not reward employees. It takes more thought and more creativity to design a reward program based on individuals and their uniqueness. This does, however, depend upon the recognition or the uniqueness of each employee.

Learn to Listen

Listening continues to be a lost art. People tend to be better talkers than listeners. This may occur, in part, due to the fact that many consider listening to be a passive activity instead of approaching it as an active process with sincere involvement and participation. The keys to active listening involve hearing not just the words that are spoken, but listening to the feelings and then responding to those feelings.

When listening, it is critical to watch and observe the nonverbal cues. Volumes are communicated nonverbally. The words actually spoken are the smallest part of the communication. To actively listen and receive the full message intended by the sender, the nonverbal components must be read. Body language or tone of voice can drastically change the real meaning of the words actually spoken.

In most cases, people who are not actively engaged in talking are spending their time thinking about what they are going to say next rather than listening. When really listening, people learn more and "plug into" others. Covey's advice in his best selling book, *The 7 Habits of Highly Effective People,* is worth noting. "Seek first to understand and then to be understood." When managers engage in active listening and attempt to understand the perceptions of others, they are generally more effective in building effective relationships.

Empowering Others

Organizations give a great deal of lip service to empowering their workforce. Some may think if they delegate the distasteful tasks to employees that they are empowering them. It is much more,

however. Those managers who truly empower others build effective relationships. But this is hard work requiring courageous personalities who trust others. To empower a workforce requires courage to give up power. It also involves rethinking the traditional perspective of power. Today's mindset that supports empowerment suggests that power be more evenly distributed throughout the organization. This also supports participative management.

While empowering others can be highly effective, it only works if others have the knowledge, skills, and abilities to be able to perform. This means that managers must invest in others—and their development. In a business environment that favors downsizing, this is a particularly important lesson. If others are to be empowered and perhaps take on additional responsibility, they can only be successful if they have the skill set to perform. If the appropriate training and development is not provided, this will not empower others, but rather will frustrate them.

A key component of empowering others also involves sharing information. Sharing information goes hand-in-hand with empowerment. It is necessary for people to have the appropriate information to make informed decisions and to perform effectively when they are empowered. Managers, then, must be brave enough to distribute information to others (rather than hoarding it in a power play).

Delegating is another critical element of empowering others. Delegation is an art in itself that is critical to building effective relationships. An inability to delegate is even said to be one of the top reasons for the failure of many managers.

Empowering others can be liberating and rewarding for both the manager who empowers others and for those who are being empowered. This communicates a level of trust in others that is usually well received—and motivating.

Building Trust

John C. Maxwell suggests in his book, *The 17 Essential Qualities of a Team Player,* that people must take the lead in serving others and trusting others. While many excuse themselves by waiting to return trust or service once it has been bestowed on them, they must instead trust others first and serve others first. Then others will trust them and serve them.

The first step in building trust is to demonstrate trustworthiness. Effective relationships depend upon trust. This requires that individuals demonstrate dependability and commitment.

Finally—Taking a Cue from *Fish!*

The Fish Philosophy provides an essential element of building effective interpersonal skills. The foundation of the Fish philosophy as proposed by Stephen Lundin and his co-authors in the best selling book, *Fish!,* is choosing an attitude. This is a daily choice each person makes. A positive attitude and enthusiasm go a long way to developing effective relationships in today's business environment. And only by developing those relationships will managers be able to get things done.

From *Supervision,* July 2005, pp. 20–22. Copyright © 2005 by National Research Bureau, 320 Valley Street, Burlington, Iowa 52601. Reprinted by permission.

Managing Employee Relations

Develop interpersonal communications and conflict-management skills to better manage employee relations.

GREG ROPER

When was the last time you took a good look at your workforce. What did you see? You probably saw a rapidly changing group of employees that is getting more diverse by the day. The accelerated growth of diversity in the workforce over the past 20 years has spawned new developments in managing employee relations, making it one of the biggest challenges facing managers.

To meet this challenge, managers must improve skills such as active listening, adaptability and decision-making. These core skills can assist supervisors and managers in tackling difficult issues that may arise within their workforce.

However, while the skills mentioned above are key, this article focuses on the two most important skills for managing employee relations: interpersonal communications and conflict management.

Interpersonal Communications

The first skill for managers to understand and practice is interpersonal communications, because it is the foundation for all actions in the workplace and it allows the supervisor or manager an opportunity to build relationships with the overall workgroup without alienating anyone in the work environment. Working with diverse groups of people requires a tremendous amount of interaction. If these interactions are positive, they can help create the right workplace climate, attitudes, beliefs and behaviors.

In addition, because interactions occur daily, it is important for managers to have the respect of their employees. If this respect is absent, the supervisor or manager will have a difficult time getting things accomplished.

In a June 2004 *Harvard Business Review* article titled "Understanding 'People' People," Timothy Butler and James Waldroop identify four dimensions to optimize interpersonal communications:

- **Influence.** This dimension is for those who thrive on constant interaction with people. The interaction allows individuals the opportunity to develop and extend their personal sphere of interpersonal influence. This provides professional satisfaction with the ability to influence,

negotiate and leverage valuable information as a method to enhance ideas. Think of these individuals as having highly developed salesmanship skills because they have the ability to constantly keep people highly motivated, no matter what the situation.

- **Interpersonal facilitation.** This dimension describes those who are perceived and known as "people persons." They are very aware of the interpersonal aspects of the work environment and are intuitive, because they are constantly monitoring the situation behind the scenes. Those who focus on this dimension pose critical questions to themselves, such as: What is going to be our strategy to ensure positive employee relations? Moreover, what employee relations issues are going to impact the business and what is the proper way to address them? "People persons" use these questions and subsequent answers to look for ways to improve organizational effectiveness through proactive solutions.

> **Listening skills are the foundation to managing conflict. Focus on what the person says, not your response to what is said.**

- **Relational creativity.** This dimension focuses on nurturing and developing relationships with diverse groups through visual and verbal imagery. An example of this would be the leader of a marketing team who develops and implements a marketing strategy designated for a particular consumer segment, or the plant manager who prepares a speech that the CEO of the organization will deliver to employees, as a method to excite employees about the organization's new direction.
- **Team leadership.** This dimension is for those who are committed to maintaining and fostering good employee relations with the workforce. They enjoy the day-to-day

interaction as a method of feeling good about themselves. Those who embrace this dimension don't care for individual tasks such as writing reports, working on a computer, or any other activity that doesn't allow them to engage others as a means to feel satisfied and fulfilled.

With respect to the four relational dimensions, it is important to note that a manager can have a profound interest in one, two, three or all four dimensions. It is also important to understand that managers need to keep these dimensions in mind when engaging diverse groups, developing people and creating employee relations strategies.

Conflict Management

The second skill for managers to leverage is conflict management. Learning to leverage this skill can help in resolving employee relations issues quickly and effectively, and can create greater satisfaction with the workgroup. There are seven components to effective conflict management:

- **Speak your mind and heart.** As a manager, you need to speak up and say what you think. As obvious as this point seems, people have a difficult time articulating their needs, wants and desires. This exacerbates the conflict because the communication gets distorted and people become frustrated. An example of this would be an employee who is very upset with their manager's management style. He goes to the manager to discuss how he feels, but, instead of focusing on the issue, the manager brings up other issues, which distorts the communication and frustrates the employee. Remember, instead of avoiding the problem, address it and speak up.

- **Listen well.** Listening skills are the foundation to managing conflict. Your focus should be on what the person says, not your response to what is said. Focus on what is positive in the conversation instead of negative, and inform the other party of what you are doing.

- **Express strong feelings appropriately.** Conflict of any type creates a surge in emotions such as happiness, anger, despair and sorrow. Your job as the manager is to manage those emotions through respect and careful examination of what the person is experiencing. Never attack the individual talking. Say, "Dave, I understand your conviction on this matter, and I am willing to work through it so that we can bring closure to the issue," instead of, "Dave, I am tired of your complaining and the poor attitude exhibited by you and your co-workers. To me, this is a done issue." Remember, you are trying to establish a relationship with your workforce.

- **Remain rational for as long as you can.** This means keeping yourself focused on resolving the conflict and remaining connected to the individual throughout the conversation. Then, summarize the situation and ask questions. For example, say, "John, I heard you say that you and Susan are having issues communicating. Allow

me to meet with Susan so that I can assist in addressing your concerns."

- **Review what has been said.** Ensure that all issues regarding the conflict are clarified, and if they are not, ask questions to get answers to the things you don't know. For example, say, "To get at the crux of the issue, I need answers to my questions. Why did Ken hurl a racial insult at Mohammed?"

- **Learn to give and take.** The conversation must be two-sided, not with you doing all of the talking. This will help provide a short- or long-term solution to the conflict. An example of this would be saying, "Linda, you made a good point, now please hear me out," instead of, "Linda, you need to listen to me. I don't need your input. I will solve this problem." Get employees involved so they buy into the process.

- **Avoid all harmful statements.** When you verbally attack, you create enemies and put individuals on the defensive. This means that you are reducing the chances of quickly resolving any conflict. Just remember the Hippocratic Oath: "Do no harm."

As stated in the seven points above, conflict management requires a great deal of listening, clearly articulating the issues, asking questions and providing solutions. Using these techniques to improve your conflict management skills will go a long way in fostering positive employee relations with a workforce.

"Employee relations in the workplace will continuously test the mental fortitude and physical endurance of managers in all industries," says Billy D. Ihrig, group director of labor and employee relations at Ryder Inc. in Miami. "Understanding the importance to getting at the root causes of employee relation issues will be the impetus for improved employee relations, increased credibility with the workforce and the establishment of a positive workplace for years to come."

The Payoff

This article has described two anchor skills—interpersonal communications and conflict management—that managers can use to improve employee relations in the workplace. Incorporating interpersonal communications and conflict management into your employee relations strategy could result in interactions that are more positive and less combative.

Remember, no organization wants to be known as one that doesn't foster strong employee relations. To survive in a highly competitive business environment, organizations want to attract and retain the best talent from all walks of life and be known as the employer of choice.

Greg Roper, PhD, is a registered organizational development professional and region director of human resources at Frito Lay Inc. with over 12 years of experience in managing employee relations and change. He has research and writing interest in diversity, employee relations and employee involvement.

Banishing Bullying

Communication training, well-publicized policies and even theater productions help reduce interpersonal aggression in workplaces.

SADIE F. DINGFELDER

The logo for the Ramsey County, Minn., government is a big red R, which stands for the county's name on building signs and letterhead. However, the R takes on a double meaning on employee identification pins: It hovers over the word "respect," and is just one way the county fosters a work environment that is inhospitable to bullying, says Don Gault, a member of the county's public health department.

"We have a policy of respect, and we back it up with trainings that teach people to listen to each other," says Gault, who also serves as a member of the county's Workplace Action Team, the group responsible for such initiatives.

In fact, Ramsey County takes a variety of approaches to preventing workplace aggression. It even occasionally brings in a theater group to illustrate the ways that miscommunication can escalate in a workplace. Such a broad strategy is probably the most effective way to address workplace bullying, observes Kevin Kelloway, PhD, a psychologist at St. Mary's University in Canada who researches the topic.

"The way you limit [bullying] behavior is not by developing an exhaustive list of things you can't do, but by taking a more positive approach, saying 'This is the way we treat other people here,'" says Kelloway.

Businesses are increasingly tapping psychologists' expertise to foster healthy, respectful workplaces, Kelloway notes. For instance, he has found that companies increasingly call him for help changing their climates. They may be motivated by a number of factors, such as avoiding lawsuits, decreasing employee sick-day use and reducing turnover, he notes.

"We are seeing a trend where there is a shortage of qualified professionals," says Kelloway. "Companies are competing for talent, and . . . people recognize they can go elsewhere instead of tolerating behavior they may have tolerated in the past."

Further support for the idea that improving work climate can decrease aggression and bullying comes from a recent Department of Veterans Affairs pilot program. In it, psychologists and other professionals taught employees communication skills using a technique known as Collaborative Action Inquiry, which encourages groups to collect data on a problem and then cycle through stages of action and reflection. After the training,

employees at the pilot sites, including hospitals and claims-processing centers, reported less aggression and increased employee satisfaction.

In one case, the intervention reduced the average time for a claim to be processed, notes project consultant Joel Neuman, PhD, a psychologist in the School of Business at the State University of New York, New Paltz. Workers accomplished this feat by listening more carefully to one another: For example, they used a "talking stick" that gave one person the floor and reduced interruptions in meetings.

"The only way to address day-to-day forms of aggression—verbal aggression, psychological aggression, emotional abuse—is to change the nature of the conversations people are having with each other," he says.

Rooting out Root Causes

Beginning in 1999, Neuman and his colleagues aimed to help 11 workplaces in the VA system increase communication and civility. But a team of outside experts can't just go into an office and tell a company how to reduce bullying, says Loraleigh Keashly, PhD, a psychologist at Detroit's Wayne State University who also consulted on the project. Unique issues contributed to disrespectful behavior at each of the VA workplaces, she notes.

"At one claims-processing center, the root causes were problems with communication and unfair promotion," says Keashly. "Favoritism was poisoning the climate there; union employees felt they weren't being heard by upper management."

So Keashly, Neuman and their colleagues asked both the union and management to nominate a group of employees to serve on an "action team" that would address the problem. The researchers then gave everyone in the center a survey that measured, among other things, how often the employees felt they were the target of disrespectful behavior, such as hostile glaring, malicious gossip and eye-rolling. The consultants then presented the results, which showed that some aggressive acts occurred more frequently there than at similar VA facilities.

With guidance from the researchers, the action teams analyzed the data and determined that rank-and-file employees were frustrated because they felt unheard by management. So they instituted an intervention program called "Flake-off Fridays," in which the center's assistant director invited a randomly selected group of employees to meet and chat with him. During these hour-long meetings, employees asked questions, brought up concerns or just enjoyed some time away from their desks.

"The only way to address day-to-day forms of aggression—verbal aggression, psychological aggression, emotional abuse—is to change the nature of the conversations people are having with each other."

—Joel Newman, State University of New York, New Paltz

After the institution of Flake-off Fridays, the researchers administered a follow-up survey and found that bullying and other aggressive behavior had decreased at the claims center. The average amount of time it took to process a claim also decreased, reports Keashly about the as-yet-unpublished data.

The researchers repeated this process of surveys, meetings, intervention and follow-up at 10 other VA workplaces with similar results, says James Scaringi, the VA's special project program manager.

Though the teams' projects were no doubt part of the improvements, the process of developing the interventions— through respectful though sometimes heated discussions—also contributed to reduced bullying, notes Keashly. During the planning meetings, the psychologists taught the action teams to, for instance, speak up when someone said something that was unfair about another employee, she notes.

"Not only was the intervention they designed having an impact, but the way they were operating was catching on with other people," she says.

Backing It Up

The public health department of Ramsey County also aims to change how people communicate with each other by running training sessions that emphasize listening and communication.

In one exercise, small groups of co-workers go through a list of behaviors, such as "You get angry, go into a private room and kick the wall," and rate how violent they are on a scale of one to 10. After considering the examples, the group members discuss their answers.

"We have done this with thousands of people, and what we have found is each time we do it people have very different responses," says Gault. "What you learn from it is that people you work with have different takes on these things. One person might think kicking a wall is a healthy way to relieve anger, while others may think it is violent."

The exercise usually leads to discussion of what behavior is appropriate at work. The goal, however, is not to come to a final definition of respectful behavior, but to expose employees to each others' perspectives, Gault says.

While such discussions are useful, having a policy that explicitly defines and imposes sanctions for bullying can help fortify attempts to improve communication, says Kathryne Dupré, PhD, a Memorial University of Newfoundland business professor who researches the causes of workplace aggression ("Bullying stems from fear, apathy"). Ramsey County has such a policy, which is stated on posters and in the employee manual, and so do many businesses that APA has lauded through its Psychologically Healthy Workplace Award, notes David Ballard, PsyD, MBA, the directorate's assistant executive director for corporate relations and business strategy. Each year, the program nationally recognizes companies that safeguard employees' health and well-being. One such example is IBM's T.J. Watson Research Center, which won in 2006 in part because of its efforts to foster cooperation and respect in the workplace, he notes. (See the May *Monitor* or www.phwa.org for a full list of the winners.)

"IBM does a variety of things to address the issue and create a culture of trust in the organization, including creating a work environment where intimidation is not tolerated and formalizing this through their core values and employment guidelines," he notes.

The company's Business Conduct Guidelines state that IBM will not brook any intimidating behavior, and the company backs that up with disciplinary action, Ballard says. In fact, IBM won media coverage in 2003 when it fired a group of factory workers who were bullying their new boss.

"It's not just the existence of a policy but the belief that the organization will enact it," Dupré says.

UNIT 4

Developing Effective Human Resources

Unit Selections

Key Points to Consider

- Organizations spend a great deal of money on training and development. Why do many organizations feel it is necessary to provide courses in-house? Why do other organizations spend money on outside programs? Why might the training programs of some firms be inadequate, even though a great deal of money is spent on them? What are some of the new techniques being used in corporate education? What are some of the old organizations using new technology? What are some of the questions organizations should be asking of their training and development operations?

- What are your career plans, and how do you plan to implement them? How has career development changed over the years? Do you think you are likely to have a number of careers in the future? What do you think will be the impact of the Internet? Are you planning on going into one of the growth areas in the economy?

- Do you think the concept of diversity is a good idea? Why or why not? How should diversity be attained? What are some of the problems with diversity?

Student Web Site
www.mhcls.com

Internet References

Center for Organization and Human Resource Effectiveness
http://www.iir.berkeley.edu./cohre/cohre.html
Discrimination and Diversity
http://www.domz.org/society/work/worplace.discriminatiorydiversity
Employment Interviews
http://www.snc.edu/socsci/chair/336/group3.htm
Feminist Majority Foundation
http://www.feminist.org

Every organization needs to develop its employees. This is accomplished through a number of activities, including formal corporate training, career development, and performance appraisal. Just as the society and the economy will continue to change, so will the human resource needs of organizations. Individuals and their employers must work together to achieve the effective use of human resources. They must plan together to make the maximum use of their abilities so as to meet the challenge of the changing environment in which they live.

American industry spends approximately the same amount of money each year on training and developing employees as is spent by all colleges and universities in the United States combined. It also trains roughly the same number of people as there are students in traditional post-secondary education. Corporate programs are often very elaborate and can involve months or even years of training. In fact, corporate training and development programs have been recognized by academia for their quality and excellence. The American Council for Education has a program designed to evaluate and make recommendations concerning corporate and government training programs for college credit. Corporations, themselves, have entered into the business of granting degrees that are recognized by regional accrediting agencies. For example, McDonald's grants an associate's degree from "Hamburger U." General Motors Institute (now Kettering University) offers the oldest formalized corporate sponsored/related degree-granting program in the United States, awarding a bachelor's in industrial management; several companies offer MBAs in cooperation with a number of universities, and a PhD program in policy analysis is available from the Rand Corporation. American industry is in the business of educating and training employees, not only as a simple introduction and orientation to the corporation, but as a continual and constant enterprise of lifelong learning so that both firms and employees can meet the challenges of an increasingly competitive world. Meeting these challenges depends on knowledge, not on sweat, and relies on the ability to adapt to and adopt technological, social, and economic changes faster than competitors do. But, for training to be truly effective and beneficial for the organization, management must be able to set priorities that will be effective and appropriate for the firm. Corporations must also take advantage of the latest in instructional technology, recognizing the value of performance simulations, computer-based instruction, as well as other new techniques and address the problems of employees who do not respond well to the new methods of instruction.

There is an important difference between jobs and careers. Everyone who works, whether self-employed or employed by someone else, does a job. While a career, which is made up of a series of jobs and positions over an individual's working life, is more than that. It is a sense of direction, a purpose, and a knowledge of where one is going in one's professional life. Careers

© Stockbyte/Getty Images

are shaped by individuals through the decisions they make concerning their own lives, not by organizations. It is the individual who must ultimately take the responsibility for what happens in his or her career. Organizations offer opportunities for advancement and they fund training and development based on their own self-interest, not solely on workers' interests. Accordingly, the employee must understand that the responsibility for career development ultimately rests with him- or herself.

In today's world of short job tenure, people will frequently change jobs and they must be prepared to do so at a moments notice. Jobs are being lost, but they are also being created. Potential employees, especially those just starting their careers, need to consider this. They must continue to learn and remain competitive or become the kind of worker whose skills will be a commodity and as with all commodities, will be employed/purchased by the lowest bidder.

One of the ways that organizations can assist in the career development of their employees is to engage in appropriate and effective performance appraisals. This process benefits both the employee and the employer. From the employers' perspective, it allows the organization to fine-tune the performance of the individual and to take appropriate action when the performance does not meet an acceptable standard. From the employee's perspective, appraisal allows the individual to evaluate his or her situation in the organization. Appraisal will indicate, in formal ways, how the individual is viewed by the organization. It is, for the employee, an opportunity to gauge the future.

One of the pressing issues today is diversity. The American, and for that matter, the global workforce is made-up of many different people with many different backgrounds. All of them have a wide degree of potential, none of which is based on race, creed, gender, or ethnic origin. It is very dangerous for any organization to ignore any potential labor pool whose talent can be used in a competitive environment, especially if that talent can be used competitively against the organization. Organizations that ignore diversity do so at their peril, a point strongly made by "The 40 Best Companies for Diversity." The next Henry Ford, Bill Gates, or Warren Buffett could come from anywhere, and given today's world, it is far less likely to be a white male, than twenty or thirty years ago. It is, in fact, far more likely to be a minority group member, or a woman as might be deduced from "The Face of Diversity Is More than Skin Deep."

To ignore the development of the potential of the employees of any organization is to court disaster—not only for the organization, but for the employee. People who have stopped developing themselves are cheating themselves and their employers. Both will be vulnerable to changes brought on by increased competition, but the workers will be the ones who join the statistics of the unemployed.

Your Co-Worker, Your Teacher: Collaborative Technology Speeds Peer-Peer Learning

In today's fast-paced business world, workers need to be able to quickly swap knowledge without waiting for a structured training initiative. That doesn't mean traditional e-learning is dead, however.

ED FRAUENHEIM

The latest trend in corporate training technology can be summed up simply: Water Cooler 2.0.

Organizations are trying to encourage the kind of informal learning that has long come from sometimes chance encounters with colleagues and industry peers. These days, however, corporations are tapping into collaborative technologies such as blogs, wikis and podcasts to allow their workers to pick up crucial information whenever and wherever they need it.

That's not to say traditional training is dead. Thanks in part to the need to comply with a multitude of regulations, demand is growing for structured learning—whether it be instructor-led classes or online courses. That means healthy business for vendors of learning management software systems that track employee course work and certifications.

But some of those vendors are upgrading their products in ways that accommodate peer-to-peer learning. Essentially, the training field is realizing that the most valuable learning moments often occur when employees exercise their curiosity on the spot, says Jay Cross, a consultant and author of a new book, *Informal Learning: Rediscovering the Natural Pathways That Inspire Innovation and Performance.*

Cross says today's accelerating pace of business all but requires letting workers quickly swap their knowledge on topics like new products without waiting for a corporate training program from on high. The traditional

---

Informal Learning Tech

Some companies are using social networking technologies to promote the sharing of knowledge and expertise among their employees. Some of the tools being used are blogs, wikis and podcasts.

Blogs

Web logs, or blogs, are Web sites where someone can post content including messages and images. Readers can respond to postings in the form of a threaded discussion.

Wikis

These are Web sites that allow multiple users to author the same content. Like blogs, they can be kept within a company's internal computer system or located on the public Internet. Changes made to the site can be tracked.

Podcasts

These are audio or video files that can be downloaded onto portable digital media players, such as iPods.

---

approach to new-product training could take months to complete, given such elements as a needs analysis, a description of the product and the creation of an interactive CD-ROM for its sales force. It was too slow, he says.

"To keep employees current, information must be transferred in weeks or days or even hours, not in months," he says.

Rise of E-Learning

The first generation of e-learning, launched about a decade ago, is often regarded as a misguided experiment, where too much content was crammed online and many dollars were wasted. Several years ago, organizations sought to restore a balance by blending instructor-led activities with online activities. Today, blended learning is coming to mean mixing formal learning—which can include in-person instruction and e-learning—with informal employee epiphanies.

Those "Aha!" moments are much more likely with the advent of the new social networking technologies, says Colleen Carmean, director of research at the Applied Learning Technologies Institute at Arizona State University. Blogs, wikis and other content that remains online and is searchable mean that employees can tap into colleagues' knowledge no matter when the entries were made. And given the way search engines rank pages by their popularity, smart ideas can rise over time, she says.

"The strength of an organization can be based on how well complex information moves up" through the ranks, she says. "These new learning technologies can really allow us to do that."

In 2006, employers budgeted $55.8 billion for formal training in the U.S., according to research conducted by advisory firm Bersin & Associates for *Training* magazine. That figure was up 7 percent from 2005, the report said, thanks partly to a new focus on talent management and employee development to address "talent gaps in the global workforce." The percentage of online learning increased as well. The Bersin study found that online self-study and virtual classrooms accounted for 29 percent of formal training delivery in 2006, up from 23 percent in 2005.

E-learning is particularly prevalent for training done to comply with company or government regulations, such as worker safety courses and sexual harassment prevention tutorials. Fully 35 percent of mandatory or compliance training is conducted mostly or completely online, the Bersin study found.

Given the rise of e-learning, technology has become a vital part of training operations, according to the Bersin research. Learning technology and infrastructure ranked as the top priority among organizations surveyed, and 75 percent of organizations with more than 10,000 employees now have a learning management system.

Health insurance provider Health Net is in the process of implementing a learning management system from SumTotal Systems. Suzanne Rumsey, Health Net's director of workforce planning, says the system will help her 10,000-person company meet compliance requirements as well as make sure workers get credit for the many courses they take. Another reason Health Net signed up for the software is to signal that it is willing to invest in people. In an era where lifelong employment is no longer expected and retirement benefits have been declining, a sound employee development program can play a key role in keeping workers engaged with the business, Rumsey says. "Learning is sort of that untapped retention tool," she says.

The Right Balance

It's hard to quantify in dollar figures the growing interest in technologies for informal learning, because vendors for such products are scattered across multiple categories.

> **Companies typically have their priorities backward. "Only 20 percent [of learning] comes in the formal way. But what do we do? We spend a lot of money on the 20 percent."**
>
> —Claire Schooley, Forrester Research

Whatever the precise figure, it's probably not enough, says Claire Schooley, senior industry analyst with Forrester Research. She says companies typically have their priorities backward by focusing on structured courses as opposed to the sorts of educational experiences that happen on the job, just as an employee needs them. "Only 20 percent [of learning] comes in the formal way," Schooley says. "But what do we do? We spend a lot of money on the 20 percent."

Research company Quintiles Transnational is trying to strike the right balance in terms of learning methods. The 16,000-person company, which manages clinical trials on behalf of pharmaceutical firms, offers a range of in-person and electronic courses. Topics include project management and clinical practice training, and many of the classes are mandated by government regulation, says Tim Toterhi, Quintiles' director of learning and development strategy. To help keep track of all the structured training, Quintiles is installing a new learning management system.

But Quintiles chose the new software partly because it facilitates informal learning activities. Toterhi declined to name the vendor of the system but said it may eventually help with an experiment in podcasting. Quintiles wants to create audio tutorials on various topics that employees can download into portable devices and learn "on the fly," Toterhi says. A Quintiles sales representative about to meet with a client might get a podcast from a more seasoned sales official that contains insights into that particular company and tips for closing deals. "The walk from the car to the customer becomes a classroom of your own design," Toterhi says.

Consultant Cross says formal learning activities typically neglect an organization's veteran key contributors. "After you've got a basic grounding, you don't want courses. Courses are for novices," he says. "Advanced people need to fill in holes in their knowledge, not be dragged through what they already know."

New software products are making it ever easier for average employees to fashion multimedia demonstrations or mini-lessons. These include Microsoft's Power-Point, software firm Articulate's Presenter application and Adobe's Captivate 2 product, which is designed to help people create things including software demonstrations and interactive simulations.

Such products have reduced the time it takes to create tutorials by a factor of three or more in just the past few years, says Glenn Greenberg, e-learning specialist at utility company Southern Co. "These tools have become rapid e-learning development tools," he says. What's more, he says, they typically don't require great technical skill, allowing subject-matter experts throughout a company to generate learning content.

Variety of Tools

One vendor betting on informal learning is Proton-Media. The Lansdale, Pennsylvania-based software firm allows clients to establish a three-dimensional "virtual world" where employees interact and can pose questions. The system matches a person's need with other users logged on, relevant courses, and blogs and wikis. Clients, who include pharmaceutical giant Johnson & Johnson, also have noticed employees deciding to hold impromptu meetings in the virtual world, says ProtonMedia president Ron Burns. "It's as if we've extended the water cooler out over a large, distributed workforce," he says.

Other, much simpler collaboration technologies can be harnessed for informal learning. Web log software enables workers to create blogs in order to share their insights or expertise, while other employees can post comments in response. Wikis are Web sites that allow visitors to add or change information.

Also helpful for peer-to-peer exchanges are corporate search engines that scour the various types of data contained in a company's computer system. IBM and Yahoo recently announced a free product designed to find information stored within an organization and across the Web.

Applications that establish intranet "portals" also can be effective. Microsoft's SharePoint software is a popular choice, says Jason Averbook, chief executive of consulting firm Knowledge Infusion. He says organizations often use SharePoint to let workers post content such as presentations. "We see it being used as a very, very significant content repository," he says.

Overall, Averbook notices corporations in a phase of assessing what they want workers to learn. In the wake of investing heavily in e-learning courses several years ago, firms want to make sure they are directing their training dollars wisely, he says. "There's a lot of money spent monitoring what your workforce needs, versus buying content," he says.

Just as companies are keen to tie their training efforts to their overall corporate strategies, niche vendors of learning management systems have been branching out to add other talent management tools to their lineup. The heavyweights of the HR software world, Oracle and SAP, already offer a broad set of applications in addition to learning management systems.

Tracking Learning

Vendors in the training tech arena are taking note of the informal learning trend. Oracle, for example, touts the way its learning products are inherently interactive and ready for employees to share ideas. "Collaborative tools have been a large part of Oracle's offerings from the beginning," says Gretchen Alarcon, Oracle vice president for human capital management product strategy. "For example, we provide built-in instant messaging capabilities, forums, chat, learner ratings and reviews."

Learning management software from SAP has similar features, including instant messaging, chat and document sharing. When it comes to informal learning, one of SAP's priorities is to make it easier for organizations to capture what employees do outside of structured courses. Lacking that information, companies are hamstrung in their ability to make smart talent decisions such as which employees are indispensable and who may be ready for advancement, says David Ludlow, the SAP vice president in charge of global product strategy for HR applications.

Among the tactics under review at SAP is looking at an employee's Microsoft Outlook calendar to see if any appointments amount to a "learning event." Meetings

Learning Vendors Branching out in Talent Management

The March of the learning management companies is under way.

Vendors that specialize in learning management software systems have been expanding in recent years into other fields of talent management, such as performance management. The idea is to offer customers more complete products, ones that can enhance the ways companies develop particular individuals and shape their overall workforce.

The most recent example of boundary pushing by learning management players came in November. Learning specialist SumTotal Systems said it acquired performance management software firm MindSolve Technologies. And it isn't done growing in terms of talent management, says Karen Hickey, senior director of marketing for SumTotal. "We will continue to fill out the functionality," she says.

SumTotal, which now offers products in the fields of learning, performance and compensation management, still lacks a recruiting product to encompass what many consider the four pillars of talent management. Talent management applications are among the fastest-growing categories of human resources software. Companies are buying these tools as they recognize the value generated by employees and focus on adapting to demographic changes on the horizon, such as the graying of the baby boomer generation.

Jason Averbook, CEO of consulting firm Knowledge Infusion, says corporations are seeing learning activities as directly tied to their efforts to prepare critical succession moves and plan what their workforce will look like in the future.

> ## "Learning is playing a bigger role in the 'people chain' than it ever has before."
>
> —Jason Averbook, knowledge Infusion

"Learning is playing a bigger role in the 'people chain' than it ever has before," Averbook says, drawing an analogy between workforce planning and the supply-chain planning companies do to optimize the creation of products and services.

Learning management systems refer to software applications for keeping track of the courses employees take and certifications they earn. Major vendors also offer applications for creating online training content.

In addition to SumTotal, learning management vendors Plateau Technologies and Saba have broadened their product offerings. Each now offers performance management and succession management products.

These three vendors are competing in a crowded market for talent management applications overall. A number of companies, including Vurv Technology and Authoria, sell multiple talent management products but not learning management. HR tech's biggest players, Oracle and SAP, offer all four of the primary talent management products, in addition to HR information systems that track essential employee data.

Both giants tout the benefits of an integrated set of talent management products with ties back to the core HR system. SAP's learning management product may not have all the features that the smaller specialists have, concedes David Ludlow, the company's vice president in charge of global product strategy for HR applications. But Ludlow argues that buying SAP's array of talent management products makes more sense than going with multiple niche products, because all the SAP applications are based on a single set of data that makes for smooth integration between the tools and the core HR system. "I think that adds more value than a long list of features and functionality," he says.

His point is at the center of a long-standing debate between the big, comprehensive vendors and smaller specialists. But the companies that have historically focused on learning management are looking more like soup-to-nuts providers. Plateau, for example, hasn't ruled out moving into other talent management areas such as compensation and recruiting, says Ed Cohen, Plateau's chief technology officer. "It's something we've looked at," he says.

such as mentoring sessions would be recorded in their learning history, Ludlow says.

Learning management vendor Plateau Systems also aims to help companies track on-the-job learning moments. It recently launched iContent, which includes a Web portal allowing companies to post content including traditional courses and internal presentations as well as link to external blogs or podcasts. When employees log on to the site, they can conduct searches and any information they access can be documented in a customer's learning management system. "It's Amazon.com-type functionality designed to work with a learning management system," says Ed Cohen, chief technology officer at Plateau.

SumTotal has discussed a software upgrade that would let organizations create wikis. Last year, it teamed tip with Google to let Google's corporate search product peer into SumTotal's learning management system to find such things as courses, class materials and presentations.

SumTotal also offers a portal where employees can post documents and carry out threaded discussions. And for several years, SumTotal's system has allowed employees to download audio broadcasts. This feature can be used by managers to deliver podcasts to employees, says Karen Hickey, senior director of marketing at SumTotal.

Challenges

Creating a vigorous and valuable climate of informal learning may not be easy. Employees themselves may hesitate to share their gems of wisdom because of the time it takes to do so and the risk they may be wrong, says Arizona State's Carmean. "The missing factor is how we get workers to shift into a cultural engagement with these tools," she says. "You have to do more than seek information; you have to contribute."

The contributions can pose their own challenges. Worker blogs can result in content that is offensive, embarrassing or highly sensitive—as a number of fired bloggers can attest.

Consultant Cross says corporate distrust of workers also can impede informal learning. "Top-down organizations are accustomed to controlling the flow of information and are not comfortable with learning that comes from the bottom up," he says.

But he and other proponents say smart companies will persevere to encourage unstructured education. According to Cross, the tactics can be as low-tech as the water cooler, version 1.0. A major Silicon Valley company once asked him for advice on how to generate more conversations among its knowledge workers. Cross recommended replacing a third of the cubicles at its headquarters with leather sofas and espresso machines.

"Informal learning will happen if you just get out of its way," he says.

ED FRAUENHEIM is a Workforce Management staff writer based in San Francisco. To comment, e-mail editors@tworkforce.com.

The 40 Best Companies for Diversity

Many companies wave diversity banners. But when crafting their succession plans, are they moving black executives into the starting lineup?

THE EDITORS

When Franklin Raines was appointed chief executive officer of Fannie Mac in 1999, he became the first African American CEO of a major corporation. Called the Jackie Robinson of corporate America, he broke through a color barrier at the highest level of the corporate suite. Just two years later Kenneth Chenault stepped up to the plate when he was appointed CEO of American Express. In 2002, Richard Parsons took the helm of Time Warner and in December of that same year E. Stanley O'Neal assumed the top spot at Merrill Lynch. Up next was Clarence Otis Jr., named the top guy for Darden Restaurants Inc. in 2004. By January 2007, the number of African American CEOs of the largest publicly traded companies had inched up to seven and included Aylwin Lewis for Sears Holdings, Ronald Williams for Aetna, and Rodney O'Neal for Delphi Corp.

But when Parsons and O'Neal announced their resignations last year and their nonminority successors were named, it appeared to be business as usual. An already small pool of CEOs of color was made even smaller. (Raines had been ousted in 2004 after an accounting scandal at Fannie Mae, and Lewis stepped down from Sears at the beginning of this year.) Today, there are four black CEOs at the largest publicly traded companies. However, the turnover in black talent in the C-suites of corporate America goes beyond the CEO's office—about a quarter of the executives ranked on our 2005 listing of the 75 Most Powerful Blacks in Corporate America have since resigned or retired from their companies. (See sidebar, "Where Are They Now?")

As we unveil BLACK ENTERPRISE's 2008 40 Best Companies for Diversity, we continue to examine, the most important elements of a strong diversity program: board representation, supplier diversity, employee workforce, and senior management. This year, however, we wanted to also highlight young executives who will be part of the pipeline of talent to eventually fill the very top spots of an organization. Although we recognize that many companies are still struggling with the implementation of viable diversity initiatives, the changing demographics of our nation are forcing corporations to create organizations that not only successfully recruit talent but develop, nurture, and groom employees for leadership positions.

"Companies are still asking for the business case to employ diversity within an organization," says Kenneth Roldan, CEO of Wesley, Brown and Battle, a New York-based executive search firm. "But if the consumers are black, brown, or women—and they are because of the changing demographics out there in the marketplace—then you better start having a company that reflects what the community looks like. But that's not happening."

Experts agree and statistics support that having a diverse mosaic across corporate leadership levels increases the likelihood of getting the very best talent possible because it creates a larger pool from which to make a selection. And it brings different viewpoints, life experiences, and thought processes to the table, helping a company to better cater to market globalization and the increased spending power among minority groups.

"Think about diversity in terms of your stock portfolio. If someone came to you and said they were going to put everything you own in Southeast Asian bonds, that's probably not what you would want to do. People want a balanced portfolio with 10% in this and 20% in that because it's understood in business that over time that is what will give you the best possible outcome," says Joe Watson, author of *Without Excuses: Unleash the Power of diversity to Build Your Business* and CEO of executive search firm Strategic Hire. "Well, how is the workforce any different? It also needs to be diverse to give companies the best possible outcome."

Despite virtual unanimity among business experts regarding diversity talk, and the examples set by past and present African American chief executives that clearly indicate the leadership capabilities of people of color, minorities are still sorely underrepresented at the CEO level. Marlon D. Cousin of The Marquin Group in Atlanta says diversity in succession planning has been challenging because of the years blacks had been locked out of the boardroom.

"You're talking about a very limited pool of people, possibly 10 to 20 African Americans and minorities who could possibly be prepared to do a C-level job because in many cases when you are talking about people who are doing C-level jobs, they have 20 to 25 years of experience," Cousin says. "Well, 20 or 25 years ago minorities weren't given an opportunity to do the jobs that would prepare them for a C-level job today and that's why the pool is so small now." He believes that succession planning for diverse employees only works when there is a commitment to grooming and developing candidates.

To increase potential CEOs of color, companies must begin to increase the number of minorities at the vice president and senior VP levels, and then ready them for the top spot. Unfortunately, many organizations lack an internal pipeline to bring minority talent up the ranks. Instead, corporations consider those already on their radar screen, which in turn creates a recycling system among those executives ready to take the helm. As a result, minority representation throughout the corporate landscape remains flat because no new blood is ever injected into the body of big business.

Programs that don't work often lack a system of measurement, says Trudy Bourgeois, founder and president of the Center for Workforce Excellence, a national consulting, training, and coaching company. "It's also about accountability. Most organizations do not hold their managers accountable for creating a succession plan that has a diversity [component] to it," she explains.

Becoming CEO-Ready

Most CEOs of Fortune 500 companies have spent significant time within the organizations that they end up running. O'Neal invested 20 years at Merrill Lynch, fast-tracking through several positions including senior banker in the junk bond division and chief financial officer. Otis spent nine years matriculating through the senior ranks of Darden Restaurants Inc., serving as a vice president, senior vice president of investor relations, and chief financial officer. And Raines served five years as vice chairman of Fannie Mae before assuming the top post of the mortgage finance giant. Corporations that want to incorporate true inclusion in their ranks groom successors

five to 10 years out by producing challenges along the way that help prepare them for the post.

But there's a lot more for candidates to consider, Cousin explains. "When you reach that level, it's really not about performance because when you're at that level, it's a given that you can perform. You wouldn't be there if you couldn't," he explains. "So, you have to look at the whole pie: performance, image, and exposure, and how much weight is given to each."

Cousin says performance accounts for 10% of the equation, while image and exposure make up 30% and 60%, respectively. Corporations base their decision in part on their knowledge of the candidate and how comfortable they are with him or her running the organization. So obtaining exposure is key.

"If you look at someone like Jim Kilts, he was chairman and CEO of Gillette, ex-president of Kraft, and one of the ex-CEOs of Nabisco. He was in the running for CEO of Coca-Cola in Atlanta. So you ask yourself, how does this one guy get recommended for all these C-level jobs?" Cousin says. "It's a given that Jim Kilts is going to give you an opportunity to grow your business and turn that company around. But one of the things that Jim does a great job of is having exposure. That's the piece that we miss, and we need to do a better job at it."

Potential CEOs of color must develop mentoring relationships, both internally and externally; identify a sponsor; and be willing to take some risks professionally. That means, Roldan says, moving out of our comfort zone and volunteering for that offbeat assignment in Omaha. But minorities must also have a sense of entitlement to the position.

"We've got to stop allowing ourselves to talk ourselves out of the consideration set," Bourgeois says.

The employees we have featured in this issue have strong performance goals for opportunities in their company. Training and development programs have helped build confidence, expertise, a solid understanding of strategic expectations, a viable network of mentors and sponsors, as well as a profile within their organizations.

And so Bourgeois recommends that young corporate aspirants stay the course. "People have to stay in the game," she adds. "But they also have to be on their game and continue to sow seeds so that the generations that come behind us can reap the reward."

How We Chose the Best Companies for Diversity

The 2008 **BLACK ENTERPRISE** Best Companies for Diversity were determined by analyzing the responses to a survey of major corporations. **BE** engaged in a comprehensive

Gloria Lewis

- **Age:** 34
- **Title:** Executive Director, Channel Delivery
- **Company:** AT&T Inc.
- **Site Location:** Dallas
- **Career Goal:** To remain in a leadership position, aspiring to a senior management position within five years, an officer position in 10–15 years

Right out of college, Lewis began her career at AT&T, then Southwestern Bell, as manager of special services in its Leadership Development program, which she credits with exposing her to crucial parts of the company's business and helping her understanding of the company culture. In 2000 she received an M.B.A. in telecommunications, and she's currently managing a team of five management associates. "Understanding corporate strategy, communicating that to team members, and managing by measurable metrics," are among the strongest lessons in her development training.

AT&T INC.

- **Location:** San Antonio
- **Type of Business:** Telecommunications
- **Diversity Contact:** Cindy Brinkley, Senior Vice President—Talent Development & Chief Diversity Officer
- **Advertising Diversity Rating:** (3)
- **Comments:** AT&T's organization and talent review develops company talent, identifying areas where specific interventions are needed and setting objectives and action plans for those areas.

Strengths

- Supplier diversity
- Employee base

Tonya Berry

- **Age:** 36
- **Title:** Industrial Engineering Manager
- **Company:** Chrysler L.L.C.
- **Site Location:** Auburn Hills, MI
- **Career Goal:** To become a senior manager in operations

Berry worked as an operations engineer at Blue Cross Blue Shield of Michigan before joining Chrysler as an industrial engineer in 1997. She has received two promotions and a variety of cross functional experiences through developmental programs. She was identified for having a talent in finance and was invited to learn that aspect of the business. She ended up pursuing an M.B.A. in finance, and today manages five teams, with a total of 20 to 30 employees. Her biggest takeaways have been "cross-functional relationships I've been able to develop and [learning] how to gain and share in decision-making across the organization."

Chrysler L.L.C.

- **Location:** Auburn Hills, HI
- **Type of Business:** Automotive
- **Diversity Contact:** Monica Emerson, Executive Director, Global Diversity Officer
- **Advertising Diversity Rating:** (4)
- **Comments:** Chrysler's Global Diversity Council meets six times per year to ensure that all organizations across the enterprise area accountable for the achievement of Chrysler's diversity initiatives.

Strengths

- Supplier diversity

Abram Mercedes

- **Age:** 40
- **Title:** Program Director, Systems Technology Group Global Service & Support Planning
- **Company:** International Business Machines Corp.
- **Site Location:** Research Triangle Park, NC
- **Career Goal:** To attain a vice president position with profit/loss responsibility

Mercedes was recruited by IBM after he received his master's of science in finance from Purdue University in 1994, and he's received seven promotions. As he manages 100 employees, his executive training and Support from "great mentors, black and white," have taught him how to effectively communicate corporate strategy and highlight professional accomplishments to key executives. One mentor told him: "Your boss needs to know what dragons you've been slaying for him."

International Business Machines Corp.

- **Location:** Armonk, NY
- **Type of Business:** Information Technology
- **Diversity Contact:** Ron Glover, VP, Global Workforce Diversity
- **Advertising Diversity Rating:** (2)
- **Comments:** The Black Technical Leaders Forum—comprised of the company's highest-ranking technical leaders—mentors technical staff, participate in development panel discussions, and hosts bi-monthly calls where protégés highlight their achievements.

Strengths

- Board of directors

Roger L. McClendon

- **Age:** 42
- **Title:** Senior Director, Global Engineering and Facilities
- **Company:** Yum! Brands Inc.
- **Site Location:** Louisville, KY
- **Career Goal:** To be general manager and run an international market

McClendon joined Yum! Brands in 1996 and has since had five promotions, currently managing a team of 30. He has participated in several development programs, including Big Leap Forward, developed and facilitated by Yum! Brands Restaurants International President Graham Allan, and Taking People With You, a program created and taught by company Chairman and CEO David Novak. "You don't achieve much on your own anymore," says McClendon of what he's learned from his training. Collaboration, nurturing talent, and recognition of contribution are key factors of leadership. "I recognize and mirror those traits."

Yum! Brands Inc.

- **Location:** Louisville, KY
- **Type of Business:** Food service
- **Diversity Contact:** Terrian Barnes, Global Diversity and Inclusion
- **Advertising Diversity Rating:** (1)
- **Comments:** Yum's supplier diversity spend has grown from 1% to 8% in the last 10 years. The company also has a rigorous succession planning process that examines diversify gaps in each function and sets action plans to achieve those goals.

Strengths

- Supplier diversity
- Employee base

outreach effort to the CEOs and diversity executives of the top 1,000 publicly traded companies and the diversity executives for the 50 leading global companies with strong U.S. operations. Following initial contact, additional inquiries were made to ensure that all companies were apprised of the opportunity to participate in this year's survey.

The companies that made the list outperformed their peers in four key categories:

- **Supplier diversity:** The percentage of total procurement dollars spent with companies owned by African Americans and members of other ethnic minority groups.
- **Senior management:** The percentage of senior management positions held by African Americans and members of other ethnic minority groups.
- **Board of directors:** The percentage of African Americans and other ethnic minority groups represented on their corporate boards.
- **Employee base:** The percentage of African Americans and members of other ethnic minority groups represented in the total workforce of the company.

BE's survey focused primarily on activities related to the participation of African Americans and members of other ethnic minority groups. According to the U.S. Census Bureau, the term "ethnic minority" applies to people from the following backgrounds: black, American Indian/Alaska Native, Asian-Pacific Islander, and Hispanic/Latino. Information provided by companies on diversity efforts on behalf of other groups, such as women, gays/lesbians/transsexuals, and the disabled, was used as a secondary, supporting criterion for inclusion on the list.

BE performed a quantitative assessment of all corporate respondents in each survey category. Based on the analysis, each company was provided a score per category, which was compiled into a final survey score. A heavier weighting was given to scores in the supplier diversity and senior management diversity categories, in deference to expertise of diversity professionals who stress that spending with minority suppliers is the diversity function with the greatest potential economic benefit to minority communities, while minority representation in senior management reflects a commitment to diversity at every level of a company, from entry level to the corporate suite. The final scores, along with the results

of reporting and research conducted by the BE editorial staff, were used to determine the 40 Best Companies for Diversity.

These scores were also used to determine BE's "Best Companies for Senior Management Diversity," "Best Companies for Supplier Diversity, "Best Companies for Workforce Diversity," and "Best Companies for Board Diversity." All companies were surveyed on a secondary category, marketing and outreach. This included advertising, promotions, community outreach, and scholarships. Using data from TNS Media Intelligence, as well as information provided by the companies surveyed, BE determined its "Best Companies in Marketing Diversity" list. These "sublists" include companies that, while failing to make our Best Companies for Diversity list, are strong in one particular category of diversity. Readers can review these sublists at www.blackenterprise.com. We will also highlight these companies in the Diversity Watch section in upcoming issues of BE.

B.E.'s Advertising Diversity Rating

Using data provided by TNS Media Intelligence, as well as information shared by respondents to our diversity survey, each company on the BE Best Companies for Diversity list is assigned a four-star Advertising Diversity Rating, based on an assessment of advertising dollars purchased through media targeting black and ethnic minority audiences.

4. **Four stars** $2 million or more in total spend with black media or ad dollars spent with black media comprising at least 5% of total spend of at least $10 million

3. **Three stars** $1 million or more in total spend with black media or ad dollars spent with black media comprising at least 3% of total spend of at least $10 million

2. **Two stars** $500,000 or more in total spend with black media

1. **One star** Less than $500,000 or more In total spend with black media and/or significant marketing efforts, outside of direct advertising, appealing to black and other ethnic minority consumer groups

Additional reporting by Wendy Harris, Sean Drakes, Annya M. Lott and Lois Barrett.

Company	Location	Type of Business	Diversity Contact	Advertising Diversity Rating	Comments	Strengths
AETNA INC.	Hartford, CT	Insurance	Raymond Arroyo, Chief Diversity Officer	2	Diverse Discoveries Programs are the main pathway to succession plans and provide career training, mentoring, and coaching.	Board of directors Senior management Employee base
AFLAC INC.	Columbus, GA	Insurance	Brenda Mullins, Second Vice President, Human Resources/ Diversity Officer	1	Aflac conducts employee satisfaction surveys and conducts surveys after diversity events to measure the success of programs.	Senior management Employee base
AMERICAN EXPRESS CO.	New York	Financial Services	Melinda Wolfe, Chief Diversity Officer & SVP, Executive Talent	3	The company's Hiring Champions program encourages diverse hires at the director and vice president level.	Board of directors
ARAMARK CORP.	Philadelphia	Food & Facilities Management Services	Nicole Johnson-Reece, Vice President of Diversity	1	The company launched a Strategic Diversity Council of Aramark executives.	Board of directors Employee base
BANK OF AMERICA CORP.	Charlotte, NC	Financial Services	Geri Thomas, SVP, Global Diversity Inclusion & Global Consumer & Small Business Banking	1	Bank of America reviews composition of the leadership ranks by gender and person of color status in each of the top areas of the company.	Supplier diversity Employee base
BURGER KING HOLDINGS	Miami	Food Services	Robert Perkins, Vice President, Inclusion & Talent Management	3	In the first quarter of 2008, the volume of minority-owned supplier business increased by 18% compared with the same quarter last year.	Supplier diversity Employee base
COCA-COLA CO.	Atlanta	Beverage	Steve Bucherati, Chief Diversity Officer	4	Coca-Cola encourages diverse candidate slates for all positions. For mission-critical roles, candidate pools are based on skills, competencies, and capabilities.	Supplier diversity Senior management Employee base

Company	Location	Type of Business	Diversity Contact	Advertising Diversity Rating	Comments	Strengths
COMCAST CORP.	Philadelphia	Cable and Communications	Brian L. Roberts, Chairman & Chief Executive Officer	1	Comcast charges senior leaders with identifying diverse, high-potential candidates for all slates.	Supplier diversity Employee base
EASTMAN KODAK CO.	Rochester, NY	Imaging	Essie Calhoun, Chief Diversity Officer and Director of Community Affairs & VP EKC	1	Eastman Kodak's Gold, a succession planning tool, tracks candidates across gender, race, and nationality.	Board of directors Supplier diversity
EXELON CORP.	Chicago	Utilities	Peggy A. Davis, VP, Diversity & Recruiting	N/A	Diversity and inclusion principles and objectives are integrated into the succession planning process through annual talent reviews.	Board of directors Senior management
FANNIE MAE	Washington	Financial Services	Stacey D. Stewart, Chief Diversity Officer & SVP-Office of Community & Charitable Giving	1	The relaunched Employee Network Groups serve as an employee resource with sponsorship from the executive officer level.	Senior management Employee base
FEDEX CORP.	Memphis	Package Delivery	Judith Edge, Corporate Vice President, Human Resources	3	FedEx is committed to diversity and inclusion through its workforce and involvement with the global community.	Employee base
GENERAL MILLS INC.	Minneapolis	Consumer Packaged Goods	Kelly Baker, VP, Diversity	4	Senior function leaders are rated via the company's diversity scorecard, which measures efforts in areas such as senior-level diversity commitment.	Supplier diversity
GENERAL MOTORS CORP.	Detroit	Automotive	Roderick Gillum, VP, Corporate Responsibility & Diversity	4	Senior management meets routinely with General Motor's affinity groups to discuss their work experiences.	Supplier diversity Senior management

(continued)

87

Company	Location	Type of Business	Diversity Contact	Advertising Diversity Rating	Comments	Strengths
JOHNSON CONTROLS INC.	Milwaukee	Automotive Systems and Building Controls	Charles Harvey, Vice President, Diversity and Public Affairs	N/A	Strategic talent reviews include a summary of minorities and women in the review process.	Supplier diversity
KELLOGG CO.	Battle Creek, MI	Consumer Packaged Goods	Sherri Toney, VP, Diversity & Inclusion	2	Kellogg's Diversity Speakers Series encourages managers to increase employee performance and retention around diversity and inclusion.	
MARRIOTT INTERNATIONAL INC.	Bethesda, MD	Lodging	Jimmie Paschall, SVP, External Affairs & Global Diversity Officer	2	In 2007, Marriott spent a record 13.6% with diverse suppliers. Also, the company promoted 11% of African Americans to manager/supervisor positions.	Board of directors Employee base
McDONALD'S CORP.	Oak Brook, IL	Food Services	Patricia Harris, Global Chief Diversity Officer	4	McDonald's provides diversity networking, mentoring, and succession planning programs to its black, Hispanic, Asian, women, and gay/lesbian employees.	Board of directors Supplier diversity Senior management Employee base
MGM MIRAGE	Las Vegas	Hotels, Casinos, and Resorts	Punam Mathur, Senior Vice President, Corporate Diversity & Community Affairs	1	The company developed the first in-depth educational program in the gaming industry, The Diversity Champions Training Program.	Board of directors Supplier diversity Senior management Employee base
PEPCO HOLDINGS INC.	Washington	Utilities	Joy Dorsey, Director, Diversity & Supplier Diversity	N/A	Pepco has launched domestic partner benefits for both same-sex and opposite-sex partners.	Supplier diversity Senior management Employee base
PEPSI BOTTLING GROUP INC.	Somers, NY	Beverage Distribution	Sherry Nolan, Vice President, Diversity & Workplace Development	1	Pepsi's efforts include an internal and external diversity advisory board, employee resource groups, and supplier diversity program.	Board of directors Supplier diversity

Company	Location	Type of Business	Diversity Contact	Advertising Diversity Rating	Comments	Strengths
PEPSICO INC.	Purchase, NY	Convenience Foods and Beverages	Ronald Parker, SVP, Chief Global Diversity & Inclusion Counsel	4	PepsiCo's Leadership Development Program offers advancement for candidates who are at or just below executive level, 50% of whom are minority.	Senior management
PG&E CORP.	San Francisco	Utilities	William Harper III, Vice President and Chief Diversity Officer	1	At PG&E, diversity and inclusion is a required leadership competency for all managers and supervisors.	Supplier diversity Senior management
PITNEY BOWES INC.	Stamford, CT	Computer and Office Equipment	Susan Johnson, Vice President, Strategic Talent Management & Diversity	1	The company has created Diversity Leadership Councils, employee groups at every level from administrative and support staff to senior management.	Board of directors Employee base
PROCTER & GAMBLE CO.	Cincinnati	Consumer Packaged Goods	Maxine Brown-Davis, Chief Diversity Officer	4	The succession planning process includes the identification of minorities to be developed for leadership positions.	Senior management
RYDER SYSTEM INC.	Miami	Transportation	Vivian Brier, Senior Manager, Corporate Diversity and Work/Life Planning	N/A	The company's recruiting and management teams work together to identify diverse candidates for employment.	
SEMPRA ENERGY	San Diego	Utilities	Shawn Farrar, Director, Corporate Diversity	N/A	Sempra Energy has increased recruiting efforts at historically black colleges and universities, working directly with the Thurgood Marshall College Fund.	Supplier diversity
SODEXHO USA	Gaithersburg, MD	Food and Facilities Management Services	Rohini Anand, SVP and Group Chief Diversity Officer	N/A	Diversity scorecard results are linked to a significant portion of management bonuses.	Senior management Employee base

(continued)

89

Company	Location	Type of Business	Diversity Contact	Advertising Diversity Rating	Comments	Strengths
STARWOOD HOTELS & RESORTS WORLDWIDE	White Plains, NY	Lodging	Shelley Freeman, Dir., Global Diversity & Inclusion and Chief Diversity Officer	1	In 2007, Starwood exceeded its supplier diversity spend goal by more than 2%. The company also launched a variety of diversity programs.	Employee base
STATE FARM INSURANCE COS.	Bloomington, IL	Insurance	Laura Haas, Assistant Vice President, Diversity and Inclusion/HR	4	State Farm has seen a 15% increase in Employee Resource Group participation. It presently has more than 10,000 members in 120 chapters.	Board of directors Senior management
TIAA-CREF	Charlotte, NC	Financial Services	Renee Alexander Sherrod, Vice President, Diversity and Community Affairs	1	TIAA-CREF has established a corporate scorecard measure to increase the pool of diverse candidates presented for employment opportunities.	Senior management Employee base
TOYOTA MOTOR NORTH AMERICA INC.	New York	Automotive	Dian Ogilvie, SVP and Secretary	4	To promote diversity, human resources meets with the executives of each organization to review and discuss talent assessments and succession planning.	Supplier diversity
UNITED PARCEL SERVICE INC.	Atlanta	Package Delivery	Allen Hill, SVP, Human Resources	2	Through ongoing training and workshops, UPS has developed a management structure to identify and develop talent.	Supplier diversity Senior management
VERIZON COMMUNICATIONS INC.	Basking Ridge, NJ	Telecommunications	Magda Yrizarry, Vice President, Workplace Culture, Diversity, and Compliance	4	In 2007, Verizon spent almost $3 billion with minority business enterprises.	Board of directors
WGL HOLDINGS INC.	Washington	Utilities	Andrea P. Adams, Director, Labor Relations	N/A	WGL Holdings actively recruits and retains professionals with expertise from varied backgrounds.	Board of directors Senior management Employee base
XEROX CORP.	Rochester, NY	Computer and Office Equipment	Phil Harlow, Chief Diversity Officer	2	Xerox is made up of more than 30% African Americans, Latinos, Asians and Native Americans.	Board of directors Senior management Supplier diversity

Where Are They Now?

Update of the Nation's Most Powerful Blacks in Corporate America

In the past year there have been a number of shifts in top corporate spots, namely the retirement of Richard D. Parsons as CEO of Time Warner (he remains chairman of the organization); and the resignations of E. Stanley O'Neal, former chairman and CEO of Merrill Lynch; and Aylwin Lewis, former CEO of Sears Retail and president of Sears Holdings, In 2005, when BLACK ENTERPRISE presented its list of the 75 Most Powerful Blacks in Corporate America, these executives were on our roster of celebrated talent.

This year, as we present the Best Companies for Diversity, focusing on the importance of succession planning and talent management, we decided to take a look back at that report and at how much the list has changed.

Executives on the Move

Steven A. Davis

- **Former:** President & COO, Long John Silver's; President, Multibranding, Yum! Brands
- **Present:** Chairman of the Board & CEO, Bob Evans Farms

Pierre E. Leroy

- **Former:** President, Worldwide Construction & Forestry, Deere & Co.
- **Present:** Director, Capital One Financial

Gary E. McCullough

- **Former:** President, Ross Products Division; Senior VP, Abbott Laboratories
- **Present:** President & CEO, Career Education

Cecil B. Pickett

- **Former:** President, Schering-Plough Research Institute; Senior VP, Schering-Plough
- **Present:** President of Research and Development, Biogen Idec

Retired Executives

Brian Anderson OfficeMax Inc.

Virgis W. Colbert Miller Brewing Co.

Jerri DeVard Verizon Communications Inc. (Resigned)

William H, Easter III Duke Energy Field Services

Ann M. Fudge Young & Rubicam Brands

Emerson U. Fullwood [5] Xerox Corp.

Isaiah "Ike" Harris BellSouth Advertising & Publishing Group

Frederick W. Hill J.P. Morgan Chase & Co.

Carl Horton The Absolut Spirit Co. Inc.

Louis Hoyes Fannie Mae

David E. Jackson Wal-Mart (Resigned two years ago)

Donna A. James Nationwide Strategic Investments

William Lamar McDonald's USA

Aylwin Lewis Sears Holding Corp. (Resigned)

E. Stanley O'Neal Merrill Lynch & Co. (Resigned)

Myrtle S. Potter Genentech Inc.

Franklin D. Raines Fannie Mae (Resigned)

Bradley T. Sheares Merck & Co. Inc.

Paula Sneed Kraft Foods Inc.

Executive Changes within the Same Company

Y. Marc Belton

- **Former:** Senior VP, Yoplait, GMI Canada, New Business Development, General Mills
- **Present:** Exec. VP, Worldwide Health, Brand & New Business Development, General Mills

Thomas K. "Tony" Brown

- **Former:** Senior VP, Global Purchasing, Ford Motor Co.
- **Present:** Group VP, Global Purchasing, Ford Motor Co.

Frank M. Clark

- **Former:** President, ComEd Exec. VP & Chief of Staff, Exelon Corp.
- **Present:** Chairman & CEO, ComEd

Reginald. E. Davis

- **Former:** CEO, Atlantic Region, Wachovia
- **Present:** Eastern Banking Group Exec., Wachovia

Darryl B. Hazel

- **Former:** President, Lincoln-Mercury, Ford Motor Co.
- **Present:** Sr. VP, Ford Motor Co.; President, Ford Customer Service Division

Paula Madison

- **Former:** President & General Manager, KNBC
- **Present:** Exec. VP Diversity, NBC Universal; Company Officer, General Electric

Dennis Maple

- **Former:** Exec. VP, Aramark Education, Facilities Services, Aramark Corp.
- **Present:** President, Aramark Education, Aramark Corp.

Renetta McCann

- **Former:** CEO, Starcom Americas
- **Present:** CEO, Starcom MediaVest Group

Rodney O'Neal

- **Former:** President, Dynamics, Propulsion, Thermal & Interior Sector, Delphi Corp.
- **Present:** CEO & President, Delphi Corp.

continued

Where Are They Now? *(continued)*

Richard D. Parsons

- **Former:** Chairman & CEO, Time Warner
- **Present:** Chairman of the Board, Time Warner

Charles E. Phillips Jr.

- **Former:** Co-president & Director, Oracle Corp.
- **Present:** President, Oracle Corp.

Debra A. Sandler

- **Former:** Worldwide Group Vice President, McNeil Nutritionals, Johnson & Johnson
- **Present:** Worldwide President, McNeil Nutritionals, Johnson & Johnson

Don Thompson

- **Former:** Exec. VP & Innovation Orchestration Leader, Restaurant Solutions Group, McDonalds' USA
- **Present:** President, McDonald's USA

Matthew Thornton III

- **Former:** Senior VP, AGFS division, FedEx Express, FedEx Corp.
- **Present:** Senior Vice President, U.S. Operations, FedEx Express

Michael A. Todman

- **Former:** President, Whirlpool Europe; Exec. VP, Whirlpool Corp.
- **Present:** President, Whirlpool North America, Whirlpool Corp.

Kevin E. Walker

- **Former:** President & COO, American Electric Power, Ohio
- **Present:** Sr. VP & Chief Information Officer, American Electric Power

Edward T. Welburn Jr.

- **Former:** VP of Design, North America, General Motors
- **Present:** VP, Global Design, General Motors

Ronald A. Williams

- **Former:** President & Director, Aetna Inc.
- **Present:** Chairman & CEO, Aetna Inc.

Chris C. Womack

- **Former:** Sr. VP, Fossil & Hydro Power, Georgia Power Co., Southern Co.
- **Present:** Exec. VP, External Affairs, Georgia Power Co., Southern Co.

The Face of Diversity Is More than Skin Deep

CATHERINE M. DALTON

Diversity. The word itself can invoke a wide range of reactions, some supportive and others less so. An intriguing aspect of diversity is that while we might achieve agreement at the macro level as to what constitutes diversity, such agreement is significantly less likely at the micro level. That is, diversity wears many faces, and the nature and character of the face looks very different depending on the individual.

For some, the face of diversity is defined by skin color. For others, it is based on gender, ethnicity, sexual orientation, or religious preference. In some ways, however, these issues touch only the surface of diversity, its meaning, and its importance. Based on my experience, diversity is complex and rich, while at the same time being quite simple and straightforward.

For me, the face of diversity is a white, male, 70-year-old Midwesterner. It is a face that few might associate with diversity; after all, by the reckoning of most, it is the face of the majority, not the face of a minority. At the surface, such a conclusion seems fair. However, on closer examination it becomes crystal clear that this face is the very embodiment of diversity. It is a face I know well; it is the face of my father.

I have learned more about the importance of diversity from my father than from anyone else, perhaps precisely because he appears to be such an unlikely advocate of diversity. We all fall victim to stereotypes, and diversity is an area that does not enjoy immunity from them. A member of the "majority" is not necessarily less likely to understand, appreciate, or advocate diversity than a member of the "minority."

My lessons in diversity started at an early age. As a young child of the 1960s, I was witness to the growth of the Civil Rights movement in the U.S. It was a time in history when taking Robert Frost's "road less traveled" could prove a challenging path. Ms. Rosa Parks, who passed away in 2005 at the age of 92, provides a moving example of an individual who bore the costs of taking the road less traveled when, after a long, tiring day at work in December 1955, she refused to yield her seat on a Montgomery, AL city bus to a white man. She was summarily arrested, and subsequently faced constant threats and lost her department store job. Her simple act, however, sparked the Civil Rights movement and demonstrated that while path breakers seldom travel an easy road, their courage paves the way for countless others who might then more easily follow.

Diversity Starts at Home

One of my earliest experiences in diversity appreciation occurred in the 1970s. Having grown up in the Midwest, in the heart of suburbia, I had little exposure to racial diversity on a day-to-day basis. It is fair to say, however, that racial integration was not embraced by most suburbanites at the time. As such, when my father, a liberal arts professor at a small liberal arts university, brought home an African priest from work one day, suitcase in hand, it provided the whole family a valuable experience in diversity, including lessons in both the costs and benefits of embracing diversity.

It would be grossly unfair of me to say that my father was metaphorically color blind. He was, and is, not; in fact, few individuals are as skilled at seeing the broad spectrum of color that life provides. That said, I suspect that my father never considered the potential costs of inviting Father Bill, a priest from Kenya, Africa, to live with us while he earned a master's degree at the university where my father worked. My father only saw an individual, in a foreign country, who desperately needed a temporary home. He did not see, first and foremost, a black man. That simple, perhaps impetuous (at least according to my mother, who received no advance warning of our guest's arrival) decision to invite Father Bill into our home bore significant costs, as most of our neighbors did not share my father's enthusiasm for our houseguest. Father Bill was shunned, my parents were shunned, and my siblings and I were shunned by many of our neighbors.

Was it worth it? Absolutely. Who else in the neighborhood received a direct education in life in an African village? Who else in the neighborhood heard personal accounts of wrestling an alligator? More importantly, who else in the neighborhood had firsthand experience with the hope that Martin Luther King, Jr. expressed for his four children: that they would be judged for the content of their character, not the color of their skin? When my family looked at Father Bill, I assure you that we saw a person, not a "color."

I had similar experiences throughout my childhood, largely compliments of my father. My family shared our home at various times with a parade of fascinating individuals that included Gina, an exchange student from Bogotá, Colombia who was studying at the university where my father works, and seven of the nine members of the Nguyen family, who were able to escape just prior to the fall of Saigon, South Vietnam. Each addition to the family created interesting challenges (e.g., while not always easy, 15 people actually can peacefully co-exist in a five bedroom house for a two-year period, even though half speak only English and half speak only Vietnamese). More importantly, each addition to our family provided lifelong lessons in the value of tolerance, respect, and flexibility.

Those lessons during my "developmental years" have served me extraordinarily well in my professional life. While I may not have embraced diversity, writ large, in the same enthusiastic fashion as my father, I certainly have an appreciation for it; in particular, the value that diversity brings to organizations.

Diversity=Survival

Biologists have long understood the importance of diversity; in fact, nature provides potent lessons in its power. Biological diversity addresses the variety of living organisms, and their relationships with each other and the broad environment. Biologists talk about diversity within specific types of organisms, diversity across organisms, and diversity of ecosystems. The organizational corollary might be diversity across individuals, departments, strategic business units, organizations, and industries.

In both contexts, a central issue is that diversity is essential for survival. In the biological world, Darwin's "survival of the fittest" attests to the need for diversity in species. With no discernible distinction in living organisms, whether plant or animal, a potent invader can lead to the death of the species. Consider the constantly growing list of extinct and endangered animals or the devastation of plant species due to pests, disease, pollution, or destruction of habitat. Each loss is a loss of resources, real or potential.

Consider also a lack of diversity in organizations. A cynic may argue that organizations can survive quite well with no diversity. Imagine, for example, an early 20th century manufacturing firm employing only young, white males. Perhaps such an organization can survive in the short-term. However, ponder that same organization in the early 1940s when countless healthy, young, white males found themselves mired, voluntarily or otherwise, in World War II. "Rosie the Riveter" filled their places, enabling those firms to survive an otherwise devastating intervention.

Competitive strategy, too, is built on the concept of diversity. Take an industry in which all firms compete on the same basis, have access to the same resources, and sell to the same customer base. This homogeneity virtually forces such firms to eventually compete on a tenuous basis such as price. As many firms in many industries have experienced, that is almost always a losing proposition in the long run. It is heterogeneity, the ability to distinguish the firm's products and/or services from those of other firms, that enables organizations to garner and maintain a loyal customer base.

The Face of the Customer

Another compelling reason for embracing diversity in organizations is to better serve customers. Consider the case of a consumer products company whose products are largely purchased by women, but whose key decision-makers are all men. Taken to the extreme, contemplate that these same male executives are all in their middle 50s, college educated largely at Ivy League schools, and from middle- to upper-class backgrounds.

What I have described is the typical large firm top management team, even in 2005. According to Catalyst, a research and advisory organization dedicated to the advancement of women in the workplace, well under 10% of top jobs in large U.S. corporations are held by women. The numbers for minorities are equally as dismal.

At issue is not necessarily that any key decision making group should include a woman or a member of a racial minority. What is at issue, however, is that there is a significant body of research on top management teams that demonstrates heterogeneous (diverse) teams tend to produce superior outcomes as compared to homogeneous teams. Diversity infuses discussions with a wider variety of perspectives and ideas, leading to greater innovation. Granted, decision processes are lengthier and more difficult to manage with a diverse group of decision-makers. However, the alternative is likely to be a quick decision process that seldom leads to change or innovation. Were customers' needs static, such a top management team composition might be viable.

Importantly, diversity must extend beyond the traditional foci of race and gender. While it is true that these factors are strong forces and visible means for achieving diversity, it is also true that they scratch only the surface of diversity. This is akin to the biologist's conception of within-species diversity. It would seem, at best, naïve to assume that all women, for example, think alike. As a woman, I can confidently assert that we do not. A central challenge for organizations, then, is to determine the types of diversity that are relevant to the firm and its customers and to ensure that the appropriate perspectives are included in the organization.

A Sprint versus a Marathon

Recent events have reminded me that achieving diversity is much more of a marathon than a sprint. In her rookie season, Indy Racing League driver Danica Patrick was publicly derided by Formula One President Bernie Ecclestone, who suggested that women had no business racing with men, despite Ms. Patrick's fourth place finish in the 2005 Indianapolis 500. He then likened women to domestic appliances, noting that they should all be "dressed in white" (I prefer clothing with a bit more variety, thank you very much, Mr. Ecclestone). Those familiar with Mr. Ecclestone's 2000 commentary on women driving in Formula One ("What I would really like to see happen is to find the right girl, perhaps a black girl with super looks, preferably Jewish or Muslim, who speaks Spanish") would likely be unsurprised by his lack of sensitivity.

Consider also Neil French, former Creative Director of WPP Group, who, following making comments about female ad executives, resigned that position in 2005. When asked at an industry dinner why he believed there were not more women represented among the ranks of creative advertising directors, Mr. French opined that "they're crap" and "don't deserve to make it to the top." Another candidate for sensitivity training.

My own experiences have provided potent reminders of how much work remains to be accomplished in the area of diversity. This is certainly true as regards gender diversity, an issue that hits the mark for me. While I own far more examples than I will burden the reader with, one that is particularly notable for its recency involved a communication I had with the Director of Corporate Relations for a major corporation. He asked me if the use of gender-neutral language in *Business Horizons,* a standard practice in many journals, is "a university PC thing." Like many others, that exchange reminded me that I had better tighten up the laces on my running shoes and strap on the water bottle, because it's going to be a long race.

R-E-S-P-E-C-T

The use of gender-neutral language in *Business Horizons* is not a "PC thing"; rather, it is, in the words of Aretha Franklin, a "RESPECT" thing. It is about creating an environment in which everyone feels welcome. That, to me, is the very essence of diversity. Too often, people get mired in a belief that diversity means they need to compromise their own value set. I believe that diversity simply means I need to understand and respect others and their choices, although I don't necessarily have to agree with them.

This belief, too, is a direct reflection of the lessons I learned from my father. He is the very model of someone who actively chooses, on a day-to-day basis, to embrace diversity in its many forms. Even at his current age, he continues to teach classes on the subject and engage in activities that will help him better understand diversity. My father appreciates that diversity can often best be understood when experienced. His own experiences have included everything from living with a group of university students in the inner city for a semester, to participating in service learning experiences in Nicaragua, Honduras, Ghana, and Appalachia, to volunteering as an assistant basketball coach for an inner-city basketball team, to serving meals in an inner-city soup kitchen.

Not only can learning, growth, and appreciation occur though such experiences, but one's comfort zone can expand exponentially. Inasmuch as we often fear what we don't understand, the more I experience, the more I understand, and the easier it is for me to respect others who are "different" from me. Imagine the power of leveraging such respect in the organizations in which we work. To do so is to imagine the power of diversity.

What do you see when you consider the face of diversity?

UNIT 5

Implementing Compensation, Benefits, and Workplace Safety

Unit Selections

Key Points to Consider

- Companies are involved in worldwide competition, often with foreign organizations with much lower wage rates. What should management do to meet this competition? What do workers need to do to meet this competition?

- When companies merge, what do you see as some of the problems that could happen from an HR perspective?

- How would you implement a merit/incentive program in a staff department such as research and development or data processing? And how would you implement it in a line department such as sales or production?

- Explain why you believe some senior executives might be overpaid. Do you feel some are underpaid?

- What strategies should employers implement to control the rising costs of benefits while still getting the maximum value for their employees? How would you address the health care crisis for an organization?

- Health and safety is one of the primary concerns facing any organization. What are some of the innovative ways that corporations have found to provide better health care while at the same time reducing costs?

Student Web Site
www.mhcls.com

Internet References

BenefitsLink: The National Employee Benefits Web Site
http://www.benefitslink.com/index.php

Equal Compensation, and Employee Ownership
http://www.fed.org

Equal Pay Act and Pay Inequity
http://www.infoplease.com/spot/equalpayact1.html

Executive Pay Watch
http://www.aflcio.org/corporateamerica/paywatch/

Job Stress
http://www.workhealth.org/news/nwprahn98.html

Social Security Administration
http://www.ssa.gov

WorkPlace Injury and Illness Statistics
http://www.osha.gov/oshstats/work.html

Money makes the world go around . . . the world go around!
—From "Money" in the musical *Cabaret*

Individuals are usually paid what others perceive their work to be worth. This situation is not necessarily morally correct. In fact, it does not even have to be logical, but it is reality. Police officers and college instructors are often underpaid. They have difficult jobs, requiring highly specialized training, but these jobs do not pay well. Other professions pay better, and many illegal activities pay better than law enforcement or college teaching.

When a company is trying to determine the salary of individuals, two markets, must be considered. The first is the internal structure of the firm, including the wages that the company pays for comparable jobs. If the organization brings a new employee on board, it must be careful not to set a pay rate for that individual that is inconsistent with those of other employees who are doing the same or similar jobs. The second market is the external market for employees. Salary information is available from many sources, including professional associations and the federal government. Of course, both current and prospective employees, as well as organizations, can easily gain access to this information. To ignore this information and justify pay rates only in terms of internal structure is to tempt fate. The company's top producers are the ones in whom the competition is the most interested, and no organization can afford a mass exodus of its top talent. Organizations must develop a "Philosophizing of Compensation."

One recent development in the area of compensation is a return to the concept of pay for performance. Many firms are looking for ways to directly reward their top performers. As a result, the idea of merit pay has gained wide acceptance in both industry and government. Pay for performance has been used in industry for a long time, most commonly in the sales and marketing area, where employees have historically worked on commission plans based on their sales productivity. Organizations are constantly looking at these types of programs, as seen in "Pay-for-Performance Should Be Fair and Clear." Theoretically, merit pay and other types of pay for performance are effective, but they can easily be abused, and they are often difficult to administer because measuring performance accurately is difficult. Sales and production have numbers that are easily obtained, but research and development is a different situation. How does a firm measure the effectiveness of research and development for a particular year when such projects can often take several years for the results to be achieved?

One issue that has evolved over the past several years is the question of pay for top executives as seen in "Pay Setters." During times of economic recession, most workers are asked to make sacrifices in the form of reduced raises, pay cuts, cuts in benefits, other compensation reductions, or layoffs. Many of these sacrifices have not been applied to top management. Indeed, the compensation for top management has increased

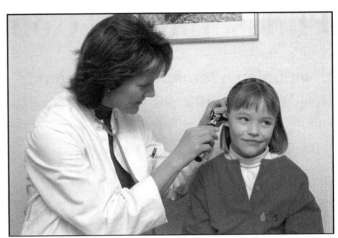

© Andrew Wakeford/Getty Images

substantially during the past several years. Are chief executives overpaid, and if so, how did they get that way, and who should set their pay?

The fastest-growing aspect of employee compensation is benefits. Benefits are expensive for any firm, representing an ever-increasing burden to employers. As a result, many firms are reducing benefits and attempting to find more effective ways to spend their benefit dollars, as discussed in "Benefits and the Bottom Line." Also, the needs of the employees are changing. As our society ages, there is greater interest in health benefits and pensions, and less interest in maternity benefits. Another facet of the issue is that employees are seeking greater benefits in lieu of salary increases, because the benefits, with some exceptions, are not usually taxed as discussed in "Employee Benefits and the Future."

Health and safety are also major concerns of employers and employees. The workplace has become more violent as workers act out against their employers for unfairness—whether real or imagined. Some firms have had to address the anger of employees and other problems. The problems facing companies may even extend beyond the workplace and employers may face liability when domestic violence comes to the workplace. Today, issues concerning safety and health in the workplace include AIDS, burnout, and substance abuse. These issues reflect not only changing social conditions but also a greater awareness of the threats presented by unsafe working conditions. An attempt to address some of these issues has been to practice what is essentially preventive medicine with wellness initiatives and other programs as seen in "Doc in the Box" and "Building a Mentally Healthy Workforce." While there was initially some doubt about their effectiveness, the results are now in, and wellness programs do work.

All in all, salaries, wages, and benefits represent a major expense, a time-consuming management task for most firms, and health and safety requirements are a potential area of significant loss, in terms of both dollars and lost production.

Philosophizing Compensation

Develop an overarching statement to ensure that your pay practices are applied consistently and effectively.

CHARLOTTE GARVEY

Most compensation philosophies have the same basic objectives: to attract, retain and motivate the best employees. But where you go from there determines whether the philosophy is a paper abstraction that sits on a shelf or a vital tool that allows you to equitably and consistently implement your compensation programs.

A well-crafted compensation philosophy "helps tell the story of who you are as an organization and what you value as an organization," says Lynne Sport, director of human resources and administration for the Carnegie Endowment for International Peace, a Washington, D.C.-based, not-for-profit think tank. Sport, who has worked in HR for nearly 20 years in a variety of sectors, including financial services and technology, says the philosophy can help guide HR compensation managers in assessing where the company fits in the marketplace when it comes to trying to attract talent.

A compensation philosophy should provide consistency in three areas: among departments, over time and as the company grows.

"Our comp philosophy is the overarching umbrella that all the compensation programs should fall under," says Karen Macke, senior vice president of compensation and benefits at The Hartford Financial Services Group Inc., a Connecticut-based insurance and financial services corporation with about 28,000 employees in the United States. "If a program falls outside the umbrella, you've got to question if the program is right for the organization."

Having a compensation philosophy can help shield HR professionals from pressures exerted by individual managers who want to customize compensation within their department or division. Without a clear philosophy in place, "you'll always be inundated by the business manager of a profitable business [line] who says, 'I want my own plan,' and you have no way of addressing that," says Paul Shafer, business leader and compensation expert with consulting firm Hewitt Associates in Norwalk, Conn.

The Hartford's philosophy identifies what the company's pay programs are trying to achieve, along with what elements must be consistent throughout the organization. The company does allow for some customization for "unique business situations," Macke notes, such as incentive plans for salespeople. But any unique programs must still align with The Hartford's business strategy and the desired culture of the organization, Macke says.

David Balkin, chairman of the management division at the University of Colorado's Leeds School of Business in Boulder and a compensation expert, suggests that a philosophy should provide a strategy "that links the different compensation programs and pieces together." Basing compensation decisions on historic company practices—in other words, the "We've always done it that way" approach—"doesn't work in a very dynamic economy with global and technological pressures," he says.

Another factor driving the decision to develop a philosophy is the size of the company, says Hewitt's Shafer.

In small companies, such as startups in the technology field, "you have a founder or a small group of senior people who tend to know everybody in the company" and who make "personal" decisions about individual pay, Shafer says. But once a company's workforce grows significantly, "those who are responsible for making the pay decisions oftentimes start losing touch with who all the people are," he notes. "They need a philosophy to be able to govern the program so it can be administered in a fair and equitable manner."

Close Collaboration

While HR generally is in the driver's seat when developing a compensation philosophy, that development often is done in close collaboration with high-level management to ensure executive buy-in and to develop a philosophy that meshes with the company's business objectives.

Kristen Vosburgh, PHR, manager of benefits and compensation at the Cary, N.C.-based business intelligence software company SAS, says that HR and compensation specialists should drive the process, "with feedback and validation from managers."

Sport adds, "HR is clearly in the best position to drive the process. We are the ones who understand the marketplace, have the compensation survey tools, have the knowledge about the jobs, understand the labor market issues and understand the legal issues." But "you can't have a process without senior management buy-in," she notes.

Once HR and top leadership are committed to developing a philosophy, Shafer says he likes to get senior leaders of the organization together to push them to identify and quantify the attributes of a compensation program that they think are important, such as the mix of pay elements. Most senior managers will tell you their philosophy should be to "attract, motivate and retain the best people," Shafer notes, but he adds, "That's too general. It really doesn't give you much guidance." Once the managers identify what they value in terms of compensation, Shafer says his firm works with the client's HR leaders to craft a philosophy statement that is acceptable to management and HR.

The process of considering changes in the philosophy also often is a collaborative process between HR and management. Vickie Davis, manager of compensation and benefits at the Babcock and Wilcox Co. (B & W), a Barberton, Ohio-based energy services company with about 1,100 employees at its U.S. headquarters, says the company's philosophy is reviewed every year prior to the salary-planning process.

While business leaders focus on possible changes relating to business objectives, it's HR's job to examine potential resource issues that might, for example, require a company to consider paying a premium for talent. If there was a scarcity in the available labor pool that would prompt a change in compensation philosophy, HR leaders "certainly would be the catalyst for that because we would be aware of it first," Davis notes.

You should put a compensation philosophy within the framework of your target philosophy.

Shafer urges HR managers to step back when considering their philosophy to look at the broader framework of attracting and retaining employees. "You should put a compensation philosophy within the framework of your talent philosophy," he says, by assessing fundamental issues such as whether the company is trying to develop homegrown talent or invest in attracting outside talent.

"It's cheaper to grow your own tomatoes than to go buy them in the market," Shafer observes. "But if it's the middle of winter and you need a tomato, you really don't have much choice."

HR needs to review how the company currently is evaluating jobs and paying employees, including consideration of market positioning of the jobs, and assess potential variances in pay compared to the market. HR managers also need to consider if current pay practices are working or whether adjustments are needed to attract and retain employees based on current wage rates, Vosburgh notes. Some of the more obvious signals that pay practices aren't working are employee turnover and an inability to successfully hire top job candidates.

Online Resources

For help creating a compensation philosophy, see the online version of this article at www.shrm.org/hrmagazine/05January. There you will find Prudential Financial's compensation philosophy statement and a new study showing that a growing number of workers indicate better health care coverage is more important than higher pay.

Company culture and business needs also must plug into the analysis, says Vosburgh. For example, she notes that at SAS, which employs about 5,300 people in North America, "We do aspire to pay our people competitively, but there is a cultural need to be egalitarian," so that need has shaped the compensation philosophy.

"Except for certain [research and development] and critical jobs where we may target base salary above the market median, we look at the local market median for the base salary," explains Vosburgh.

'Intangible Compensation'

Innovative companies are developing philosophies that communicate all that their workplaces have to offer. Vosburgh says SAS's philosophy focuses only partially on pay. "We have not given up on the paycheck. Base salary is important," she says. "However, our benefits, annual company contribution to profit sharing, a 401(k) safe-harbor contribution and on-site amenities are also a significant portion of the package."

The University of Colorado's Balkin notes that SAS has been included on many "best places to work" lists in part because of this broader compensation philosophy that emphasizes total rewards.

Similarly, as a not-for-profit organization, the Carnegie Endowment for International Peace does not offer high pay, Sport notes. What it does offer is the "intrinsic value" of working for an organization that emphasizes quality of life and robust benefits, including generous retirement and vacation programs. "We place a really high value on quality of life," she says, suggesting that a pleasant work environment perhaps should be considered "intangible compensation."

'Transparency and Clarity'

Once a philosophy is in place, many companies work hard to communicate it to their employees across the board. "For us, transparency and clarity in communication are critical to employees," says The Hartford's Macke. "The philosophy that helps define the comp program can't be motivating to employees if it isn't understood."

At B & W, enhanced communication turned out to be crucial in getting managers and employees to understand the company's new emphasis on pay for performance, which resulted in better performers receiving a larger proportion of salary and bonus dollars.

"Managers had difficulty embracing the philosophy at first," says B & W's Davis. Although the pay-for-performance system had rolled out several years earlier, Davis says it became clear by 2002 that more aggressive communication measures were needed to bring about increased acceptance of the approach.

Davis worked with B & W's communications staff to write a basic philosophy statement and to post it on the company's intranet. HR managers also began coaching line supervisors and providing them with talking points to help them in salary-related discussions with employees.

"The driving force behind putting [the philosophy] out there is the feeling that the employees needed to see it in writing, needed to understand it, so that they would understand it wasn't arbitrary," Davis says. Managers have achieved "a better comfort level" in discussing compensation with employees but, she acknowledges, it has been an evolution.

"We've gone from a culture that didn't talk about compensation to one that does," she notes. Employees "may not agree with how it has impacted them, but they do at least understand that it's not arbitrary, there is a process, there is a philosophy that everyone is trying to adhere to."

Possible Problems

But communicating openly with employees could leave companies vulnerable. The University of Colorado's Balkin, who has appeared as an expert witness on behalf of plaintiffs in pay discrimination cases, urges caution when considering just how open to be. The philosophy could come back to haunt the employer if the employer has failed to abide by it, he suggests.

In a litigation setting, "If I know what the compensation philosophy is and I see [an employee] who was treated as an exception to that policy, I would use that as additional evidence that discrimination took place," he says. "If you don't act consistently [within an open system], there's a liability there."

In addition, if those you expect to communicate the philosophy to the rank and file are not up to the task, think twice about how far you spread the word, says SAS's Vosburgh. "If the managers are not equipped to effectively communicate the philosophy, then the philosophy should be limited to management only," she says, adding, "Managers should possess basic compensation knowledge before a stated philosophy is publicized companywide."

The reality of many workplaces is that some jobs are valued more, and therefore are compensated better, than others.

Compensation often is a hot-button issue among employees, and the compensation philosophy should be constructed to address potential problems. The reality of many workplaces is that some jobs are valued more, and therefore are compensated better, than others.

When employees ask why jobs are ranked differently, "those are hard, hard questions to answer," says Sport. "But if you put together a good philosophy, they're very defensible." When she worked at a boutique financial services firm, she says, "we placed a very high value on talent, and that talent was unique." As a result, the key people in financial positions were very well compensated in terms of salaries and bonuses, while other employees were paid about market rate.

"But it was justifiable," Sport notes, because the compensation philosophy emphasized the value of those employees. "Without those key financial people, we wouldn't be in business."

CHARLOTTE GARVEY is a freelance writer, based in the Washington, D.C., area, who reports on business and environmental issues.

Do Your Employees Qualify for Overtime?

The Answer May Surprise You

DEE GILL

She's well compensated. He's a manager. They're all on salary. These are some of the common reasons employers give to explain why they do not pay their employees overtime. But in many cases these reasons are not legally valid.

That's something business owners have been learning the hard way. Indeed, the number of overtime lawsuits has exploded over the past couple of years. In 2005, class-action suits involving wages surpassed discrimination cases as the most widespread work force class action, according to a recent study by Chicago law firm Seyfarth Shaw. During the same year, the Department of Labor collected $166 million in back wages, mostly overtime pay—a 26 percent increase from 2001. Large companies, such as Cingular Wireless, have doled out millions in back overtime wages recently. Smaller companies are being forced to pay up as well.

The litigation has been fueled, in large part, by changes to the Fair Labor Standards Act in 2004. The Department of Labor updated the antiquated act, which first came into effect in 1938, in order to eliminate references to outdated jobs (think straw bosses and keypunch operators) and establish guidelines for contemporary workers. Among other changes, the agency determined that employees must make at least $455 a week to be ineligible for overtime pay, a sharp increase over the previous benchmark of $250 a week. As a result, 1.3 million workers suddenly qualified for extra pay, according to the DOL.

But the effects of those changes are really being felt now. Not only are more workers "aware of the changes, but employment lawyers are increasingly on the lookout for potential overtime suits. "What we're seeing now are claims that are driven by an increase in awareness," says Paul DeCamp, administrator of the Wage and Hour Division at the Department of Labor. "All of a sudden, people are realizing that they have rights to overtime that they didn't know about." Paul Lukas, partner at Minneapolis law firm Nichols Kaster & Anderson, says that most clients come to his office complaining about wrongful termination or discrimination. But he ends each initial interview with questions about overtime pay, with an eye toward building a class-action case. And he's not alone. The revised overtime laws, Lukas says, have created a cottage industry. "Nothing wakes up lawyers faster than someone else making money on a certain kind of case," he says. "The word is that FLSA cases are lucrative cases."

Employers have been caught off guard by the rise in overtime disputes. "Employers frequently don't appreciate the value of spending time on these issues until it's too late," DeCamp says. Case in point: Eloy Torrez, president of SEI Group, an engineering firm in Huntsville, Alabama. Torrez thought he was being a good boss when he devised a pay plan that allowed him to avoid layoffs by adjusting his employees' salaries along with the ups and downs of government contracting. When business was flush, he paid staffers a salary, plus the equivalent of one hour of pay for each hour worked in excess of 40 hours a week. In a good year, he doled out as much as $30,000 extra per employee. But when contracts from clients like the U.S. Army and the Department of Homeland Security slowed down, Torrez scaled back some salaries, treating his staff of engineers, architects, accountants, and program managers as part-timers—paying them only for the hours they worked—but with full health benefits.

Torrez figured the system was great because it eliminated temporary layoffs and gaps in health coverage. But unbeknownst to him, it was also illegal. Because SEI's professional staffers were not receiving consistent salaries, they qualified for overtime pay—at least one and a half times their regular hourly wages—for every week they worked more than 40 hours. Last October, after an audit that lasted months, the Department of Labor ordered SEI to pay two years of back overtime wages totaling $464,342 to 103 of its 126 employees. "That's about half of this year's earnings," Torrez says. "This has been a huge burden for us."

Like many business owners, Torrez assumed that his staffers were ineligible for time and a half because they received salaries. But the updated overtime rules make it clear that salaried workers such as computer programmers and account executives

Excuses, Excuses

If you're using one of the following justifications to explain why you're not paying overtime, you could be breaking the law.

1. "He's on salary." Even salaried workers may have to be paid overtime if their jobs meet certain exemption criteria. The rule of thumb: If they don't make many independent decisions, they may qualify for time and a half.
2. "Longer hours are in her contract." Some employers try to avoid paying overtime by building extra hours into employment contracts. But employees can't opt out of overtime pay.
3. "He makes a lot of money." White-collar workers who earn more than $100,000 a year and meet the "independent judgment" criteria are ineligible for overtime only if they make at least $455 a week in guaranteed salary. In many cases, bonuses don't count.
4. "He's an outside sales rep." Outside salespeople are generally exempt from overtime pay. But if they spend more than half their time in the office, they may actually qualify.

may be eligible for overtime if their jobs meet certain exemption criteria. Those criteria are numerous and detailed, but the philosophy behind them is simple: Workers who do not spend most of their days performing tasks that require them to exercise "discretion and independent judgment" probably qualify for overtime pay. That could include anyone from a secretary who answers phones all day to a loan officer who relies on computer algorithms to determine an applicant's eligibility. Even managers and job site foremen who do not have strong input into hiring and firing decisions may be eligible to collect overtime.

Many employers realize they're in violation of the revised overtime laws only after they've been contacted by the Department of Labor. Most audits are the result of a complaint from a single worker that blows up into a companywide investigation. "If the DOL visits you, it will rarely be to look at the one employee complain," says Steve Trent, chairman of the labor and employment practice at Baker, Donelson, Bearman, Caldwell & Berkowitz in Johnson City, Tennessee. Audit results are rarely good news for companies. Those found to be in violation must pony up two years of back overtime wages, in addition to fines for repeat offenders. Lawsuits tend to be even more damaging: Lukas, for example, typically sues employers for two years of back overtime pay. If he can demonstrate that a business knowingly broke overtime laws—which he frequently does—his clients may be entitled to a third year of back wages.

To stay out of trouble, consider paying a labor attorney a few thousand dollars to vet your pay policies. And take a hard look at what your employees do all day, regardless of their job descriptions. If they don't make many independent decisions, there's a good chance they qualify for overtime pay. Also, think twice about offering flextime to hourly workers. If an employee with a flexible schedule works more than 40 hours in a given week, regardless of how much he or she worked the previous or following weeks, that person may qualify for overtime.

To learn more about the rules governing overtime pay, visit the Web site of the Department of Labor's Wage and Hour Division (wagehour.dol.gov) or call the DOL hotline (1-866-4-USWAGE).

Of course, you might not like what you discover. And correcting overtime mistakes isn't easy. Workers will probably ask about back wages when they find out they are eligible for overtime. To avoid a pricey lawsuit and bad press, some companies bite the bullet and hand over two years of back wages and pay overtime going forward.

Torrez, for his part, isn't sure how the Department of Labor found out about SEI's pay system. He recently switched his work force to guaranteed salaries with no overtime pay. When business slows down, Torrez says, he'll be forced to lay off workers. He's gotten plenty of complaints from staffers about the new system. "No one is happy about it," he says.

Pay-for-Performance Plans Should Be Fair and Clear

SUSAN MEISINGER

In recent years, corporate operations have come under increased scrutiny. Pay for senior executives, particularly CEOs, is often the focus of discussions about corporate excesses. Much of the debate is centered on pay for performance, especially since many poorly performing organizations have made huge, highly publicized payouts to executives.

Shareholders are shining a light on executives' compensation and their overall accountability for the success of their organizations. And workers are now weighing in on the issue, as revealed in a recent survey, *Rising Above the Average: 2007 Compensation and Benefits Report,* by the HR consulting firm Hudson.

Thirty-nine percent of workers surveyed believe senior executives are paid too much, and nearly half (48 percent) think the pay disparity between corporate leaders and average employees is too great.

Like shareholders, workers expect their leadership to be held to performance standards—64 percent think executive pay should be tied to organizational performance. Employees—many of whom are compensated on the basis of *their* performance—want to see the level of executive pay justified by the impact these leaders have on their organizations.

The Hudson survey indicated that the connection between pay and performance is not reaching all levels of many organizations. While 56 percent of managers said employees who do a better job get better compensation, only 32 percent of non-managers agreed. Furthermore, nearly half of the employees surveyed said their performance has often been reviewed against goals that were not previously communicated.

These findings highlight a common failing of many pay-for-performance plans: a failure by employers to communicate clearly and a lack of transparency on how the review process is conducted and its impact on workers. The result: Many employees don't have a clear understanding of how their employers link pay to performance.

A previous Society for Human Resource Management (SHRM) study, *2006 HR Practices in Executive-Level Compensation Survey Report,* examined the role of HR in determining pay practices for top-tier employees. The SHRM study found that a perceived lack of fairness in compensation policies created resentment among workers, concluding: "It will become harder to justify to a workforce where pay for performance is the expected norm that highly paid executives are not being held to the same standard."

HR professionals must ensure that executive pay packages adhere to organizational governance standards and performance objectives. HR also has a responsibility to establish clear and regular communication that not only explains when reviews will occur and how they will be structured, but also ensures that employees at every level—including senior management—understand how individual performance can affect their compensation.

For any compensation plan to be effective, it must be perceived as fair by employees at all levels. To achieve this perception, it must be clearly *understood* by everyone involved.

Pay Setters

Chairmen of compensation committees give the lowdown on why executive pay keeps going up.

FRANK MALEY

T om Smith ran a big grocery chain for 13 years and was paid handsomely for it. In 1998, his last full year as CEO of Salisbury-based Food Lion Inc., he earned $3 million, according to the formula Business North Carolina uses to calculate executive pay. Adjusted for inflation, that would have been equal to about $3.6 million in 2005. That would put Smith at 20th on this year's ranking of CEO pay at the 75 largest public companies in the state.

He also starred in some of Food Lion's television commercials, so couch potatoes around the state quickly grew familiar with—some, perhaps tired of—his boyish mug interrupting their favorite shows. Since retiring in 1999, he has dropped out of the public eye but not completely out of corporate boardrooms. These days, Smith helps set pay for executives at Concord-based CT Communications Inc. as chairman of its compensation committee.

He's not unusual. Eight of the 10 highest-paid CEOs on the list—compiled by the Charlotte office of human-resources consultant Findley Davies Inc.—run companies where the compensation-committee chairmen are current or former CEOs. Four are, or were, CEOs of public companies. The theory is that few know as much about CEO compensation as CEOs. Few have reason to care as much. But is it wise to let CEOs, past and present, set their peers' pay?

"There are two points of view there," says Paul Hodgson, a compensation specialist at The Corporate Library, a Portland, Maine-based company that researches corporate governance. "One is that it is the fox guarding the henhouse and that they're unlikely to be harsh with their fellow CEOs and say, 'We need to be more modest about our pay levels here.' Alternatively, they may actually have more authority in that situation and therefore be able to stand up to another CEO."

Whether it's the best practice, CEOs often are judged by their peers, and in any given year their pay could go either way. Twenty-three CEOs on our list took pay cuts in 2005, sometimes even when their company produced a positive total return, but 46 got a pay boost—seven even though their companies produced negative returns. The median pay change for CEOs at the state's 75 largest public companies was 13.1% in 2005. That's

Working for Their Keep

Even though he was the top-paid CEO, Ken Lewis was a bargain for his shareholders, Paul Anderson worked just for dividends.

CEO/Company	Total Compensation (000s)	Net Income Per Dollar of Compensation
1 Paul M. Anderson, Duke Energy	$ 0.0	nm
2 Kenneth D. Lewis, Bank of America	$26,524.4	$620.7
3 G. Kennedy Thompson, Wachovia	20,396.4	325.7
4 Robert A. Niblock, Lowe's	9,428.8	293.9
5 Susan M. Ivery, Reynolds American	3,677.8	283.3
6 Robert P. Ingle, Ingles Markets	101.0	263.2
7 John A. Allison IV, BB&T	7,748.7	213.4
8 Christopher J. Kearney, SPX	5,514.0	197.7
9 Daniel R. DiMicco, Nucor	7,297.4	179.6
10 Robert B. McGehee, Progress Energy	4,115.3	169.4

a smaller increase than the previous year but larger than the median total return in 2005—measured from the first trading day of the fiscal year to the last—of 6.4%. And with a median pay package of $1.4 million, those CEOs won't get much sympathy from their shareholders.

To get fat pay packages, though, CEOs don't need shareholder sympathy, just their acquiescence and a strong demand for their talents. "Our system operates on the basis of the free market and of competitiveness," says Bill Holland, former CEO of United

Dominion Industries, a Charlotte-based maker of industrial equipment, and compensation-committee chairman at Lance Inc., a Charlotte-based snack maker. "Top-level executives command a lot of money. That's just a fact."

Setting CEO pay is a complicated process that usually takes several months and is part of a larger task of deciding what to pay all of a company's top executives. "I do not like to see these incentives for the CEO much different than ones for the other top executives," Smith says. "The amounts might be different, but the same things that guide him or her need to guide the other executives."

At CT Communications—a local phone company that has branched into Internet access, wireless communications and long-distance service—discussion of CEO Michael Coltrane's 2005 pay started in mid-2004. The compensation committee instructed Findley Davies to launch a survey of compensation at companies in the same industry—preferably eight or more. "The way I like it is if you can knock out the upper and lower extremes and still have a good listing of companies to balance out, because you never find a company that you can match up with exactly," Smith says.

In most years, CT's consultant presents the completed survey to the committee in September and fields questions about it. The committee may request additional information. In November, the full board of directors discusses the company's goals. Around the first of December, the committee meets again and tries to translate those goals into a pay package that will motivate top executives and place them in the right spot on the industry spectrum. "If you've got a CEO and your company is doing average, I think you should pay him near the median," Smith says. "But if you've got one that's producing results better than those other eight, or better than seven out of the eight, then you should move the CEO higher."

As at many public companies, CT's Coltrane receives a fixed salary plus a bonus and other pay based on performance. In 2005, his annual bonus was contingent on the company hitting goals in, among other things, operating revenue; operating earnings before interest, taxes, depreciation and amortization; operating free cash flow; and customer growth. His long-term incentives were based on three-year growth in operating revenue, operating EBITDA, earnings per share and total shareholder return compared with a peer stock index.

The process varies from company to company. But many rely on consultants and try to peg CEO pay to company performance within its industry. The process is more detailed and defensible at many than it once was but still can produce results that are puzzling when pay is compared with company performance in the same year. Coltrane, for example, got a 57% raise in 2005, when CT's total return was a paltry 1.4% and its net income dropped slightly. Most of the increase came from an option grant and long-term incentive payouts aimed at boosting future performance and weren't influenced only by 2005 results.

Company performance can be affected by industry trends, long-term goals and extraordinary circumstances. CT's bottom line was stagnant, but it's in an increasingly competitive industry—with long-distance carriers, cell-phone companies and cable-television operators wanting bigger shares of local phone markets—and net income took a hit from the cost of laying more fiber-optic cable, which Smith says will help it compete long-term.

Likewise, it's hard for outsiders to easily understand the deal Lance gave David Singer. He received about $6 million in 2005, ninth on our list. That's more than six times what his predecessor, Paul Stroup, made in 2004 and more than seven times what Singer made in 2004 as chief financial officer of Charlotte-based Coca-Cola Bottling Company Consolidated. It was 35% more than Holland made in his penultimate year as CEO of United Dominion, though Lance is less than a third the size United Dominion was in Holland's day, before it was purchased in 2001 by SPX, now based in Charlotte.

Lance didn't exactly sparkle in 2005. Its total return was a minuscule 1.1%, and net income dropped 26%, though part of that decrease stems from the purchase of Tom's Foods, a Columbus, Ga.-based competitor, for $38 million in October, Holland says.

Singer's pay had to be big, in part, to lure him from Coke Consolidated, where he was CFO 19 years, Holland says. Besides, Lance historically hadn't paid well. Most of Singer's 2005 pay was in restricted stock that won't vest for five years. "A great deal of his compensation was equity-based and will either pay out or not pay out. It's valued at a point in time. But based on how the company performs, he may or may not earn that money."

Although he once did the same kind of executive work as Singer, Holland is certain he can be impartial. After all, he answers not to Singer but to the company's shareholders. "If a particular board or a particular committee is not in step with what their shareholders think they should be able to kick them out. And that happens." It's more difficult at Lance than at some companies because its directors aren't voted on annually, but staggered terms for directors also can help prevent precipitous purges by shareholders, Holland says.

Since it passed in 2002, the Sarbanes-Oxley Act has made boards and CEOs more accountable for corporate finances and more conscientious about explaining CEO pay. In July, the U.S. Securities and Exchange Commission issued rules that will force companies to clarify executive compensation even more. Among other things, they must report a dollar value for all equity-based compensation and a total compensation figure comparable with those at other companies. The new rules will close most loopholes companies have used to avoid disclosing full CEO compensation, Hodgson says, but he doesn't expect them to give complete details about the performance measures used to set pay.

He would like shareholders to have a stronger voice in setting CEO pay, such as nonbinding votes on compensation-committee reports. A negative vote wouldn't overturn the decision but would send a message to board members. Holland says such a vote could set bad precedent and blur the lines between shareholders, directors and management. "You could get down to saying, 'Is the company setting the right capital-expenditure budget? Are they aggressive enough in their growth plans?'"

No matter how fully it's disclosed, CEO pay isn't likely to go down soon. People capable of running big public companies are in short supply, and heightened interest in CEO pay could, paradoxically, lead to more pay, says Hank Federal, principal and Southeast compensation-practice leader for Toledo, Ohio-based Findley Davies. "With the ever-increasing scrutiny around the businesses and what they do and how they pay these executives, they have less and less room for any kind of error. Therefore, it is contracting the pool of very qualified CEOs. When you've got people demanding and needing high-qualified CEOs and a shrinking pool, what does that typically do? It raises prices."

Doc in a Box

Wellness specialists credit health-monitoring kiosks with saving time, money and lives.

DAWN S. ONLEY

Automated health screening stations at Frank Fuentes' workplace are helping keep him off blood pressure medication and out of the doctor's office.

Fuentes, an office equipment coordinator at American Honda Motor Co. in Torrance, Calif., credits the noninvasive, computerized monitoring stations with giving him and other Honda em-ployees the key to managing their own health: timely information.

Fuentes says he has used the screening stations consistently over the past decade to monitor his blood pressure and to get alerts when he has picked up weight. "I was on medication once before. They told me I couldn't get off it until I lost weight," Fuentes says, adding that he checks his blood pressure every few days now at one of the stations. "By doing the reading, I can tell whether I need to exercise."

Computerized Screening Inc. (CSI) of Sparks, Nev., sells the Health Station used by American Honda and other employers to help employees like Fuentes get fast health assessments at their worksites.

American Honda has used the stations for more than 10 years. Workers in the security department requested that the machines be installed in the workplace after seeing how they were used in supermarkets.

American Honda safety specialist John Duehring says that at first the company leased the kiosks, but they proved to be such a major hit, with thousands of uses each month, that officials decided to purchase them to complement a corporate wellness structure that includes an on-site fitness center, wellness seminars and free exercise classes. Honda now owns 11 Health Stations spread across more than half a dozen major facilities and plans to buy nine more stations, Duehring says. Employees use the stations in cafeterias and break rooms.

Touch-Screen Testing

The Health Station comes in basic and advanced models and measures users' blood pressure, heart rate and weight noninvasively. To use the machines, employees sit down at what resembles a combination workbench and mini-entertainment center with touch-screen computers that will walk users through a variety of tests.

To measure blood pressure, users put their arms into a standard blood pressure cuff and rest their elbows on a table in front of them. In some models, a scale built into the seat measures weight. Health Stations, depending on the options purchased, also can monitor other signs such as spirometry, the measurement of lung strength and capacity used by physicians treating breathing issues such as asthma.

Other tests, driven by question-and-answer sessions with the computers, look at users' lifestyles and health choices, such as their level of exercise or smoking habits. The answers help the station generate a personalized health risk appraisal, which places users in government-defined health risk categories.

Bob Sullivan, CSI's executive vice president, says an upgraded version offers enhanced features including Internet links, through a secure server, to let users reach their health care providers or pharmacists on the web. This model also features a drug encyclopedia and a database that ensures medications are compatible. Some models include connectivity that allows videoconferencing right at the station. Stored in the stations are hundreds of health tips and educational videos on everything from alternative medications to nutritional supplements and herbal remedies.

The stations contain customized information on local health care providers including physicians, hospitals and crisis centers.

Use of the Health Station is "completely patient driven," Sullivan says. "The patient is involved in his own health care. This is giving people the ability to understand what their health status is."

In keeping with medical information privacy law, neither employers nor the vendor can access employee-specific information in the kiosks.

Prices for Health Station models range from the Model 3K at $3,495 to the Model 6K at $6,995. Options, such as more tests and information databases, vary depending on the employer's needs, Sullivan says. CSI has 3,500 stations in workplaces, supermarkets and other locations across the United States and Canada. According to the 26-year-old company, its health-monitoring stations are in about 60 percent of *Fortune* 500 companies.

There is at least one other manufacturer of such health monitoring machines. Medical Screening Services Inc. of Niles, Ill., markets its Vita-Stat health stations, which measure blood pressure, heart rate and weight, calculate body mass, and provide educational information on hypertension, exercise, weight and diet.

Fuentes says he likes being able to monitor his blood pressure. But he says he wishes his company machine gave users a weekly or monthly tip on what they should eat as well as on new medical discoveries.

Some employees are skeptical of the station's readings, Fuentes adds. "Some of the people are not aware that the machine gives you a true reading. People are a little apprehensive about trying to use it. They can have high blood pressure without knowing it."

Keeping Data Private

CSI's Health Stations also allow users to establish their personal medical records in the station's system. The user can bring in records of doctor's visits, hospitalizations or prescription drug use and load that data into some models.

Employees need not worry that their bosses could peruse their personal medical information, Sullivan notes. The Health Insurance Portability and Accountability Act (HIPAA) requires increased security for employee health information and imposes criminal and civil penalties for employers that don't comply. In keeping with HIPAA, Sullivan says, neither employers nor CSI can access employee-specific information. The Health Station encrypts such information, and users can access it only with a personal identification number known solely to the employee.

Employers can choose how their Health Station model stores data, Sullivan adds. Some stations are truly stand-alone, with all data stored at the station at the employer's site, while others store data on servers based at CSI. "But we do nothing with the patient-identified data internally, nor do we have access to it," he says.

Although employers cannot access an employee's individual data from the stations, employers can get aggregate data to see what employee populations are using the monitoring stations and what their health concerns are. Then employers can use that data to develop health programs to address issues identified in the data, according to Sullivan.

For employers who wonder if they might be liable should an employee use a monitoring station and then fall ill, Sullivan notes that each time a CSI Health Station gives a user a measurement such as blood pressure, it also displays a disclaimer that points the user to a physician or health care professional for any follow-up.

Cost-Effective Wellness

About four years ago, a blackjack dealer at the Cal-Neva Resort & Spa in Lake Tahoe, Nev., suffered a heart attack and passed out at work. The dealer survived, but the incident prompted senior wellness officials at the upscale casino and resort to take additional steps to promote employee wellness.

The resort, which had long mandated CPR classes for managers and had external defibrillators on-site, was already proactive about employee health, but after the dealer's heart attack, officials felt they could do even more, says Rick Talbot, Cal-Neva's chief of security and director of employee wellness and safety. Cal-Neva purchased a Health Station to give employees and resort visitors a way to monitor their health.

That move may have prevented another calamity last October when the resort's director of engineering, who felt under the weather, decided to test his heart rate. The director, who suffers from ongoing heart problems, sat down at the Health Station and quickly learned that his heart rate was racing at more than 200 beats per minute.

Cal-Neva is considering purchasing another monitoring station. Talbot, who acknowledges he's in a high-stress job, says he uses the station daily to monitor his own blood pressure and heart rate. About 3,000 users each month access the resort's station. Talbot adds that the station helps not only employees but also resort guests, many of whom are unaccustomed to the high altitude of Lake Tahoe.

"We're at 6,200-feet elevation, and the air's a little thin," Talbot explains. "We get older folks here. I've taken guests, complaining of shortness of breath, to the machine myself."

Sullivan recalls the story of a man at another workplace who was noticeably red in the face and was told by another employee to check his blood pressure at their company's health-monitoring station. When he did, he learned it was off the chart, and he had to have immediate bypass surgery, Sullivan says.

Talbot believes the stations save his employer money and increase productivity, although Cal-Neva doesn't keep statistics on how much it believes it saves due to the stations.

"This is saving health care dollars. Just think of what you save if you save [on] hospitalization for cardiac arrest [if the machine catches heart irregularities before an attack]. It's a real lifesaving possibility," Sullivan says.

While American Honda also doesn't have any metrics in place to measure whether the monitoring stations have helped reduce absenteeism or increase productivity among the workforce of 3,040, Duehring says user feedback shows that employees use the kiosks widely. For example, just at the company's headquarters, there are 1,000 uses of the machine a month. And Duehring says he hears from employees all the time—asking for more machines.

"All we go by is how many people are using the machines," he says. "We know that when we have the machine set up in one area and we move it, we get a lot of phone calls."

AstraZeneca, a pharmaceutical manufacturer headquartered in Wilmington, Del., is another employer using the monitoring stations. Amy Milhorn, senior manager of corporate health services, says the three CSI Health Stations her company owns definitely have saved her and her staff time. Milhorn has three full-time and two part-time nurses on her staff who don't have to do as many blood pressure readings and other tests as they used to.

"Instead of employees coming to the nurses to get readings, they use the machines," Milhorn explains.

We provided a complete wellness program to the entire staff of our corporate headquarters at minimal cost and great efficiency.

"CSI provided the basis for a program that enabled us to cost-effectively reach all employees," says Milhorn, whose company has 5,500 employees. "We provided a complete wellness program to the entire staff of our corporate headquarters at minimal cost and great efficiency. We spent far less than if we hired additional health care practitioners, and [we] reached a much greater number of people in a lesser amount of time."

DAWN S. ONLEY is a Washington, D.C.-based freelance writer who specializes in technology issues in private-sector and federal workplaces.

Building a Mentally Healthy Workforce

Psychologists highlight effective interventions to help counter the rising cost of mental health problems in the workplace.

Melissa Dittman

Psychologists and occupational health leaders highlighted programs aimed at alleviating work-family conflicts and workplace stress at a recent conference organized by the National Institute for Occupational Safety and Health and more than 20 co-sponsors, including APA. The 2004 Steps to a Healthier U.S. Workforce Symposium brought together leaders from the occupational safety and the health promotion communities to explore ways to improve employees' health and safety.

One session at the event included promoting employee well-being through such means as flexible work schedules and team-based employee problem-solving.

The need is evident: The number of employees nationwide reporting psychiatric disabilities is steadily growing and costing companies in lost productivity and employee absenteeism, according to psychologists who spoke at the session.

For example, at Bank One—now J.P. Morgan Chase—employees' mental health issues from 2000–2002 accounted for the second leading cause of short-term disability and were second in total of days absent from work—behind only pregnancy.

Depression, in particular, is the most reported psychiatric disability, and contributes to the most absences, limiting employees' cognitive reasoning and interpersonal skills, said clinical psychologist Daniel J. Conti, PhD, an employee assistance program director at J.P. Morgan Chase. By 2020, depression is expected to rank second in leading causes of worldwide disability; in 1990, it ranked fourth, according to the "The Global Burden of Disease" (Harvard University Press, 1996).

As such, Conti said companies need to not only take into account the productivity lost through employee absenteeism due to such mental health problems, but also the productivity lost while an employee is present but limited at work due to health problems—which he referred to as "presenteeism." He stressed the need for companies to change management and organizational work methods to help decrease such losses.

Doing that requires workplaces to examine returns on mental health components of their medical plans, and it requires employees to shift their work attitudes and behaviors, Conti noted.

Employer flexibility is also key to minimizing mental health problems among employees, said Lynne Casper, PhD, of the National Institute of Child Health and Human Development.

"Workplace policies can have an effect on people's health, how they live their life and their ability to manage their work and family obligations," she said.

Team-Building Interventions

Indeed, tedious job tasks, job insecurity or inflexible work schedules can demoralize some employees or lower their motivation, speakers noted.

To address such issues, psychologist David M. DeJoy, PhD, director of the Workplace Health Group, conducted a study on healthy work organization in retail. DeJoy and his colleagues surveyed employees at 21 stores—all part of the same company—to identify employees' concerns about issues such as their work schedules. From there, the researchers formed a team of eight to 12 employees at each store to develop store-specific interventions to respond to those concerns. Such interventions included programs geared to build skills to enhance employer and employee communication, improve morale, manage conflict and solve problems related to, for example, customer-service issues.

> **"Workplace policies can have an effect on people's health, how they live their life and their ability to manage their work and family obligations."**
>
> —Lynne Casper
> National Institutes of Health

According to self reports from employees and employers, the interventions led to better communication as well as improved employee satisfaction with work schedules, job content and feelings of increased involvement in workplace decisions, said DeJoy, a professor of health promotion and behavior at the University of Georgia. The team-based intervention also had some positive effects on store sales and employee turnover.

Working Parent Programs

Researchers have shown that programs—such as Triple P (Positive Parenting Program)—geared to help working parents balance work and family life also can contribute to improved employee mental health.

Triple P provides evidence-based support strategies for parents of children from birth to 12 years old, said psychologist Ron Prinz, PhD, Carolina Distinguished Professor at the University of South Carolina. The program features individual or small group sessions focused on helping parents better plan and prioritize their family and work responsibilities and gain confidence in their parenting skills. Australian psychology professor Matthew Sanders, PhD, and his colleagues at the University of Queensland developed Triple P.

Triple P, in particular, derives from research showing that parents with high work stress tend to have low job self-efficacy, less positive parent-child interactions, less parental satisfaction and more coercive parenting styles, Prinz said.

Triple P can counter some of that, according to preliminary data. Parents who participated in Triple P group sessions at work were able to reduce work stress and child behavior problems and also improve their overall self-efficacy, Prinz said.

However, child care isn't the only source of family life stress. At IBM, for example, the company found a 200 percent increase from 1986 to 2001 in employees needing elder care for aging loved ones. To help, the company created a national referral and resource service to help employees find elder care.

Flexible Work Schedules

IBM also introduced flexible work schedules—such as giving many employees the option to work part-time or at home—based on another of its survey findings that such scheduling contributes to improved worker satisfaction. Now one-third of IBM employees do not work primarily at a traditional IBM office. Working from home, in particular, has gained acceptability among employees and employers, said Michael D. Shum, IBM's director of Global Workforce Diversity Operations.

Indeed, IBM researchers have found that employees who work at home have the least difficulty with motivation and retention and are more willing to put in extra effort in their job. Plus, 55 percent of the employees surveyed agreed that working from home at least one day per week is acceptable, and 64 percent said they are likely to work from home in the next five years.

"This whole face-time culture of a manager having to watch a person work is changing," Shum said. "We still have a long way to go, but we're making progress."

Employee Benefits of the Future

Melissa Proffitt Reese, Linda Rowings, and Tiffany Sharpley

Employee benefits provide a significant portion of an employee's total compensation and are an important element in any employee's job satisfaction. To maximize the positive impact of benefits on employees, employers must reconsider benefit packages and how such benefits are communicated to employees. This will help ensure they meet the needs and wants of the four generations of individuals who will be working side by side. This article:

- describes the generations that will be working together and what businesses will need from each generation;
- examines ways employers can attract and retain different generations;
- discusses ways in which employers can and should consider the costs associated with providing benefits; and
- provides design ideas for an employee benefit package that will motivate multiple generations.

Which Generations Will be Working Together in the Workforce?

Historically, businesses have relied on the ability of multiple generations to work together to make the business a success. Typically, there have been at least two, if not three, generations working simultaneously in the workforce. In the near term, business communities will have four generations working together in the workforce. The generations are commonly known as: the "Traditionalists," "Baby Boomers," "Generation X," and "Generation Y." Although experts express differences as to who falls within these different categories, generally the Traditionalists were born prior to 1946, the Baby Boomers were born between 1946 and 1964, Generation X-ers were born between 1965 and 1977, and Generation Y-ers were born between 1978 and 1989.

Traditionalists

The Traditionalists are expected to retire within the next five years. They lived through World War II and appreciate security. Traditionalists typically have historical knowledge of their business industry and company and tend to be loyal to their company.

Traditionalists are known for positive traits such as: stability, attention to detail, thoroughness, loyalty, and hard work.[1] Other less flattering characteristics include dislike of ambiguity and change, reluctance to buck the system, being uncomfortable with conflict, and reticent when they disagree.[2]

Baby Boomers

The Baby Boomers are known for being hard workers and making the necessary sacrifices. Baby Boomers are very busy growing their organizations and their own individual careers. Baby Boomers are often viewed (especially by Generation Y-ers) as primarily focusing on money with "lip service" paid to family/work/life balance. Many Baby Boomers are "empty nesters" and have significant discretionary income, while others are struggling to simultaneously work, raise children, and assist aging parents. Baby Boomers are positively described as service-oriented, driven, willing to "go the extra mile," good at relationships, eager to please and good team members.[3] However, Baby Boomers are also known to be uncomfortable with conflict, reluctant to go against peers, overly sensitive to feedback, judgmental of those who see things differently, and self-centered.[4]

Generation X

Generation X is smaller in number than the Baby Boomer generation and has generally struggled more with the work/life balance issues. This generation is seen as feeling more of a need to actually achieve a work/life balance, which did not seem achievable by the Baby Boomer generation. Generation X-ers tend to be self-sufficient and are technologically literate. Generation X-ers are positively described as adaptable, independent, unintimidated by authority, and creative.[5] This generation's less attractive qualities include impatience, a lack of people skills, inexperience, and cynicism.[6]

Generation Y

Generation Y, also known as the Millennials, is the up-and-coming generation. Generation Y is expected to very shortly outnumber Generation X and perhaps the Baby Boomer generation in the workforce. This generation prides itself on spending more time with family and less time at work. Generation Y individuals not only understand technology, but are truly experts with respect to using technology. Also, Generation Y-ers are expected to change jobs repeatedly over the course of their careers. Generation Y is positively known for collective action, optimism, tenacity, and multitasking capabilities.[7] Generation Y is also thought to need supervision and structure and lacks experience, especially with respect to handling difficult people.[8]

What Does Business Need from Each of the Generations?

Each generation described in the previous section brings a unique set of skills to the workforce. The Traditionalists provide historical knowledge of the industry as well as experience and wisdom from the past that needs to be shared with the next generations. The Baby Boomers are currently leading and managing their companies and focusing on their own careers. Generation X individuals provide strong support to the Baby Boomer generation and perform duties very independently with a strong work ethic. Generation Y is expected to fill the gap that will be left when the Baby Boomer generation retires. As mentioned above, Generation Y is very large in population (unlike Generation X). Therefore, companies will rely on Generation Y for their futures. Unfortunately, Generation Y is not seen as independent as Generation X, and has a need for supervision and structure. Therefore, since the labor, and ultimately the leadership, of Generation Y will be necessary to maintain the workforce, organizations need to focus now on mentoring and training Generation Y to prepare them with the skills that the business will need in the upcoming decades.

What Can an Employer Do to Attract and Retain the Different Generations?

Employee benefits are such a large cost for employers that it is imperative to spend these dollars effectively. Thus, benefits should be designed and communicated to address the different generations' needs and desires. The "one size fits all" approach of the past will not be effective for such diverse generations.

Furthermore, according to the Bureau of Labor Statistics, the American workforce is expected to grow only one percent annually over the next decade, meaning that finding qualified workers will be an ongoing issue for employers. Offering a more flexible workplace and benefits will make it easier to attract and retain the right workers.

Flexible Scheduling

Despite their differences, a common characteristic of all generations of workers is a desire for more flexibility. For example, many Traditionalists wish to ease into retirement, while Boomers are frequently responsible for caring for aging parents, Generation X-ers often desire time for participating in school

activities with their children, and numerous Generation Y-ers want time for community service. Many employers have found that they can increase work schedule flexibility while maintaining productivity.

One of the more common approaches to increasing work schedule flexibility is flextime. Most flextime programs require the employee to be present for certain "core" hours, such as from 9:00 A.M. to 3:00 P.M., while providing the opportunity for an employee to elect a start time as early as 7:00 A.M. and a departure time of 3:30 P.M. or as late as 9:00 A.M. with a departure time of 5:30 P.M. While flextime makes scheduling meetings more problematic, it can provide better service to customers in other time zones. Somewhat similar to flextime, compressed work week programs allow employees to work four 10-hour days each week, or nine nine-hour days per two-week period, with the tenth day of the period off. Typically, employees are expected to schedule medical appointments and home maintenance on their days off, which increases productivity; skeptics, however, have expressed concerns that productivity decreases during the longer days.

Another approach is job sharing. Job sharing frequently involves two employees, each working 2½ or three days per week to perform a single job. This allows the employees to perform a full-time job on a part-time basis. If the job-sharing workers have different strengths and the job is structured to utilize each person's particular skills, the employer will also benefit from the job sharing. A key element to the success of this approach is the ability of the sharing employees to communicate effectively with each other. Typically, benefits for those who job share are prorated. Each worker would need to meet the applicable eligibility requirements to receive retirement, life, health, and disability benefits.

Telework has grown in popularity in recent years, due to employee interest, as well as concerns about pollution and gas prices. In addition, improvements in technology have made it possible to perform many jobs without physically being in the office one or more days per week. Many federal government agencies use telework. The federal Web site *www.telework.gov* has a number of helpful elements, including a telework guide, frequently asked questions, and telework training sessions for employees and managers. If an employer is considering implementing a telework program, it should consider what equipment it will provide, policies regarding use of that equipment by family members (which may raise privacy and security concerns), approval of overtime, supervision, training, and worker safety. Employers who have implemented telework programs have found that many at-home workers miss the social interaction of the workplace, and thus implement monthly on-site meetings and schedule on-line meetings to alleviate the loss of interaction. Telework also reduces opportunities for mentoring and may further erode the social skills of the on-line generation (*i.e.*, Generation Y).

To avoid the high cost of replacing valued workers, a number of corporations (notably IBM and PricewaterhouseCoopers) have implemented extended leave and sabbatical programs (for as long as five years).[9] While mothers of small children are the most frequent users, younger employees often appreciate the ability to complete higher education degrees on a full-time basis.

Unique Benefits

While some employers have found success with adding flexibility to work schedules, others have added unique "perks." Employers seeking to attract and retain younger workers may want to consider free food or beverages on a daily or weekly basis, casual dress every day, movie tickets and small gift certificates, and tuition reimbursement. Employers seeking to attract and retain older workers may want to offer free financial planning, elder care assistance, and wellness programs. Employers targeting families might offer monthly on-site celebrations for the whole family, lactation rooms, adoption assistance, child care referrals or on-site day care, paid maternity or paternity leave, child care reimbursement for overtime or business travel, and infertility assistance. Other creative employers have offered group legal, auto, and homeowners insurance (and allowed their employees to payroll deduct the premiums), subsidized fitness center memberships, paid parking and mass transit passes, domestic partner benefits, pet insurance, rest areas (complete with pillows and blankets), and concierge services, such as on-site dry cleaning, oil changes, and massages.

Traditional Benefits

With respect to more traditional employee benefits, Traditionalists want and expect benefits that reward longevity, such as defined benefit pension plans. Conversely, Generation Y-ers, who anticipate multiple job changes over the course of their careers, prefer portability in the form, for example, of 401(k) or profit-sharing plans with short vesting schedules and health savings accounts, which will allow them to preserve and take with them their retirement and medical savings as they move from job to job.

What Do the Differences in Generations Mean to Benefit Communications?

Traditionalists and Baby Boomers expect significant direction from their employers on benefits matters, and are less than comfortable with technology. For these groups, the traditional handouts, booklets, and meetings are most effective. If on-line enrollment and Internet-based education is used, employers need to be certain these groups are comfortable with the processes needed to access the information.

Generations X and Y, in contrast, have great faith in technology and their own decision-making abilities. The individuals in these generations have grown up with computers. These groups demand Internet-based education and a variety of options. Employers need to be mindful of the large amount of misinformation readily accessible through the Internet, and need to make sure that their message is disseminated and received. Benefits departments must (if they have not already) implement electronic methods of communicating with participants, provided employees have computer access at work. For companies with employees without computer access (*e.g.,* employees who are on the road or who work in a manufacturing plant), print materials mailed to homes may still be most effective.

Another impediment to electronic (and effective) communications is the current Internal Revenue Service and the Department of Labor requirements for providing plan information to participants. Current requirements limit the instances in which communications can be given electronically and require that very technical information be included. Thus, summary plan descriptions and certain notices that go to employees are too technical and complicated to grab the attention of the younger generations, and frequently overwhelm the older generations. The best type of communication is a cross between the "Highlights" type of information employees often receive at times of open enrollment, and a summary plan description which includes specific details as regulated by the Department of Labor. In the future it will be most effective to communicate using a combination of print and electronic methods (*e.g.,* postcards, booklets, newsletters, text messages, e-mails, podcasts, Webcasts, etc.) and in a way that minimizes the complexity of the material.

What Do the Costs of Offering Employee Benefits Mean to Your Business's Bottom Line?

The first step in evaluating an organization's employee benefit package is to take inventory of the benefits (and costs of these benefits) currently offered. When calculating the cost, an employer should be sure to include the administrative cost of the benefit. For example, under a retirement plan, costs include not only the funding of the plan, but also the cost of plan administration (regardless of whether a third-party administrator or an internal administrator manages the plan). In addition, there may be actuarial costs and legal costs, such as costs incurred to provide proper plan documentation, submissions to the Internal Revenue Service, notices to participants, and other areas of compliance. A review of costs should be conducted for each employee benefit that is provided to employees (including vacation days, approved leaves, retirement plans, group life, health, and disability, and perks). Once the benefit costs are determined, an employer can begin to evaluate what is truly important to each particular generation, and determine which benefits should be maintained or enhanced and how they should be changed or modified. To a large extent, the benefits offered by U.S. employers are shaped by tax favorable treatment. As employers go through this evaluation process, they may find a need to lobby Congress or state legislatures to modify the tax or legal requirements associated with the benefits being offered.

What Do Employee Benefit Packages Designed to Motivate Four Generations of Employees Look Like?

The overall objective when designing employee benefit packages for the future should be to empower employees to make their own decisions for benefit packages that fit their needs and lifestyles. Traditionally, employee benefit packages have been designed with a paternalistic approach. Instead of providing choices for employees, employers have historically dictated what the benefits package will be—the "employer knows best" approach. This has meant the employer presents the benefit and the employee's choice is simply whether or not to sign up for a particular benefit in the benefits package. Unfortunately, this approach has become obsolete with the advent of two-income families, single-parent households, and a multi-generational workforce. To maximize the impact of the employer's benefit contributions, employees should be given an opportunity to choose the benefits that are most meaningful to them. For those who worry that employees cannot or will not handle choices appropriately, this empowerment concept is not untested with respect to employee benefits. The key to success, however, is strong and consistent communication from the employer regarding options and issues to consider when selecting benefits.

Let's discuss some possible options for employers to consider:

Option 1: Elimination of "Traditional" Employee Benefit Plans. An employer could simply terminate all of its benefit plans and replace those benefits with a specific dollar amount to each employee to use as the employee sees fit. For example, an employer could provide employees with $15,000 a year extra in compensation to cover any health care, retirement, PTO leave, or other employee needs. This approach provides the ultimate flexibility to employees and completely eliminates employer involvement for employee benefit plans. While superficially attractive, under the current U.S. tax structure, the employee and employer would lose significant tax advantages, thus leading to an increased tax liability and potentially decreasing compensation for the employee overall. Additionally, if employees were required to find their own individual coverage, under the current benefits system, individuals with medical problems could have significant difficulty obtaining coverage. Given this country's poor savings rate, the pure compensation approach also raises issues about how to handle those who fail to purchase individual health, life, and disability coverage or save for retirement.

To the extent this lump-sum approach is attractive to employers and employees, Congress should be approached to create a tax-advantaged method to providing additional flexibility for employees to pick and choose the benefits that are most valuable to them, while freeing the employer from the time of administration of benefits and the pressure to spend funds to provide under-appreciated benefits. In addition, third-party administrators and other vendors that currently provide employers coverage for employees would need to create products that could provide such *ad hoc* individual coverage on a tax-free basis (assuming Congress passed the necessary legislation).

Option 2: Maintain Current Employee Benefit Plan Structure with Modifications. The least radical strategy to motivate the multiple generations in the workforce would be for an employer to make modifications to its current employee benefit plan structure. For example, if an employer has a traditional health plan, the employer could consider offering health reimbursement arrangements (HRAs) or health savings accounts (HSAs), either as an option or as the sole health plan. To help bridge the increased deductible gap from a traditional health plan to an HRA or HSA, the employer should use at least a portion of the premium savings from purchasing a high deductible health plan to initially fund the HRA or HSA. HRAs and HSAs shift significant costs and responsibility onto the consumer (*e.g.,* the employee), but currently it is very difficult for employees to know the cost of medical expenses and how best to shop around for the best price and treatment option. An employer could assist by lobbying for increased disclosure of health care costs and outcomes.

Option 3: Non-Traditional "Unique" Employee Benefits. In addition to modifying their "traditional" employee benefit plans (Option 2 above), employers could offer unique benefits to attract the new generations and retain their older workers. As discussed earlier in this article, an increasing number of employees are demanding a flexible work schedule and work environment, and employers are finding that allowing these employees to work remotely from home (which may or may not be located in the same city as the "office") is feasible. Video chat rooms can be used for business meetings or just socializing with colleagues. Ensuring that all documents needed by employees are available electronically (*e.g.,* 401(k) enrollment forms, health plan enrollment forms, flexible benefit claim forms, summaries of material modifications, etc.) is essential for employers who have telecommuting employees.

Working Women recently published a list of benefits/perks offered by companies voted the "100 Best Companies." The perks offered by the best employers to work for include a number of the non-traditional benefits mentioned above, such as elder care and child care resource and referral, massage therapy, dry-cleaning service, take-home meals, parental leave *beyond* the Family Medical Leave Act requirements, paid adoption leave, infertility treatment assistance (*in vitro*), child care reimbursement for business travel, and emergency sick-child care.[10]

Conclusion

The options discussed above are only the beginning of the benefit designs that can be (and should be) considered as organizations move into the new era of a four-generation workforce. The emphasis should not be as much on the options, but on embarking on a new way of thinking about employee benefits. Organizations should no longer rely on the traditional benefit plan structures and features. To be competitive and attract the best and brightest workforce, employers must create innovative benefit packages that appeal to a broad range of workers.

Notes

1. Ron Zemke, Claire Raines, and Bob Filipczak, *Generations at Work* 46 (2000).
2. *Id.*
3. *Id.*
4. *Id.*
5. *Id.* at 110.
6. *Id.*
7. *Id.* at 144.
8. *Id.*
9. *The Best vs. the Rest,* Working Mother, October 2006, 82.
10. *Id.* at 74.

MELISSA PROFFITT REESE is co-managing partner of the law firm of Ice Miller LLP. **LINDA ROWINGS** is senior counsel, and **TIFFANY SHARPLEY** is an associate, at the firm. Residing in Ice Miller's office in Indianapolis, the authors can be reached at melissa.reese@icemiller.com, linda.rowings@icemiller.com, and tiffany. sharpley@icemiller.com, respectively.

From *Employee Benefit Plan Review,* January 2007, pp. 21–25. Copyright © 2007 by Aspen Publishers. Reprinted by permission of Wolters Kluwer Law & Business.

Benefits and the Bottom Line

Take a good, hard look at your benefits package to make sure you're doing what's best for employees and your company.

Phillip M. Perry

Controlling the rising cost of employee benefits is a challenge that never seems to get easier. Though escalating health insurance premiums get the lion's share of attention, business owners must consider the full range of worker benefits, which together comprise 37.2 percent of the average payroll, according to the U.S. Chamber of Commerce.

Of course, doing away with benefits is not an option. Hourly workers and salaried staff demand them as part of the employment agreement. The challenge is to offer attractive plans that encourage quality employees to remain on board while maintaining a healthy bottom line.

To do this, make sure you aren't paying for benefits your staff doesn't need, advise various consultants. Being all things to all people is more expensive than narrowing in on what your employees really want. To find out the latter, survey your employees. This will help you put your energy where there's 'value added,' as opposed to offering a little bit of everything.

Web to the Rescue

Your goal is to select the most affordable quality plans and administer them as cost effectively as possible. Technology can help.

"A number of new Web-based services offer plans and quote prices so certain choices can be made over the Internet," says Tim Harrington, a principal with Mercer Human Resource Consulting, a Chicago-based consulting firm that has tracked benefits costs for more than 25 years.

The automation inherent in the Internet allows Web-based services to offer comparison-shopping of products from a broad range of carriers. They can also reduce the overhead involved in processing employee claims, educate new employees on your benefits plans, and answer common questions.

Various Web services handle benefits such as health insurance and retirement plans, and offer clients the opportunity to create custom Web pages for use by their employees. In many cases these services allow employees to access information on the plans without having to call their human resources departments, saving your business time and money.

Health Insurance

Health insurance, by far the most popular benefit, is offered by 96 percent of employers, according to Business and Legal Reports, a human resources research organization based in Old Saybrook, Conn. Premiums for such coverage rose an average 7.7 percent in 2006, a rate more than twice as great as workers' wages (3.8 percent) and overall inflation (3.5 percent). The figures were announced in the 2006 Employer Health Benefits Survey from the Kaiser Family Foundation.

When containing costs, your first line of defense is to join purchasing groups.

"When you join forces with other employers you bring more leverage to the negotiating table," says Larry Boress, president of the Midwest Business Group on Health, a Chicago-based consortium of 80 employers.

The second step on the cost savings journey is to shift costs to employees. Cost sharing occurs when employees make greater co-payments and/or pay higher annual deductibles for services received.

Employees become more prudent consumers of health care when they pay a greater portion of the costs. At the same time, insurance companies fund less of the total annual health care expense. Both phenomena translate into lower risk for the carrier and lower premiums for the employer.

Life Insurance

Life insurance is both inexpensive and popular, with 89 percent of employers offering it. Because it's a commodity item, employers should shop around for the best rate. You may find you can save money by purchasing group life from one carrier and accidental death and dismemberment from another. Be aware that some life carriers have divisions that compete with each other. One division may offer both life and AD&D while another may offer just life. The prices of the life insurance may differ in the two divisions, so shop around.

A common but costly error is to save time by purchasing different forms of insurance from the same broker. If you don't have time to comparison shop and need to use a broker, ask other employers which ones have proven to be highly knowledgeable about carriers.

Workers Compensation

Workers compensation is a mandated benefit that can erode your bottom line if you don't watch it carefully. Premiums are increasing nationwide at about 10 percent to 15 percent annually, according to a spokesperson for Sullivan Curtis Monroe, an insurance brokerage in Irvine, Calif.

"It's starting to hit businesses in the pocketbook," he reports. "They are asking 'What can we do now?' "

Premium increases represent only one part of your cost. Other, indirect costs can be two to three times as great. They include the overhead to administer a claim, supervisory time in investigating an accident and lost time from the injured individual. Here are suggestions for cost containment measures:

- **Run physical tests for applicants.** Include "range of motion" tests for jobs that require much lifting, stopping and standing.
- **Improve your workplace.** Adjust work stations to reduce claims that result from repetitive stress injuries.
- **Choose an experienced carrier.** Don't just buy insurance from the carrier with the lowest price. Choosing the cheapest carrier can end up costing you more when it fails to handle claims properly. Instead, look for a company with a good claims-handling history. Meet with the individuals who will handle your claims, and determine their operating philosophy. And get feedback from other businesses that have experience with that carrier.

You can also reduce premiums, or keep them from increasing unnecessarily downstream, by taking some proactive steps.

"Overcharges by insurance companies are very common," says Edward Priz, principal of Advanced Insurance Management, Riverside, Ill.

To keep them from occurring, Priz says you need to audit your own classification codes to assure accuracy with the workplace conditions to which your personnel are exposed.

You also need to assure the accuracy of your "experience modification factor." That term refers to the number used to modify your charges, based upon the accident history of your workplace. Consider having an outside auditor review your records.

Disability Income

Workers compensation protects your workers from financial disaster if they're injured on the job. But what if the injury takes place outside of work? That's where long- and short-term disability comes to the rescue. It can be a valuable benefit, offered by 68 percent of employers nationwide.

How can you control the rising costs for this insurance? The Washington Business Group on Health, an organization that assists businesses in this area, has three suggestions:

- **Form early "return to work" policies.** You want to encourage people to return to work as soon as possible. That's because the costs of an illness go far beyond disability payments and insurance premiums. They also include lost productivity, overtime for employees required to accomplish the missing person's work, and re-training time.
- To encourage early return, develop workplace programs that will accommodate workers who suffer from temporary disabilities. Many employers have these in place for staff members covered by workers comp, but have not extended the programs to cover people absent under short-term or long-term disability. Now is the time to do so.
- **Pick the right plan.** Be aware of policies that encourage workers to stay home longer. For example, some plans allow no payments unless a person stays out for two weeks, at which time the payments become retroactive to the first day. Under these plans, individuals often stay out longer because it is in their self-interest.
- **Select your carrier wisely.** Not all insurance companies are equal. Select a company that will help you increase your productivity by helping injured people return to work more quickly.

Ask the right questions of any prospective company: Do they spend money on rehabilitation? Do they have good medical resources? Do they have doctors and nurses on staff? What training do they provide their people? Check with other businesses in your area to discover what insurers they use and their level of satisfaction.

Finally, put disability insurance in context. It's all about productivity. You can push down cost by choosing a plan that is less expensive, but the result may be longer periods of time during which people are away from the workplace. The savings you pick up on the health side can be cancelled out by losses on the productivity side.

Cohesive Approach

Left uncontrolled, the rising costs of employee benefits can erode your bottom line and lead to staff discontent when draconian measures are needed to cap spiraling expenses.

Take action now to review your entire benefits package. Survey your staff to find out what benefits they really want, in important. And finally, share information on costs with your employees. When employees know the effect benefits have on the health of your company, they'll be more willing to help by cost sharing and responsible utilization of benefits.

Internet Services

Here are some Internet services that can help employers reduce employee benefits costs by streamlining the recordkeeping process.

- www.employease.com [Variety of benefits.] Services include maintaining a centralized database of employees, managing enrollments, issuing benefit statements, and allowing employees 24-hour access to data. Claims it can be used with any carrier.

- www.benefitmall.com [Health insurance, payroll, other benefits.] Maintains a network of brokers who sell products from more than 100 health insurance carriers. Allows employers to visit sites and compare prices and features of various health insurance plans.

- www.healthmarket.com [Health insurance.] This service offers self-directed health plans that by-pass the usual managed care organizations. Employers and employees each contribute a set number of dollars annually to the plans, which have signed on doctors and hospitals.

From *Industrial Distribution,* Vol. 96, No. 1, January 1, 2007, pp. 32+. Copyright © 2007 by Industrial Distribution. Reprinted by permission of Reprint Management Services.

UNIT 6

Fostering Employee/ Management Relationships

Unit Selections

Key Points to Consider

- Taking disciplinary action is often one of the most difficult and unpleasant activities that a manager must do. If you were a manager, how would you take disciplinary action? If you were the employee being disciplined, what would you do? What would you do about an employee who suddenly lashes out at another for no particular reason?

- What are some of the advantages of hiring temporary employees? Why is it good for the employer? And how is it good for the worker?

- Should managers be concerned about ethics? Why or why not? Do you think that unethical behavior can be economically justified? Why would a manager knowingly engage in unethical and/or illegal behavior and think they can get away with it?

- There is a labor market that is essentially unregulated and out of the reach of the law. Do you think this should be controlled? Who do you think is responsible for this?

Student Web Site

www.mhcls.com

Internet References

Management, Leadership, and Supervision
http://humanresources.about.com/od/managementandleadership/

The American labor movement has a long history dating back to the start of the Industrial Revolution. That history has been marked by turmoil and violence, as workers sought to press their demands on business owners, whether represented by managers or entrepreneurs. The American labor movement exists because working conditions, pay, and benefits were very poor during the early years of the Industrial Revolution in both the United States and the rest of the world. It should be remembered that the American labor movement is only a small part of a broader, worldwide labor movement that includes most Western, European societies. The working conditions under which the first American industrial workers labored would be unacceptable today. Child labor was common. There are documented instances of 6- and 7-year-old children, chained to machines for 12 hours a day, 6 days a week, who threw themselves into the machines—choosing death over life in the dehumanized and mechanized existence of the early factory. Conditions in some factories in the North prior to the Civil War were so infamous that Southern congressmen used them as a justification for the institution of slavery. Slaves sometimes lived in better conditions than the factory workers of New England and many other Northern states.

Unions exist because workers sought a better working environment and a better standard of living. Companies often took advantage of employees, and the government sided with management and the owners, frequently quelling strikes and other forms of labor protest initiated by the workers. Such incidents as the Pullman Strike, the Hay-Market Square Riot, and the Homestead Strike exemplify the struggle of the American labor movement to achieve recognition and success in the attempt to improve the lives of all workers, whether unionized or not. The victories of labor have been hard fought and hard won. But, labor has not been without blemish in the struggle for worker's rights. The Marion County Turkey-Shoot, in Southern Illinois, probably the most violent day in American labor history, involved coal miners deliberately chasing, and killing strikebreakers from the mines.

During the past hundred years, the fortunes of the American labor movement have varied, and now their fortunes may be taking an even deeper downward turn, with attempts at unionization even more difficult. Unions have been able to achieve their gains through the mechanism of collective bargaining. The individual has very little bargaining power when compared to a company, especially huge companies such as General Motors or General Electric. Collective bargaining allows workers to pool their collective resources and power to bargain with the corporation on a more equal footing. Unfortunately for the unions, many of the industries in which they are strongest are in decline. New leadership is necessary if the American labor movement is to survive and rebound in the next century, and if it is to serve as a useful organ of society.

© BananaStock Ltd.

A union's ultimate weapon in contract negotiations, the strike, represents a complete breakdown of discipline from management's perspective. Disciplinary situations are almost always unpleasant, and today they can often lead to court cases, with all of the attendant legal questions and problems. A key to effective disciplinary action is documentation of employees' actions and the steps that were taken to correct them. How to go about "Setting Up a Disciplinary Procedure" is outlined in the article of that name. Management needs to implement procedures and policies to assure employees are treated fairly and equitably in the workplace as discussed in "Poor Performance & Due Process."

The American labor movement has come a long way since the first strike by printers in Philadelphia in 1786. The journey, though difficult, has led to greater justice in the workplace and an increased standard of living for the nation as a whole. Unions have experienced both declines and increases in membership, but they have endured as a powerful social, political, and economic force. Whether or not they will again successfully "reinvent" themselves and adapt to a changing environment is a major question.

During the past fifteen years, primarily as a result of the dislocations in the job market, temporary workers became available to organizations. There are certain advantages to this situation for the employer, but employers must manage these temporary employees on a permanent basis. These special problems are analyzed in "Working with "Temps" Is Not a Temporary Job."

There is also the issue of ethics. How companies treat their employees and their customers is going to be of increasing concern in the future. Ethical behavior will be at a premium, and managers know that it will be part of the job. Unfortunately, some managers of organizations will always make the economic/legal calculation that doing something that is illegal or unethical at best will benefit them, if not their shareholders, customers, and/or employees. "Business Ethics: The Key Role of Corporate Governance" will always be a problem no matter what the laws may be or the enforcement of those laws. Someone will always try to get away with some sort of illegal, unethical, or dishonest gain. Flawed human nature will always play a role.

The underground and lower end labor market also plays a role in the ethical treatment of employees. With an estimated twelve-to twenty-million undocumented aliens in the United States, these people have to work somewhere and often for less than minimum wage. They do it because they work for unethical employers, who know that they are in the United States illegally and therefore are not protected by employment laws; and so the workers are exploited. This is creating an underclass of workers who perform at below the legal wage. This is not only subsidizing these unethical employers, but it is giving them an unfair advantage in the marketplace by lowering their costs when competing against employers paying legal wages, and driving down the wages of legitimate workers in the economy.

Employee management relations are always going to be complicated. There will never be a simple solution because people are complicated and their needs and wants will be in constant flux. Dealing with these changes will present human resource professional constant challenges.

Setting Up a Disciplinary Procedure

CHARTERED MANAGEMENT INSTITUTE CHECKLIST

Introduction

This checklist is aimed at those wishing to implement a disciplinary procedure within their company or organisation.

It is essential that an employer acts reasonably in dealing with misconduct and ill-discipline. A fair and thorough disciplinary procedure can help protect an employer against an unfair dismissal claim and the ensuing costs of a successful claim. Legislation aside, it is good personnel practice to deal with employee ill-discipline quickly and fairly, and to offer guidance on improving behaviour, so that problems do not fester and grow.

Although this checklist focuses on the mechanics of a disciplinary procedure, it is important to remember that good management, for example spotting problems before they become serious and identifying development needs to improve performance, can prevent many cases reaching this stage.

National Occupational Standards for Management and Leadership

This checklist has relevance for the following standards:
B: Providing direction, Unit 8; D: Working with people, Units 1 and 2

Definition

A disciplinary procedure provides employers with a structured approach for dealing with ill-discipline at work. The procedure defines the types of ill-discipline it covers, the presentation and documentation of warnings, representation at disciplinary interviews, time limits for investigation, and rights of appeal.

Action checklist

1. Designate a Disciplinary Procedure Management Committee (DPMC)

The Committee should include, depending on the size of the organisation, at least one person from the personnel department, and from each level of management within the organisation, and a representative from each trade union to which employees belong. The Committee will manage the design, implementation and running of the disciplinary procedure. Appoint a coordinator (preferably a member from personnel, but certainly someone with project management experience who commands respect, has excellent communication and negotiation skills and can get things done) to oversee the project.

2. Define the terms of reference

Identify the employees covered by the procedure (for example, all non-directors) and the managers who will be responsible for the disciplinary interviews. Define ill-discipline (both minor and serious misconduct), clarify legal obligations, and agree on the process which can lead to dismissal.

3. Draw up the procedure

Use the experiences, soundings and research of the Committee to devise a procedure. Try to obtain samples of procedures used in other organisations and remember to write as simply as possible so that it is easy to understand. If necessary, consider using external expertise.

The procedure should contain the following:

- **Purpose.** An initial paragraph giving the reasons for having a procedure, highlighting the benefits to employees of a consistent set of rules and the importance of discipline in the workplace.

- **Types of misconduct.** This should give staff an indication of the type of misconduct that would invoke the disciplinary procedure. Distinguish between minor offences and those which are serious or may constitute gross misconduct:

Minor	Serious
Smoking (where appropriate)	Vandalism
Time-keeping	Fraud
Misuse of company facilities	Alcohol/Drugs
Dress	Violence, bullying

- **Warnings.** Depending on the seriousness of the offence an employee will be faced with a series of warnings:

  Oral (confirmed in writing)
  Written
  Final written

  The ultimate penalty after this will be dismissal, although sanctions short of dismissal such as transfer, demotion or loss of pay may be considered.

The warnings will be given to the employee after an interview, usually with the employee's line manager. Many procedures stipulate a length of time after which, if the employee does not re-offend, the warning lapses, but this can leave the door open to abuse of the system. For this reason it is best not to set a time limit, and to keep the warning on file. Remember that the disciplinary procedure should not be invoked unless informal warnings from the line manager have had no effect, or unless the offence is considered to be so important that instant disciplinary action must be taken. In cases of gross misconduct an employee may be suspended from work, on full pay, pending an investigation, then dismissed.

- **Representation at meetings.** A colleague or trade union representative can, by right, accompany or represent the employee at each warning interview. Consider stipulating that the union should be involved unless the employee specifically objects. On occasions when the offence also constitutes a criminal offence, a solicitor should be allowed to be present.
- **Investigations.** All abuses of discipline must be investigated before a warning of any kind is issued. At the very least this involves hearing the employee's side of the story. It is possible to suspend the employee on full pay while the investigation is taking place.

Set a time limit to carry out investigations into gross misconduct, such as deliberate malpractice. This should be not more than 10 days after the offence was committed.

- **Documentation.** Detailed minutes should be taken at all interviews and kept along with copies of any investigation into the misconduct and any warnings issued. This documentation is not only useful for checking whether an employee's behaviour improves; it can also be used as evidence, in the event of an industrial tribunal, that correct procedures have been followed.
- **Plans of action.** In the case of minor offences every effort must be made to help the employee overcome problems, obviating the need to pursue the process further. The procedure should make it clear that plans of action will be agreed between the employee and the line manager at each interview to enable improvements in discipline. A date will be given for an evaluation interview, at which, if progress has not been made, a more severe warning can be issued.
- **Appeals.** Employees should be given the right to appeal against any warning they receive, as long as it is made in writing to their line manager within five working days of the issue of the warning.

4. Draw up an implementation timetable

In a large organisation it is often better to pilot the disciplinary procedure on one site or in a large department before full implementation.

5. Provide training for managers and supervisors

Training should be given to all managers and supervisors who may have to deal with disciplinary issues. Ensure that they understand the mechanics of the procedure and try to make sure that there is a consistency of approach. Give training not only in conducting a disciplinary interview effectively but also on general discipline and control; this will help solve as many problems as possible without the need for the full procedure.

6. Communicate the procedure to all employees

If you have disciplinary rules, by law they must be notified to employees. Ensure that staff are aware of the procedure (a letter should be sent to all employees along with a copy of the procedure), and know when the procedure will come into effect. Explain that the procedure has been introduced to benefit employees by providing them with a consistent way of dealing with ill-discipline. The same information should be given to new recruits and included in the staff manual.

7. Implement the procedure

Ensure a member of the DPMC is available to answer any questions that may arise, especially during the critical period following the communication of the procedure.

8. Evaluate the procedure

Regular evaluation of the procedure will contribute towards improving it. The number of times the procedure is used should be recorded, and any managers who seem to have difficulty in handling discipline should be identified. Employees who have been disciplined under the procedure should be asked for their views on it.

9. Make changes and give feedback on the results

Changes should be made in the light of the evaluation. These may include extra training for some managers, or re-writing some of the steps or phases. Communicate the changes made to employees.

Managers Should Avoid:

- Taking disciplinary action until the case has been investigated.
- Setting the procedure in stone by ignoring the need for regular reviews.
- Allowing the procedure to replace the need for good management.

Poor Performance & Due Process

T. L. STANLEY

An employee with, habitually poor performance can drive a supervisor to the brink and drain an organization of valuable resources. Even though highly motivated professional managers and supervisors have the capacity to deal with a chronic poor performer, management energy would be better used to increase organizational efficiencies.

Sometimes, it's tempting to quickly just rid an organization of a poor performer. However, everyone has a right to due process. The employee I employer relationship rests on the notion that due process and fairness will be the cornerstone of all workplace interactions.

Being afforded due process in union and nonunion work environments means that the employee is provided a procedural fair hearing when being evaluated or disciplined for shortcomings. Within this context, organizations must make sure every employee is treated fairly.

In collective bargaining agreements, due process is included contractually for the purpose of affording employees a fair hearing. In nonunion work environments, organizations that have a commitment to professionalism will also be equitable in dealing with employees. Needless to say, employees in employment-at-will situations lack the protection of due process contractually. But, all employees expect to be treated fairly. The litigious nature of all workplace relationships requires that supervisors and managers treat each employee with respect and afford each and every employee due process and a just hearing.

In order to make sure that organizations are being fair to everyone, reasonable standards of performance will be established by supervisors and managers. Then, the standards of performance will be administrated in a fair-minded fashion. Being fair-minded means that supervisors and managers must demonstrate integrity beyond reproach when dealing with all aspects of employee performance.

There is no room in employee relations for a subjective application of standards of performance. The standards of performance should be applied in such a way that every employee is treated fairly. High quality supervisors and managers will purge all signs of favoritism.

Unfortunately, misunderstandings and poor communications between a supervisor and a subordinate can happen. In extreme cases, a heated personality conflict can develop. Regardless, high quality supervisors and managers will make sure that fact-based objectivity overrides opinion-driven subjectivity.

Proper training must be provided to employees, so each and every employee has the opportunity to team their job thoroughly. Any doubts about the employee receiving the proper training should be addressed with additional training.

A poor performer must be given help to overcome a deficiency. Even if a poor performing employee has been trained, it is wise to retrain. This may be redundant. Regardless, it's best to always give the employee the benefit of the doubt and provide remedial training when poor performance lingers. If the poor performing employee can be turned around and meet the standards of performance, the time and energy spent in retraining will be worth the expenditure of resources.

Work deficiencies and poor performance may be deceiving. For instance, an employee may not meet the standards of performance, because production equipment is outdated or malfunctioning.

An incomplete reporting system can also distort an employee's job performance. Highly technical reporting systems might not account for certain workplace characteristics. A report may indicate an employee is a poor performer, but the work being assigned may be the most difficult type of work.

It's common for reporting systems to be quantitatively driven with little regard for qualitative measurements. A poor performing employee may be producing the highest quality work in the organization, but many computer driven reporting systems would not account for this reality. Therefore, supervisors and manager must investigate apparent poor performance thoroughly.

Sometimes, an employee can just get labeled as a poor performer. This may be based on past workplace behavior or a personality conflict between a supervisor and employee. With this in mind, it's essential that evidence of current poor performance is absolutely objective and based on up-to-date information.

There is no reason to bring past deficiencies and personality conflicts into the mix. If an employee had a history of poor performance but has corrected past shortcomings, evaluate the employee only on current performance.

Give every employee a chance to overcome their past. Holding an employee hostage over past shortcomings is unjust. This may cause an employee to continue performing below expectations. Furthermore, by holding a struggling employee in contempt over past poor performance, a supervisor can lower performance even further.

Spiteful or vindictive behavior by a Supervisor or manager will have a negative impact on the organization as a whole. Because, employees will not trust management. Regardless of performance, supervisors and managers must give every employee respect.

Sometimes, it's appropriate for a supervisor to consult with another supervisor or manager not close to the troubled employee. Because, emotions and personality issues may cloud a supervisor's evaluation of a poor performer. Therefore, an impartial supervisor or manager detached from the heat of personalities, standards of performance, and other workplace demands may be able to shed a different perspective on the situation.

Supervisors and managers must use a fairness doctrine when applying all standards of performance. The question must be asked: Are all employees held to the standards of performance?

Objectivity is a must in applying standards. There is no room for subjectivity or a random implementation of standards of performance. Applying the standards of performance must include a careful evaluation of the quantity and quality of work.

All deficiencies should be addressed in a timely manner. Employees must be aware of heir shortcomings in order to correct them. And, all supervisors have a duty to notify employees who are deficient as soon as the shortcoming is evident.

Based on the negative legal environment of our workplace today, taking serious disciplinary action against a poor performing employee can be a minefield. When considering suspending or terminating a poor performing employee, it is essential that supervisors and managers consult with the appropriate labor law professional or human resources representative.

Due process runs into complications when an employee is involved in workplace violence. Research suggests that aggressive behaviors such as intimidation, bullying, sabotage, vandalism, and fighting have grown in organizations. Employers have an obligation to prevent workplace violence. And, when workplace violence happens, employers must deal quickly and effectively with the employee instigating or causing violence in the workplace. Developing a zero tolerance for workplace violence is an effective way to deal with this alarming situation.

There is little argument over the need to provide a strict policy to deal with workplace violence. First, organizations must identify and communicate what constitutes workplace violence. The policies should make it clear what behaviors will not be allowed in the workplace. The prohibited behaviors should include physical violence, threats, bullying, and harassment. Second, possession of a weapon of any kind should not be allowed on company property. Third, the consequences to the employee should be spelled out clearly for instigating or participating in workplace violence. Forth, once expectations have been communicated, managers and supervisors must enforce the rules consistently. Normally, dysfunctional behavior should be addressed by progressive disciplinary action directed at changing behavior.

Due Process Checklist

1. Have the standards of performance been communicated clearly?
2. Are the standards of performance reasonable and fair?
3. Did the employee receive the training necessary to meet the standards of performance?
4. Is everyone required to meet the standards of performance?
5. Has there been a thorough evaluation of the deficiency?
6. Has the evaluation been objective?
7. Has another impartial manager been consulted for objectivity?
8. Are other employees with similar deficiencies treated the same way?
9. Has the deficiency or shortcoming been addressed in a timely manner?
10. Has human resources or legal department been contacted prior to suspension or termination?

Needless to say, all cases of aggressive behavior or violence in the workplace should be investigated thoroughly. This investigation should be objective. Accused employees should be treated fairly and presumed innocent until all evidence has been assessed. If an employee is found to be culpable in perpetrating violence in the workplace, disciplinary action should be forthcoming.

Balancing a zero tolerance for workplace violence and still affording employees due process is a challenge. Issues of fairness may be difficult to balance. Regardless, employees must be provided due process.

A rush to judgment by a manager may result in severe legal repercussion. In many cases, disciplinary action against offending employees have been overturned by a judicial process. With this in mind, the lack of due process and harshly crafted policies can doom the employer.

Researchers have found that overly strict and unyielding zero tolerance policies may make workplace tension worse. Thus, an environment for workplace violence may be intensified. Furthermore, the degree of disciplinary action must be appropriate. This means the punishment must fit the crime.

Mitigating circumstance should be considered. For example, was the incident isolated and without malice. Or, was the incident one of many hateful and aggressive actions directed intentionally toward another employee. All information should be considered. And, managerial action should be taken based on all factors.

Supervisors and managers must balance the need to direct a productive and safe organization with granting every employee a fair hearing. Progressive organizations provide every employee with due process.

How to Investigate Workplace Misconduct & Avoid the HP Syndrome

Jason E. Reisman, Esq

Rooting out misconduct in the workplace requires the completion of an effective internal investigation. Whether allegations of sexual harassment, stealing, or simple policy violations are involved, employers of all sizes are faced with the dilemma of how to respond. Employers increasingly place themselves in harm's way by rushing the process and skipping steps when confronted with such situations or by employing unethical tactics. Rather than taking the time to strategize and utilize the all-important "process" or "means" of an investigation, employers often find themselves jumping to conclusions and seeking to quickly get to the "ends." Unfortunately, their failure to take a step back and strategically, methodically proceed to investigate an issue before meting out discipline, for example, leads to unprotected actions, which ultimately result in a substantial risk of liability in a subsequent lawsuit. Short-cuts in or altogether shortcutting investigations leave an employer vulnerable. Investigations, though time-consuming, must be standard protocol in today's workplace.

The importance of incorporating investigations into the fabric of the workplace is on par with conducting them efficiently, ethically, and within the confines of the law. Though normally conducted behind the scenes without much fanfare, internal investigations recently came to the forefront of corporate America's thought with the intense media analysis of Hewlett Packard's efforts to identify the source of a media leak emanating from its board of directors. By most news accounts, HP employed controversial and possibly illegal practices in its investigation to find the leak, including spying on its own directors and duping phone company or financial institution employees into revealing someone's private information. HP's investigation did identify the source of the leak, but also has led to a formal inquiry by the SEC, several criminal indictments, and undoubtedly a tarnished reputation.

With the added attention to corporate investigations generated by the HP scandal, now more than ever, employers must re-focus on the proper handling of internal investigations of misconduct. Fortunately, the timing could not have been better. Indeed, today's employers are in need of a stern reminder and more detailed instructions on this critical topic. The combination of this important reminder to "investigate, investigate, investigate" and the incredible continuing boom in workplace harassment dictate the need to reevaluate how employers handle internal complaints of misconduct. The most prevalent and recognized incident of misconduct in the modern workplace continues to be harassment. Harassment at work continues to grow at a record pace, especially since the events of September 11, 2001, which have generated a significant increase in claims of religious and national origin backlash discrimination and harassment. Though EEOC statistics confirm the sustained growth in workplace harassment, the statistics alone fail to portray the true explosion, as countless incidents go officially unreported as they are handled internally and never reach the EEOC, state agencies or the court system.

Why Investigate—To Search for "The Truth"

Employers use internal investigations in an effort to find "the truth"—who did what to whom. That is the goal, at least preliminarily or theoretically, in every investigation. The quest for the truth, however, can be an all-encompassing, consuming effort. More importantly, there can be different kinds of "truths" sought. For example, for HP, the "truth" being pursued was the identity of the board member leaking information to the media. On the other hand, in harassment investigations, the "truth" sought is whether inappropriate conduct (i.e., harassment) occurred in violation of company policy.

These different "truths" cause a severe divergence of the paths of the resulting investigation methods and concerns. HP sought the "real" truth—that is, the identity of the source of the leak, which led to deceptive, unethical, and arguably unlawful practices. To HP's board of directors, the investigation would fail if the source of the leak was not identified. That pressure for an absolute result, the "real" truth, caused the orchestrators of the investigation to ignore the professional bounds of investigating. In contrast, harassment investigations seek "a" truth, but not necessarily the "real" truth. From both legal and practical business standpoints, which may not always overlap or be intertwined, an employer need not find the "real" truth. Instead, the process of the harassment investigation is at least as important as the result. The "process" involves conducting an immediate, thorough internal investigation. The "result" is making a good-faith determination about what happened that is based on the information gathered during the investigation. Though a definitive result or conclusion will be reached, the "real" truth may not be discovered—amazingly, that fact is somewhat unimportant in the harassment setting.

"You Can't Handle 'The Truth'"—and You Likely Will Not Need To

Under the law, especially in defending against discrimination and harassment lawsuits, the investigation process is paramount. Understanding why involves understanding the existence of what has become popularly known as an employer's "good faith belief" defense. This concept, developed by courts around the country, offers a virtual bullet-proof defense to any type of wrongful discharge claim by an alleged harasser or discriminator who is discharged. The defense operates as follows: if an employer conducts a timely, thorough investigation of the harassment situation and takes remedial action to discharge an employee whom the employer in good faith believes acted inappropriately, the courts will not second-guess the employer—in essence, the employer's decision will be protected and upheld. On the flipside, even where an employer investigates and cannot substantiate allegations of harassment, that same investigation, process will be used successfully by the employer to defend against any harassment lawsuit filed by the complaining employee.

From the practical business standpoint, or, what is referred to as the "employee relations" view, how important is the "real" truth? In reality, the answer is, "not very important." The bottom line is that employee relations success involves rooting out the so-called "evil" of harassment or discrimination. Of course, the primary means to achieve such success is identifying the harassers and eliminating them and their, conduct from the workplace. More often than not, however, an employer cannot definitively identify or be "certain" it has found the harasser. Therefore, demonstrating a properly conducted investigation and implementing swift and effective remedial action (when needed), to both eliminate the harassment and prevent future recurrence, is the best alternative. Although not necessarily the same as catching a guilty harasser, the investigation process serves as an obvious deterrent, especially to the harasser who is not caught, because it demonstrates that the employer: (1) has an anti-harassment policy, (2) adheres to its policy, (3) takes harassment issues seriously, and (4) will act to address situations without hesitating and will implement measures designed to root out harassment and eliminate it. The "employee relations" perspective is often more important than the legal perspective because it transcends the routine legal issues of liability and damages, and encompasses a more workplace-centric analysis. "Employee relations" incorporates concepts such as building and maintaining employee morale and the enhancement of employee management relations.

Experiencing Failure Is Not a Required Precondition to Being Successful

Whereas the HP investigation failed on several levels, an employer faced with a complaint of harassment can ensure success. Not only did HP compromise the integrity of its investigation internally with, at best, questionable tactics, it caused morale and loyalty issues and the potential serious deterioration of internal employee and executive relations. HP's controversial investigation will have long-lasting implications for corporate America and potential civil and criminal consequences for HP's current and former executives and agents. On the other hand, attentive employers can avoid failure when conducting an investigation. Upon receiving a complaint of potential harassment, the employer need only focus on the process—conducting a thorough investigation and responding as outlined below. Following that simple framework alone ensures "success" on both a legal and employee relations level, without having to employ any questionable or controversial tactics and without actually having to find the "real" truth.

In conducting an internal investigation when, for example, faced with a complaint of harassment, the basic steps to success are simple and do not call for any questionable tactics:

1. Be open to, and encourage complaints of harassment, discrimination or other inappropriate conduct.
2. Treat all complaints seriously.
3. Immediately investigate all such complaints by interviewing the complaining employee, the alleged harasser, and all potential witnesses.
4. Document the investigation interviews.
5. Review personnel files and other relevant company documents for the involved employees, looking for an indication, for example, of potential improper motives or prior history of similar problems.
6. Evaluate the information gathered, make a determination about what is believed to have happened (i.e., what your perception of the "real" truth is) based on that information, and document the determination.
7. If needed, implement (and document) remedial measures designed to eliminate the existing problematic conduct and prevent similar conduct in the future.
8. Communicate the results of the investigation to the complaining employee and alleged harasser.
9. Follow-up to ensure "workplace healing," including checking in periodically with the complaining employee and the alleged harasser (if still employed), and monitoring the ongoing workplace relationships, productivity, and morale that may have been affected.

"The Truth" Is Not Necessary to Set You Free

Important issues in the workplace arise and require attention on a daily basis. Employers cannot afford to devote all of their resources to investigating each and every issue in order to root out all evil and find the "real" truth, which can be difficult to pin down. Instead, employers must be attentive and efficient, devoting the appropriate time and resources to such issues. Some situations, such as harassment complaints or other workplace misconduct, will require a full-blown, in-depth investigation. Other minor incidents, such as a short but heated verbal exchange or sarcastic comment between co-workers, also require an investigation, but on a lesser scale. Regardless of the severity of the incident or situation, the key is the necessity of undertaking an investigation. Properly conducted, timely investigations, from a legal standpoint, serve essentially to provide a cloak of invincibility to an employer that is subsequently sued for harassment or wrongful discharge. From the employee relations perspective, the incredible impact of such an investigation upon employee morale and productivity as well as confidence in, and trust of, the management team cannot be underestimated. Though the quest for "the real truth" may ultimately fail, the value of the investigation transcends that quest.

JASON REISMAN, Esq. is a partner in the Philadelphia-based law firm of Obermayer Rebmann Maxwell & Hippel LLP, where he specializes in all aspects of labor relations and employment law and exclusively represents management. His email address is JR@Obermayer.com

Working with "Temps" Is Not a Temporary Job

While many warehouse and DC managers think of temporary employees ("temps") as an afterthought, assuming that the full responsibility for their selection and performance rests with the local temp agency, managers who reap the best results are ones who devote a great deal of time to selecting and managing temporary workers.

WILLIAM ATKINSON

I f you visit some warehouses and DCs around the country early in the morning, you may see prison busses pulling up and unloading convicts, who enter the warehouses and spend the next eight hours working inside, being picked up at the end of the day by the busses and transported back to prison. No, this isn't the plot of some strange Hollywood movie. It's reality. "Some sheriff's departments around the country have programs where prisoners are allowed to work during the day," says Daniel Bolger, P.E., president of The Bolger Group (Millersport, Ohio, www.bolgergroup.com), a management consulting firm. "The sheriff usually arranges to drop the workers off in a bus and pick them up at the end of the shift. A portion of their earnings go back to the sheriff's department to cover incarceration costs." Most of these programs are managed through local temp agencies, which take care of workers' compensation issues, etc.

A good idea? It depends. "Most of these programs work with prisoners living in community transition homes, which tends to be low security," says Bolger. "These are not mainstream prisoners."

That's one way to get temporary workers. There are others. And these days, warehouse and DC managers are looking for as many different options as possible, because some previously reliable sources have dried up, and un employment figures are low in many parts of the country. "There was a time when it was common to hire school teachers and shiftwork firefighters as temps," says Bolger. "As pay scales have increased, though, these people tend to be less available for temp work."

Some managers work with local colleges and hire students as temps. However, according to Bolger, because of benefits programs, workers' comp, liability insurance, etc., it may make more sense to work through a professional temp agency.

One exception to working through an agency, though, might be to consider hiring family members of full-time employees. "For example, your full-time workers may have children who are available to work during the summer or other times when you have a need for temps," says Bolger. The benefit here is that, if the full-time workers are reliable, there's a good chance they will make sure their children (or other relatives) will be equally reliable.

Agency Options

Of course, when it comes to hiring temps, the most common route is to work with traditional temp agencies, which will work to fill requirements of a number of different job positions for companies in a number of different industries. But it's also worthwhile to consider some specialty agencies.

One of these is AfterCollege, Inc. (San Francisco, Calif., www.aftercollege.com), the largest college Web-based employment network in U.S., which works with individual academic departments to help their students connect with employers. "For warehouse and DC workers, we work with college logistics and supply chain departments," says Roberto Angulo, CEO. Warehouses and DCs can post their job openings on the agency's website for entry-level jobs part-time throughout the year, during the summer, and even for internships.

One benefit of hiring college students as temps, according to Angulo, is that you end up getting people who are eager to learn about your specific industry, since this is what they are majoring in in college. "For this same reason, the program provides an excellent source of people to consider for permanent jobs, who can even move up in your organization," he says.

Another specialty agency is Lift Temp Industrial (Mississauga, Ontario, Canada, www.lifttemp.com), which has offices in Canada and the U.S. The company offers positions for general labor and lift truck operators, as well as all other warehouse positions. The agency specializes in providing certified and experienced lift truck operators. "We have our own lift truck training center, where we train, qualify, and certify operators," says Sheri Brimley, president. Some of the people are trained in distribution, shipping/receiving, and some are trained in supervision and management.

"We won't place temporary employees with a client until we have done a full tour of the facility ourselves," says Richard Jones, vice president. "We want to make sure the work environment is safe. They are our employees, so we have a responsibility for them, and we want to ensure their safety."

To get the workers off on the right foot when they start the job, Lift Temp provides training, but the client is expected to provide an orientation of their workplace, training on the specific work procedures, and information on their health and safety policies.

"When selecting a temp agency, look at value, not just cost," says Brimley. "For example, damage to product and equipment will be far less with a trained and competent lift truck operator." And, according to the company, the benefits of using trained temps are that the retention tends to be higher, the workers are more satisfied, safety is better, product damage is reduced, and maintenance costs of equipment are reduced.

Good Shepherd Work Services (Allentown, Pa., www.goodshepherdrehab.org) has been in existence for 50 years. Among its many services, it helps place individuals with disabilities into the workplace. "Walgreen's is one large company that uses our workers in many of its distribution centers," says Tim Hayes, administrator. "We have been working with them for over ten years, and many of our workers have eventually been hired by Walgreen's."

Good Shepherd provides employers with information on any specific work accomodations that the workers may need. There is a misconception that these accomodations tend to be very expensive, according to Hayes, but that is rarely the case. "Most of them are simple, easy, and inexpensive to implement," he says.

According to George Wells, coordinator, transitional employment services, for Good Shepherd, research shows that people with disabilities compare favorably with the general population in terms of work skills, work traits, loyalty, attendance, and productivity, as long as there is good matching.

Wells cites some benefits: "When we send a work crew of four to seven people to a warehouse, we also arrange to send a lead worker, who is responsible for supervising the crew and also does the same work," he says. This reduces the need for the client to arrange for in-house supervision. Good Shepherd also has access to certain funding streams that allow it to provide training and coaching to the workers, at no charge to the clients. "There are also federal and state tax credits for employers to hire people we provide," he says. In some cases, employers can even get certain pieces of equipment free of charge, up to $15,000, if the equipment is going to be used by workers with disabilities.

On-the-Job Supervision

Once you have the right temps on the job, the next step is to make sure they are properly acclimated and then able to perform the necessary tasks.

Temporary Warehouse Managers

When warehouse and DC executives think about hiring temps, they almost always think in terms of hiring line workers. However, according to Rene Jones, founder and principal of Total Logistics Solutions (Burbank, Calif., www.logisticsociety.com), it may not be a bad idea to leave the option open for hiring temporary supervisors and managers as needs dictate. One of the services that Total Logistics Solutions offers is a "rent a supervisor" program.

For a number of years, the company worked with several clients helping them implement warehouse management systems. In so doing, it found that many of their supervisors weren't prepared to make the necessary technological changes. The result was that the warehouse was often without a supervisor for two to three months, and it then took another three to six months to get the newly-hired supervisor up to speed.

"This led us to begin offering temporary supervisors to these clients to help make the transition until they could find new permanent supervisors," says Jones. These are experienced consultants who work for Total Logistics Solutions. "We also help clients find the new supervisors," he says. "Then, the temporary supervisor helps the new supervisor to transition into the job."

The best way to begin, according to Don Cook, president of Cook and Associates (New Brunswick, N.J., www.cookpep.com) is to design your operations properly. "You have minimum training time available to bring temps up to speed, so you need to structure work tasks in advance as much as possible, so temps can be brought in to do very simplified portions of the tasks," he says. For example, you may want to have them focus on packing or unpacking, rather than using electronic scanners for checking in merchandise.

How can you determine if temps are "earning their keep"? According to Cook, when you look at labor costs, be sure to include temp costs. "Some companies have work and productivity measurement programs for their regular employees, but don't include temps in the program," he says. Cook and Associates offers Productivity Evaluation Program (PEP), which includes performance measures for temps. Certainly, though, you can't expect temps to meet the same standards as regular employees. "We tell clients that it is OK for them to expect temps to perform 10% to 20% lower than regular employees," he says.

After the temps have been measured, the program provides the client with a list of the names of the temps who should no longer be acceptable to the client. This list can be kept on permanent file so the client doesn't end up hiring those same temps again from that or an other agency. "We also provide a list of high-performing temps, which the client can then consider for hiring," says Cook. The program also keeps track of temp productivity by temp agency. One client using PEP told temp agencies that it would give more business to the agencies whose employees had the best productivity, which was an incentive for the agencies to send their best workers.

Core e-Business (Fairlawn, N.J., www.coreebusiness.com) is another company that provides warehouse worker performance software. Not only does the software measure engineered labor standards for fulltime employees and temps to compare them, it also measures temps against each other, so clients can identify the best ones and consider bringing them on as fulltime workers.

Howard Mintz, chief operating officer of Core e-Business, offers a recommendation for getting the most from new temps: "Integrate them into the workforce efficiently," he says. "For example, if you utilize RF technology and manual paper-based processes, it may make sense to have fulltime workers use the RF technology and have the temps use the paper-based processes."

Temps in Action

APL Logistics is one company that actively utilizes temps in its warehouse and DC locations in the Americas. Because it is so large, APL has national accounts with some temp agencies. However, not all of them have been able to fill its needs in all of its locations. As such, if an APL location is able to use one of the national contracts, it does. However, if not, the location is free to use a local temp agency.

Currently, about 42% of APL's warehouse manhours are filled by temporary employees, according to Dixie Brock, national warehouse safety manager, who is located at APL's Bloomington, Illinois, office. "Some locations use mostly temps," she says. "Others only use them on occasion for special projects."

Training and acclimating are very important to APL and the temp agencies with which it works. "Some temp agencies actually bring the temps to the warehouse in advance to show them what the work will be like," she says. "This lets the temps know in advance whether it will be work that they would want to do." Some of them decide this isn't a job they want to do before they even start, which helps reduce turnover and other problems from the beginning.

"We also discuss training with the temp agency right up front, and they address much of the training before the temps even come in the door, including general warehouse safety requirements from OSHA," she says. The agency actually brings the temps to the warehouse for this training before they start work. Then, once the temps actually start, APL provides training that is more specific to the individual warehouse. "We also have monthly training for all employees, and temps participate in this, too," she says.

APL tracks the performance of its full-time employees and its temps in each of the warehouse locations. "While 42% of our manhours are filled by temps, only 27% of our injuries occur to temps," says Brock. "This shows that they are getting the training that they need."

From *Materials Handling Management,* August, 2007. Copyright © 2007 by Penton Media Inc. Reprinted by permission.

Business Ethics: The Key Role of Corporate Governance

With growing global pressure for enforceable business ethics and social responsibility, what role should a board of directors play in setting the corporation's tone and policies? Worldwide, the authors find that boards have been on the leading edge in making business ethics an effective priority for companies.

JOHN D. SULLIVAN, PhD AND ALEKSANDR SHKOLNIKOV

Although concern with ethics has always been a part of doing business, business leaders today are beginning to think about ethics as a set of principles and guides of behavior rather than a set of rigid rules. In this sense, business ethics is not only an attempt to set a standard by which all of the employees of a company can know what is expected, but it is also an attempt to encourage employees, managers, and board members to think about and make decisions through the prism of a shared set of values.

Business ethics and corporate governance have become key factors influencing investment decisions and determining the flows of capital worldwide. In part, this is the result of scandals in both developed and developing countries. However, in a more positive sense, the growing demand for good governance also flows from the lessons learned about how to generate rapid economic growth through market institutions. From this perspective, the emphasis on anti-corruption and good governance is based both in moral standards as well as utilitarian considerations of improved market performance.

While ethics and an ethical business culture are at the heart of the corporate governance framework, the two are approached somewhat differently. Corporate governance is concerned mainly with creating the structure of decision-making at the level of the board of directors and implementing those decisions. In this sense governance can be thought of as steering the corporation. In fact, the very word governance itself comes from the Greek word for steering.

Moreover, corporate governance is about accomplishing the core values of transparency, responsibility, fairness, and accountability. Because these values are also key concerns for business ethics, the two can be seen as being directly related. However, the corporate governance aspect deals with setting up the structures through which these values are attained, while

ethics is both a guide for behavior and a set of principles (or a moral code).

In its most basic form, corporate governance is about creating a set of principles and a decision-making system to govern the modern corporation. A key challenge of governance is to ensure that the owners, or the stockholders, could control and demand accountability from the hired management. Following the Asian financial crisis and other international crises, the Organisation for Economic Cooperation and Development (OECD) came to develop the "OECD Principles of Corporate Governance" that today are accepted as the international standard.

The implementation of the OECD Corporate Governance Principles requires a whole set of supporting and enforcing market institutions. On the one side, corporate governance demands the participation of private actors, including auditors, accountants, and credit rating agencies. On the other side, it involves the functions of government, securities regulators, capital market authorities, and the like.

> **The relationship between ethics codes and corporate governance has surged to the fore. Just having a code is not enough—it must be enforced on a day-to-day basis.**

The relationship between ethics codes and corporate governance has surged to the fore. In the governance principles of the World Bank, for example, ethics, although not directly listed, is an unstated assumption that runs through many pieces of it. The New York Stock Exchange (NYSE) has released new corporate governance rules that specifically declare that "listed companies must adopt and disclose a code of business conduct and ethics for directors, officers, and employees, and promptly disclose any waivers of the code for directors or executive officers."

This was done in response to Enron and other major corporations, where the board of directors waived a substantial code of ethics. What happened at Enron shows a determining factor in all ethics codes—simply having a code is not enough. It is just as important to enforce that code in day-to-day operations. The NYSE provision, in that regard, focuses on both aspects of an ethics code—definition and implementation.

Business ethics sets out a standard by which all employees can know what is expected. It also encourages them to make decisions through a shared set of values.

Given the new mandates on business, companies find themselves pressed to develop strong codes of ethics to guide the behavior of board members, managers, and employees. Multinational corporations are also being required to set standards for those in their supply chains, in some cases higher standards than the laws of the countries in which they do business.

As noted earlier, business ethics is an attempt to set out a standard by which all of the employees can know what is expected. Yet it is also an attempt to encourage employees, managers, and board members to think about and make decisions through the prism of some shared set of values. What then are the sources from which these values can be derived?

Laws and regulations of the countries in which companies operate constitute one of these sources. Another is the notion of social responsibility or *corporate citizenship,* which is the preferred term in the business community. Corporate citizenship involves building a decision-making system that takes into the account not only internal operating procedures, but also the impact of corporate behavior on its stakeholders—employees, investors, and communities.

One starting point to consider in developing initiatives to strengthen business ethics is the difference between bright lines and values. This is a relatively new distinction. Bright lines are those standards that attempt to set out specific and very finite rules which companies and individuals cannot break. Examples include the OECD Anti-Bribery Convention, which can be translated into national laws and rules on anti-bribery standards. Companies could take a considerable amount of time to develop these bright line standards or to try to identify them themselves.

Transparency International (TI), working with major corporations, has developed its own set of bright line standards called the TI Business Principles, applicable to companies of various sizes, industries, and geographical locations. Similarly, the International Chamber of Commerce (ICC) has also developed a set of rules of conduct to combat extortion and bribery. Although bright line rules are often very specific, each company still needs to develop accountability practices to ensure that employees are indeed following these rules.

In terms of general guidelines for behavior, there are a number of different sources for business ethics programs. Historically, one of the more prominent is that developed by Reverend Leon Sullivan, which began with the anti-Apartheid movement in South Africa and has since evolved into a global set of principles (*www.GlobalSullivanPrinciples.org*). Reverend Sullivan's principles have been adapted and expanded by the United Nations' Global Compact into 10 principles. The U.N. Global Compact goes considerably beyond the bright line rules and deals with the larger issue of values.

Another similar set of principles was developed by the Caux Round Table, an organization where business leaders from different countries came up with a set of general principles for business behavior. Another set of guidelines, the OECD Multinational Corporation Guidelines, go even further, attempting to encourage or mandate corporate behavior in a variety of areas, ranging from the environment to contributions to society and providing leadership in developing a nation. (The OECD Guidelines can be found at *www.oecd.org.*)

Codes of corporate ethics, codes of corporate conduct, and codes of corporate governance overlap in many ways, with many different organizations offering guidance and advice. The most encompassing list comes from the Ethics Resource Center located in Washington, D.C. *(www.ethics.org),* which provides guidance on the issues companies should address.

The various codes and sources of corporate ethics try to capture three core areas:

- Existing laws and regulations.
- Building good business relations.
- Key concerns of society and improved corporate citizenship.

Corporate citizenship starts with a corporate code of ethics. A code of corporate ethics outlines the values and beliefs of an organization and ties them to its mission and objectives. A good code not only describes an operational process and regulates the behavior of managers and employees, but it also sets long-term goals, communicates the company's values to the outside stakeholders, and motivates employees.

A code of ethics is more than simply a statement of a company's moral beliefs. A well-written code is a true commitment to responsible business practices in that it outlines specific procedures to handle ethical failures. Codes of ethics today address a variety of issues including work environment, gender relations, discrimination, communications and reporting, gift giving, product safety, employee/management relationships, involvement in the political sphere, financial practices, corruption, and responsible advertising.

To be effective, codes of ethics should be more than just a document on a shelf. They need to be created in a way that ethical behavior is encouraged and that employees take pride in making ethical decisions. Codes of ethics should provide guidance into relationships between stakeholders and corporate decision-making. More importantly, employees at every level must strive to uphold the standards put forth by the code of ethics and the top management should exemplify those standards.

Over the past several decades we have witnessed profound changes in the way business operates in countries around the world. One of the more notable areas is the business community's treatment of corruption-related issues. The private sector has become one of the leaders in global efforts to curb corruption, developing landmark and far-reaching transparency and accountability standards as well as mechanisms to enforce them. While ethical codes play an important role in driving transparency and accountability, other initiatives that extend beyond internal rules have also made their mark in combating corruption.

One source for ethical values is the laws and regulations of countries in which companies operate. At the same time, quality of laws and regulations (as well as their enforcement) has a direct bearing on the levels of corruption in a particular country. The World Bank's *Doing Business* survey of more than 100 countries, for example, clearly showed that heavy business regulation and procedural complexities in the judiciary are associated with higher levels of corruption. The Heritage Foundation/Wall Street Journal annual Index of Economic Freedom also illustrates that higher degrees of economic freedom are correlated with lower corruption.

The Conference Board has conducted a study of business ethics around the world and the role of boards of directors in carrying out board oversight of ethics programs. The Conference Board identified the following elements in the role of the board:

- Codes of conduct.
- Communication of standards through training.
- Methods to encourage employees to report possible violations to management.
- Enforcement mechanisms (investigation and discipline).
- Oversight and review to achieve ongoing improvement.

In fact, the Conference Board found that not only were these elements quite common, but in many countries the program was actually established by board resolution. In the United States, 66 percent of American companies established the ethics program as the result of the action of the board of directors, while in Japan 96 percent took a similar stance.

Boards of directors should develop ways of monitoring compliance and ensuring that these ethics codes are not simply a standard put on the company's Web site, but not communicated and implemented throughout the company. One of the ways to do that is by carrying out program audits.

In U.S. companies, some 45 percent have carried out program audits (this can be expected to increase). In contrast, in Japan 64 percent of such companies have carried out program audits. The number is even higher at 67 percent in India, and in Western Europe, where it is over 75 percent.

Directors' ethics training is becoming quite common throughout the world, with many multinationals routinely offering ethics programs for their boards.

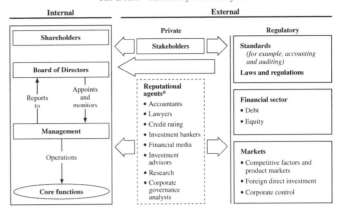

Who Sets Your Ethical Course?
The Board—And Many Other Players

*Reputational agents refer to private sector agents, self-regulating bodies, the media, and civic society that reduce information assymmetry, improve the monitoring of firms, and shed light on opportunistic behavior.

Source: The World Bank.

Complementing these program audits is the concept of directors' ethics training. The Conference Board survey found that directors' ethics training is becoming quite common throughout the world, from a low of 42 percent in Western Europe to a high of 94 percent in Japan. Many multinational companies are now routinely offering ethics training programs for their boards. The subjects covered include:

- Fiduciary duties.
- Corporate opportunities.
- Principal regulations governing company business.
- Personal liability.
- Corporate law.
- Stock exchange regulations.
- Insider trading.
- Business secrets.
- Employee training programs.

The role of the board, therefore, is seen as central to establishing and maintaining a corporate ethics program, and by corollary is a central feature in overall corporate governance guidelines and codes. This trend can be expected to continue, driven both by national legislation, international conventions, and the expectations of investors.

Debates in coming years will center on the relative roles of business, government, and non-governmental organizations in establishing codes of conduct and in reporting requirements as well as individual industry standards.

From the point of view of the business community, however, the major issue to consider is the central importance of corporate governance and business ethics in maintaining a market economy. Adam Smith, David Hume, and other philosophers and early economists were very much concerned with the role of ethics and the role of business behavior.

We can look at ethics as the solution to one of the central problems of development. In the move from a "cash and carry" or barter economy to an economy where transactions can be conducted over time and distance, business ethics are central to ensuring that contracts are adhered to. Ethics hold down the costs of doing business and improve the flow of capital to emerging markets.

Still, business should be mindful, as should nongovernmental organizations, that too much pressure is not put onto the multinational corporations to enforce laws and regulations which are actually the concerns of national government. For example, the emerging trend to hold business accountable for human rights violations in developing countries is worrisome.

In some cases, it may deter multinationals and other sources of investment from investing in an emerging market. We have to find a way to meet high ethical standards and, at the same time, ensure that the risks assumed by corporations do not inhibit the further development of the emerging markets.

JOHN D. SULLIVAN, PhD is executive director of the Center for International Private Enterprise (CIPE). **ALEKSANDR SHKOLNIKOV** is a CIPE program officer. [www.cipe.org]

From *The Corporate Board*, January/February 2007, pp. 1–5. Copyright © 2007 by Corporate Board. Reprinted by permission.

Supporting Ethical Employees

With the right training, employees can learn to make ethical decisions when issues aren't simply black or white.

JEAN THILMANY

A short time after Best Buy Co. of Richfield, Minn., officially adopted its code of ethics in 2000, the company began providing annual ethics training for its 140,000 employees across the United States and Canada.

But nothing is ever easy, and settling on a training method that best suited the retailer's culture and workforce took time, says Kathleen Edmond, who became the company's chief ethics officer in 2002 and oversaw its first ethics training program in 2003. "It was only minimally effective," she says. "It didn't take place at the time employees had questions about something going on in the workplace. It happened out of context."

Undaunted, Edmond started training around specific work issues. The first year's theme was high-stakes conversations—how to initiate them, what to say and how to listen. This time, the content fit the company's culture, she says, but the training methods didn't. Traditional stand-up delivery, where a trainer speaks to an audience, and sign-in style training, requiring attendees to sign in and document that they've received training, weren't always effective. "At some companies, that works, but check-the-box training doesn't work for us."

Today, all new Best Buy employees receive some form of ethics training during orientation—stand-up training to quickly get administrative employees up-to-speed and computer-based training for retail store employees.

Edmond spearheads an effort to update the company's code of ethics and to develop new, decentralized ethics programs to be offered in its eight U.S. business territories. Programs in Canada will follow.

As Edmond discovered, for ethics training to be effective, its form has to mesh with a company's culture, size and workforce requirements. Human resource departments that develop strong ethics programs can help companies protect their reputations and strengthen employee loyalty.

According to research conducted by the Kenexa Research Institute, working within a strong ethical culture can have a positive effect on an employee's level of pride in an organization, confidence in its future and overall satisfaction. The institute is a division of Kenexa, a recruiting software and services provider in Wayne, Pa.

Elevating Ethics

For many companies, especially those operating globally in places where standards of workplace conduct may vary, ethics training has become a high priority. In a 2005 Society for Human Resource Management Weekly Survey, 32 percent of HR professionals indicated that their organizations offer ethics training. Of those, 31 percent offer training to executives and senior managers.

Keith Darcy says corporate training programs "have become even more robust" since passage of the Sarbanes-Oxley Act of 2002. He is executive director of the Ethics and Compliance Officer Association, a 1,400-member organization with headquarters in Waltham, Mass.

Even though the federal law doesn't require employers to provide ethics training, under federal sentencing guidelines, doing so can reduce mandatory fines imposed on companies found guilty of wrong-doing. Yet many companies still lack formal programs to train their employees in ethics.

"The first goal of training is to develop a common language for what ethics is and what the company espouses as its values," Darcy says. "It's useful to spend time during any training taking people through the language of ethics and values. You want to reinforce the values, code and resources the company has and to maintain that focus."

Can you actually train an employee to act ethically?

Can you actually train an employee to act ethically?

Human resource professionals interviewed say no amount of training will ensure that employees will choose the desired behavior in every situation. After all, the most ethical response to a situation often isn't black or white, Darcy says.

But training can start a useful dialogue about right and wrong behavior that employees could remember when murky situations arise, says Deborah Haliczer, director of employee relations at Northern Illinois University in DeKalb, Ill.

Under a 2004 Illinois law, all state employees are required to receive annual, computer-based, state-prescribed ethics training. "The training has raised awareness about [employees'] personal behaviors,' Haliczer says, citing an example: "They can't use departmental fax machines to fax notices about selling a house or having a garage sale."

Ethics trainers strive to give employees a solid framework for their reasoning, so they can figure out the right thing to do in particular situations, says Bob McKinney, deputy general counsel at EnPro Industries Inc., a company headquartered in Charlotte, N.C., that makes industrial products such as seals for air compressors and engines. "We emphasize skills development." he says. "There'll always be gray areas. But we want to develop a skill set that employees can use to think about ethical issues after training ends."

Guiding Ethical Decisions

After laying out the company code. many managers turn to interactive exercises to help reinforce the ethics message and give employees a way to think creatively about ethical responses. Companies often find that Internet-based scenarios—either purchased from a vendor or produced in-house—can help employees weigh choices and make decisions in situations where answers aren't always clear.

Take Caterpillar, the Peoria, Ill.-based manufacturer of construction and mining equipment. During annual ethics training, the company's 95,000 employees consider a series of questions presented to them either via the Interact or—for factory-floor employees without computer access—on paper, says Nancy Snowden, director of Caterpillar's office of business practices. The scenarios, written in-house, encourage employees to ponder the best ways to behave in particular situations. They can consult the code of ethics as they consider their responses.

Caterpillar contracts with a vendor to ensure that all employees have taken, and passed, the training each year.

Scenarios and questions vary, depending on employees' job duties, Snowden says. For example, plant-floor employees might be presented with the following scenario: "I've noticed another group now uses a cleaning agent that works well for them. I've recently started adding the agent to my solution, and I've found it helps with cleaning. Can I continue?"

Potential answers might include:

- No, this isn't part of the job description.
- Do whatever it takes to get your job done.
- Check with an environmental health and safety group to ensure the combination is safe.

"We're really trying to train the people to do things we'd like them to do. So we try to include situations they would deal with," Snowden says.

Internet-based scenarios are also the norm when the human resource department at EnPro carries out annual ethics training.

The company purchased special training software from LRN, a Los Angeles-based provider of corporate ethics software applications, says Sheri Tiernan, director of human resources. LRN often tailors questions to EnPro's needs, she adds.

To ensure tangible results, employees must retake the course—answering different questions each time—until they score 100 percent.

Keeping up with Changes

Later this year, Lubrizol Corp., a specialty chemical manufacturer in Wickliffe, Ohio, will roll out a revised ethics guideline. The guideline was introduced in 1980 as a one-page document, was updated many times and is now a 36-page pamphlet, says Cathy Engel, ethics manager. To complement the revision, she'll oversee training all employees on the changes.

Because employees learn in different ways, Engel, after her talk about the revision, will initiate a game modeled after "Who Wants to Be a Millionaire"; it will help reinforce the changes, she says. The software, Game Show Pro 3, is from Learning-Ware of Minneapolis.

"We divide groups into two teams so they play against each other, and they have a lot of fun with it. It makes a nice variation from the straight lecture," Engel says. Teams are questioned on certain aspects of the guideline and choose among four answers.

Taking Lessons Overseas

It can be particularly challenging to communicate a company's ethical practices and guidelines across cultures. Ethics training can help define behavior expected of an employee who might not be aware of differences between U.S. and overseas workplaces, Tiernan says. EnPro has grown through mergers and acquisitions and now has operations in Brazil, China, Europe, India and Mexico. And executives expect to double the company's size in the next five years.

Ethics training can help define behavior expected of an employee.

"We're a very dispersed organization without the ability to touch employees on a personal level," Tiernan says. "It's important we send common and consistent messages to explain to employees in other countries what is ethical behavior from our standpoint."

That's why EnPro supplements its annum ethics training with quarterly software modules that give an overview of a particular issue as it's seen in the workplace. Overseas organizations often can choose to learn about a specific topic. Recently, for example, employees received programming on diversity and workplace harassment after requesting the modules.

"In a particular country, there may not be a legal statute that prohibits harassment like there is in the States, but it's important [that] people in those countries know there's a standard we hold our employees to," Tiernan says.

European employees were particularly interested in a program that gave an overview of the Sarbanes-Oxley Act of 2002. "Most everyone in North America knows Sarbanes-Oxley, but in Europe that was the first class they wanted," Tiernan says. "They'd heard so much about it, but they didn't know what it was."

Improving Success

How do you ensure your company's ethics message really resonates? HR professionals have some tips:

- **Give employees a way to air ethics questions anonymously.** EnPro operates a hotline that employees can call and, without identifying themselves, raise questions about sticky situations. Let's say a salesperson wonders if it's appropriate for a potential client to pay for a business dinner. The salesperson calls the hotline, leaves the question and calls again 10 days later to receive a response.
- **Find ways to keep the ethics policy in front of employees all year.** To remind employees about the ethics policy even when training isn't in session,

Lubrizol maintains an ethics page on its intranet and distributes pamphlets on policies such as appropriate use of e-mail and other technology. Parts of the company's ethics code are displayed on bulletin boards, posters and screen savers.

- **Hire and promote employees who demonstrate behavior in line with the message.** Caterpillar makes sure its employees demonstrate company values. But how can human resources know which candidates are likely to do that? Snowden recommends asking the right questions during the job interview. Have the applicant talk about a time someone asked him to take an action that made him uncomfortable. What did he do?

Lubrizol maintains an ethics page on its intranet and distributes pamphlets on policies.

At Best Buy, as at Caterpillar, job advancement comes after a values assessment. Edmond says 20 percent of an employee's performance review is weighed on the ethics and company values the employee has demonstrated during the year. During the review, employees discuss situations where they've put company values in play as well as specific goals they'd previously set in these areas.

Corporate Best Buy values include showing humility and respect. All employees are encouraged to brainstorm on ways they can demonstrate the company's values.

But all the training in the world won't take root, Snowden says, unless a company's code of ethics is presented dearly and is accessible to employees so they can refer to it daily.

"Everything cascades from that code to the values, behaviors and actions people should take," she says.

JEAN THILMANY is a freelance writer based in St. Paul, Minn.

UNIT 7

International Human Resource Management

Unit Selections

Key Points to Consider

- How does the smaller world affect the practice of human resource management?

- How do you think developed societies should respond to outsourcing of jobs to lesser developed societies, and what can or should they do to help individuals whose jobs have been outsourced?

- What are some considerations of transnational firms in the human resource area?

- How would you expect organizations to view the market in the future for potential employees?

- How would you expect organizations to view compensation of international employees?

- How should multinational firms treat their employees?

- How does off-shoring affect the U.S. economy?

Student Web Site
www.mhcls.com

Internet References

Cultural Globalization
http://www.inst.at/studies/collab/breidenb.htm
Globalization and Human Resource Management
http://www.cic.sfu.ca/forum/adler.html
India Finance and Investment
http://www.finance.indiamart.com
International Business Resources on the Web
http://www.globaledge.msu.edu/ibrd/ibrd.asp
International Labour Organization
http://www.ilo.org
Labor Relations and the National Labor Relations Board
http://www.snc.edu/socsci/chair/336/group2.htm

The world is changing and getting smaller all the time. At the beginning of the twentieth century, the Wright brothers flew at Kitty Hawk, and some 25 years later, Charles Lindbergh flew from New York to Paris, alone, nonstop. In 1969, the spacecraft *Eagle One* landed on the moon, and Neil Armstrong said, "One small step for man, one giant leap for mankind."

Indeed, the giant leaps have become smaller. The world has shrunk due to transportation and communication. Communication is virtually instantaneous—not as it was during the early part of the 1800s, when the Battle of New Orleans was fought several weeks after the peace treaty for the War of 1812 had been signed. For centuries, travel was limited to the speed of a horse or a ship. During the nineteenth century, however, speeds of 60 or even 100 miles an hour were achieved by railroad trains. Before the twentieth century was half over, the speed of sound had been exceeded, and in the 15 years that followed, humans circled the globe in 90 minutes. Less than 10 years later, human beings broke free from Earth's gravity and walked on the Moon. The exotic became commonplace. Societies and cultures that had been remote from each other are now close, and people must now live with a diversity unknown in the past.

A shrinking world also means an expanding economy, a global economy, because producers and their raw materials and markets are now much closer to each other than they once were. People, and the organizations they represent, often do business all over the world, and their representatives are often members of foreign societies and cultures. Human resource management in just the domestic arena is an extremely difficult task; when the rest of the world is added to the effort, it becomes a monumental undertaking.

Workers in the United States are competing directly with workers in other parts of the world, as discussed in "Roots of Insecurity: Why American Workers and Others Are Losing Out." Companies often hold-out for the lowest bidder in a competition for wage rates. This often forces the wage rates down for higher-paying countries, while only marginally bringing up the wages of the lower-paying societies—a development that is bound to have a direct impact on the standard of living in all of the developed countries of the world. In the United States, immigration has become a major issue as more illegal immigrants from lesser developed countries pour into the United States to take the low-end jobs, creating an almost separate society within the country.

As more firms become involved in world trade, they must begin to hire foreign workers. Some of these people are going to stay with the firm and become members of the corporate cadre. In the global economy, it is not uncommon for Indian employees to find themselves working for American or European multinational corporations in, say, Saudi Arabia. This presents the human resource professional with a problem of blending

© Digital Vision/Getty Images

the three cultures into a successful mix. In this example, the ingredients are a well-educated Asian, working in a highly traditional Middle-Eastern society, for a representative of Western technology and culture. The situation involves three different sets of values, three different points of view, and three different sets of expectations on how people should act and be treated. A people strategy that spans the globe is necessary to any organization doing business on a worldwide scale. There is bound to be a blending of ideas on such issues as compensation, benefits, and pensions. Not only on a regional level, such as the EU or NAFTA, but, probably on a global level in the more distant future as organizations vie for top talent, no mater where they may originally come from.

American industry does not have a monopoly on new ideas in human resources. Other societies have successfully dealt with many of the same problems. While U.S. firms certainly will not adopt every idea (lifetime employment as practiced in Japan seems the most obvious non-candidate), they can learn much from organizations outside the United States. Human resource managers need to engage in learning from their overseas counterparts if they are going to meet the needs of their employees and contribute to the success of the corporation as seen in "Collaboration Is Key to Effective Outsourcing."

Faster and better communication and transportation are leading to a more closely-knit social, cultural, and economic world, where people's global abilities can make the difference between the success or failure of an organization. But this closer world is also a more dangerous world. The recent events of the War on Terror have demonstrated the dangers associated with doing business abroad, outside the confines of one's home country. Family and personal security have become a far larger issue than they were in the past, and security is now a consideration for all individuals whether they are working domestically or outside of their home country. But we cannot turn our back on the world. The world, because it is the one largely created by the success of western culture, ideas and technology, is going to come to the United States and Europe whether the West wants it or not. The only alternative is to be ready for it. As it says in the *Art of War,* "That which you cannot change, accept with open arms."

Throwing the Switch

Take precautionary steps before switching outsourcing vendors so you don't get derailed.

Susan Ladika

When it comes to switching outsourcing vendors, nothing drives an HR department's decision more than pain. If the pain is like "a nagging toothache," the client will wait for the contract to expire before switching providers. But if it's a pain "like a broken leg," the client will do whatever it takes to ease the ache. Even a contentious transition phase or hefty financial penalties are a small price to pay for a remedy, says Jim Sowers, national HR practice leader for Buck Consultants.

Sowers cites the example of a major San Francisco Bay area retailer that outsourced health and welfare and defined benefits to a major provider, and just months later was preparing to jump ship. The systems weren't up and running properly, retirees were seeing mistakes in their benefits statements, and employees were complaining. "Essentially everything was going wrong. They're desperate for a solution," says Sowers, who is based in Houston.

When any company switches outsourcing vendors, "there's a great deal of pain because both sides are invested in a business relationship," Sowers says. But the pain can become overwhelming if service levels are so bad that they impact employee relations, costs soar, or the technology doesn't function.

The leading reason for making the switch is frustration over service levels.

Indeed, the leading reason for making the switch is frustration over service levels, says Daniel Vander Hey, senior consultant and West Coast practice leader for Watson Wyatt, based in Los Angeles. In such cases, what is actually achieved falls short of the HR professionals' expectations. "There's frustration that compels them to say it didn't work out."

In some cases, changes in business models, mergers and acquisitions, or divestitures can leave companies searching for new outsourcing providers. Regardless of the reason, when a company reaches the point of no return with a vendor, HR can make a smooth transition to a new provider, if it takes some preparatory steps.

Seeking Satisfaction

Towers Perrin, which conducts an annual study of HR outsourcing, has found that respondents are generally pleased with the cost savings derived from outsourcing but are often dissatisfied with the quality of service they receive, prompting the company to switch vendors.

Glenn Nevill, a principal with Towers Perrin who is based in Dallas, says satisfaction is generally quite high and switchover low in areas with longer histories of outsourcing, such as payroll and benefits. In those areas, clients and vendors are both well-versed in the processes and practices. But in more recent additions to the field of outsourcing, such as recruiting, compensation and training, satisfaction drops.

But, because of the difficulty involved in switching vendors, "unless there is another driver, they are not going to switch," Nevill says. Other such drivers could be when two companies merge, or an HR department requires a broader range of services than the current vendor provides.

A 2006 survey by Empagio, a mid-market human resource outsourcing firm based in Atlanta, found that of the 209 HR and financial executives surveyed about payroll and tax issues, more than half outsourced at least one payroll process, and nearly one-quarter of those said it was likely they would switch outsourcing providers.

Although the survey didn't specifically ask why executives planned to switch providers, 74 percent of respondents said they had some concerns about outsourcing. Most frequently cited were lack of responsiveness, at 43 percent, and lack of customer service, at 35 percent.

If a company has a contract with a vendor to handle multiple functions, as is often the ease these days, it is not uncommon for an HR department to switch one or two functions to another vendor and leave the other functions where they are. It might be that a particular area is not a strength of the primary vendor, so the client looks elsewhere to fill that niche, Nevill says.

Learn from the Past

If an HR department decides it's time to switch vendors, particularly if the first relationship turned sour, it's crucial "to look to the past before looking to the future" and analyze what went wrong, says Steve Garrett, senior vice president of sales and business development at Empagio.

Otherwise, clients may very well make the same mistakes or have the same issues that cropped up the first time through. It's important to take the time to document all that is expected from the provider so problems aren't repeated, Vander Hey says.

And although it's easy to blame past problems on the previous vendor, that may not be the case. In some instances, the HR department itself may be to blame. If the HR department is struggling in-house with poor data, weak communication or leadership changes, those problems need to be addressed before assuming a search for a new vendor. Certain organizations "have reputations such that vendors know as well what is going on," Vander Hey says.

At the same time, vendors can't hide their track records either. The HR world is small enough that most organizations know who worked with whom, he says. "It's impossible for vendors to escape the legacy of their success or failure."

Finding a New Partner

When selecting a new vendor, it's imperative to examine the cultural fit between the two organizations, especially if culture played a role in the demise of the former relationship. Garrett urges HR professionals to ask: "Is the vendor a partner or are they a vendor?"

On some occasions, Empagio has turned down potential clients because of their style differences. Garrett cites one organization that was inflexible about setting meetings and dates even at the beginning of the process, so Empagio walked away from the deal. "We're not going to set ourselves up to fail," he says.

Online Resources

To learn more about managing outsourcing vendor relationships, see the online version of this article at www.shrm.org/hrmagazine/07March. There you will find links to:

- An *HR Magazine* article on managing vendor relationships.
- An SHRM Online HR Outsourcing Focus Area article on bad vendor relationships.
- An SHRM Online HR Outsourcing Focus Area article on renegotiating outsourcing deals.
- An SHRM Online HR Technology Focus Area article on recognizing the signs of a bad vendor relationship.
- Towers Perrin research on HR outsourcing effectiveness.
- An Empagio study on payroll and tax outsourcing results.

An acquisition prompted Andrea Singer, director of human resources for Excel Polymers, a Solon, Ohio-based provider of customized, high-performance elastomer materials and additives, to look for a new provider.

In 2004, Lion Chemical Capital LLC and ACI Capital Co. Inc. purchased the PolyOne Elastomer and Performance Additives Group and created Excel Polymers, which has about 1,100 employees.

Singer seized the chance to find a vendor that could provide better service.

Before the acquisition, an outsourcing firm handled benefits, and HR information was managed by a complex enterprise resource planning system. But there was no electronic interface between the company and employees, and no means to enroll the employees in benefits programs online, Singer says.

So Excel Polymers opted to contract with Employease, which could combine the two functions, and could also handle employees who work extended hours and speak other languages at its call center. In two months, Employease was able to develop a system that met Excel Polymers' needs and "did so seamlessly," Singer says.

Employease was selected at the recommendation of Excel Polymers' consultant, who had a partnership agreement with the provider. With a longer time frame to get the new system up and running, Singer admits the company would have done greater due diligence in selecting an outsourcing provider. Fortunately, she has been happy with the decision so far.

Generally, though, doing thorough due diligence when selecting a new vendor is crucial, experts say. This could include issuing a request for proposals and hiring a third-party consultant to help vet prospective outsourcing providers. An HR manager also might want to visit the vendor to get a first-hand look at its corporate culture to try to determine how it might mesh with the company's.

Sharlyn Lauby, SPHR, president of ITM Group Inc., an HR consulting firm based in Fort Lauderdale, Fla., recommends networking to find others who have used that particular vendor, and not relying only on the references the outsourcing provider gives you. "Let's face it: All of our references say we walk on water."

HR managers may also want to look at the vendor's current customers, as well as those who have left, and talk to those whose businesses are similar to their own. So a manufacturer could look for providers who serve other blue-collar customers, and a bank could look for those with white-collar customers in their client base, Nevill says.

HR professionals also should take their time when making the decision to go with a new provider, he says. Often the decision is driven by a date on the calendar of the end of a budget period. With a seven- to 10-year relationship in the balance, spending an extra few months making a decision "will pay huge dividends on the back end," says Nevill.

Large organizations should start thinking about the switch up to two years before the contract's expiration.

He also says large organizations should start thinking about the switch up to two years before the contract's expiration, while smaller organizations should start 12 to 15 months in advance. The larger the company, the more complicated the transition, Nevill explains.

The Transition

While selecting a new vendor may be a major effort, it's only the start of the process. It can be even more time-consuming and emotionally taxing to switch over to another vendor. There are no guarantees that the old vendor will play nicely with the new one, or with you.

"You're not the first call they return," says Scott Lever, a managing consultant at PA Consulting Group, based in Boston. The old vendor may be unavailable, delay meetings or threaten legal action against the client for a breach of intellectual property. While attorneys counsel clients to write language into contracts that addresses this type of behavior, nothing really prevents it, Lever says. Instead, the client may offer financial incentives or promise the vendor other business to smooth the transition. Another incentive might be the promise of a good reference from the client who is making the switch.

During the transition period, the old provider is likely to move resources to other remaining clients, while the new vendor may insist it can't guarantee service levels during the transition. So Lever says it's imperative that a company "be very clear about who is delivering service at what level at each moment."

Two of the biggest stumbling blocks are usually technology and intellectual property, says David Lewis, president of OperationsInc., an HR consulting and outsourcing firm based in Stamford, Conn. The contract with a vendor might include forms, documents and databases that the service provider actually owns, meaning the HR department "might have to rebuild a lot of what they thought was theirs."

In some cases, a company might hang onto a "lousy vendor" because the thought of having to deal with the data issues is "an absolute nightmare," Lewis says. The way data are housed often is proprietary, rather than off-the-shelf. If the vendor has done a good job with the software, "it has become part of your culture, part of your process." Instead, he recommends that an HR department purchase its own technology and have the outsourcing provider manage it. Of course, hindsight is 20/20, so keep in mind that technology may impede the transition process if the vendor controls it.

Vander Hey says conversion fees can be quite costly to get data back into a form an organization can use, running from hundreds of thousands to millions of dollars. He cites one organization with 30,000 employees that was asked to pay $2 million in conversion fees. The organization refused, and eventually the fees were negotiated down to $500,000.

A typical contract guarantees a vendor a certain amount of money for the first three years of the agreement, regardless of whether the client bows out, he adds.

Paul Rubenstein, a principal in human capital advisory services for Mercer, based in San Francisco, cautions HR professionals: "Don't vilify the outgoing vendor. Avoid it becoming an emotional decision. Three or four years from now, if business changes, you might be going back to them."

It might also occur as consolidation takes place in the industry. Sowers says that for large firms with more than 50,000 employees, there are only about a half-dozen choices when it comes to outsourcing providers, giving the vendors more leverage and clout.

Getting the Word Out

Before the switch comes, it's imperative to convey the changes to your employees. They need to know what to expect during the transition phase, as well as afterward.

Singer says that before Excel Polymers switched outsourcing providers, employees were briefed on who the new vendor would be, and what they could expect. They also received training on how to use the new online system to enroll in the benefits program.

Lauby recommends holding detailed meetings with groups of employees about why the change is being made, the benefits it will bring, and how the changes will occur. By having groups of employees plugged in, they become your "on-floor cheerleaders."

Having employee buy-in is key. "Employees are very wary. They are painfully aware of issues that existed with the previous vendor," Vander Hey says.

If questions arise, workers may not turn to the HR department for information, but may be more willing to ask employees who have already been briefed. Those "cheerleaders" can counter any misinformation that might exist, Lauby says. "This is one of those moments in time when you can utilize informal networks within the organization to a tremendous advantage."

SUSAN LADIKA has been a journalist for more than 20 years, working in both the United States and Europe. Now based in Tampa, Fla., Her freelance work has appeared in such publications as *The Wall Street Journal-Europe* and *The Economist*.

Roots of Insecurity

Why American Workers and Others Are Losing Out

HORST BRAND

In 2004 the International Labor Office (ILO) published a voluminous though mistitled report called "Economic Security for a Better World." This is in fact a treatise about the economic insecurity that has been afflicting the world's working people for the past several decades. It is also an argument criticizing the "liberalization context" of insecurity and the policies that have deliberately fostered it. Liberalization, says the ILO, is the objective of policies formulated by international financial institutions in concert with the U.S. Treasury—policies that are based on the "Washington Consensus."

The ILO defines liberalization in terms of certain "key policy commitments," all of which affect the situation of workers, though at times only indirectly. One of the crucial commitments is a reduction in the size and role of the public sector of given countries, which usually results in cutbacks in public employment and productive public assets and the elimination of much of the state's regulatory capacity. Other key commitments include unobstructed capital mobility, regardless of the effects on the value of a country's exchange rate and ability to finance domestic business (hence to sustain employment levels), and labor market "flexibility," a euphemism for removing (or restricting) such labor market "distortions" as trade unions and minimum wage laws and, in brief, subjecting workers to the dictates of supply and demand.

The Washington Consensus does not, in fact, govern the economies of the leading industrial countries, but its doctrines are broadly shared by their leading economists. The rights of labor and various labor standards are seen as "rigidities," to be modified or if possible removed. In his *Global Labour Flexibility*, Guy Standing, a senior economist with the ILO, writes, "In the 1980s . . . those favoring the cold bath approach were back in ascendancy, and it is no coincidence that in the latest era of insecurity no fewer than eight Nobel Prizes have been awarded to economists from the University of Chicago, where . . . the Chicago school of law and economics depicted regulations as impediments to growth. . . . In the 1980s and 1990s, security has been derided as the source of "rigidity" and dependency. . . ." This "neo-classical paradigm" is the very antithesis of what the ILO stands for—thus another ILO writer: "It essentially ignores the value of labor standards as instruments of social justice."[1]

Nelson Lichtenstein notes the disdain with which this concern is viewed by top government representatives. "At a 1998 meeting of the G-8 industrial nations in Cologne, a delegation of trade unionists, representing virtually all the big labor confederations in the developed world, found themselves completely stymied when they tried to put international labor standards, financial market regulation, and compensatory help to displaced workers on the agenda. In any national context, such initiatives would have been long-standing elements of mainstream politics." These ideas were now "considered anathema . . . to the principles of free trade . . . and even to political parties—like those then running Great Britain, Germany, and the United States—that relied on the labor vote for their very survival."

The attitude of the G-8 officials is more explicitly conveyed by Alan Greenspan, then chair of the Federal Reserve's Board of Governors, in words that go to the roots of job insecurity—though this was not their intent. At a symposium in 2000, attended by high officials of international financial institutions and economists, Greenspan said that it was "remarkable how far economic opinions . . . have shifted since the 1970s. At the risk of some oversimplification, there has been a noticeable reversion in thinking toward nineteenth century liberalism, with the consequence that deregulation and privatization have become policies central to much government reform." Greenspan further remarked that although "the value standards of our societies that developed out of the Great Depression" have given rise to "some government regulations practiced virtually everywhere," it is now well understood that "government actions often hinder incentives to investments by increasing uncertainties, boosting risk premiums, and raising costs. . . . Many attempts to tame such regimes are not without cost in terms of economic growth and the average living standards of a nation."[2]

The "regimes" in that last sentence, which we once thought needed taming, are the "unbridled forms of capitalism." But "unbridled" is now a good thing: Greenspan immediately proceeded to discuss the contrast between the lower level of high-tech capital investment in Europe and Japan relative to the United States. And he attributed Europe's lower level of such investment to legislative protection of its workers against the "presumed harsher aspects of free-market competition." The difference between Europe and Japan on the one hand and the United States on the other is all the more important, he averred, inasmuch as the return (profit margin) from newer technologies results chiefly from a reduction of labor costs. When firms cannot "really implement" such reductions—that is, "release" workers—rates of return will be lower. And this will blunt incentives to invest and result in lower productivity gains—gains that are "clearly evident in the United States and other countries with fewer impediments to implementation."

Indeed, few impediments to "releasing" employees exist in the United States. It is the only advanced industrial country that does not legally constrain employers to hire or fire at will (except on grounds of race or gender). The 1988 Worker Adjustment and Retraining Notification Act hardly provides even a modicum of job security. It mandates notification of plant closing or mass layoff where fifty or more employees are affected; it does not bar the discharge of employees. Without labor-management contracts restricting an employer's right, "workers have little entitlement to protections against loss of work."[3]

But layoffs also occur for reasons other than technological changes that make workers redundant. "Shareholder value" has motivated some large-scale discharges. For example, a Kodak company spokesperson explained why a planned layoff was raised from ten thousand to sixteen thousand persons because of Wall Street dissatisfaction with the previously announced lower number. "You cannot ignore important constituencies like shareholders," he said, according to the *New York Times*. That the "constituency" of property owners should take precedence over the interests of productive working people and their livelihood—and this case is by no means unusual—betrays a corruption of some fundamental moral values.

As regards Greenspan's claim that rates of return on technologically advanced plants and equipment in the United States have exceeded comparable rates in the European Union (EU)—although pertinent data are not at hand—it is unlikely that this is related to the greater protection of European workers. According to data published by the Economic Policy Institute in *The State of Working America, 2004/2005*, the growth rate of labor productivity (output per hour worked) averaged 1.7 percent annually between 1989 and 2000 for the United States, which is about the same as in France, Germany, Italy, and the United Kingdom. Nor did *levels* of the gross domestic product per hour worked differ significantly when figured in relation to the United States. For a number of EU countries (such as France and Germany), those levels exceeded that of the United States.

Deregulating Terms of Employment

These European countries, however, have been plagued by very high rates of unemployment—which have been attributed largely to labor market "rigidities" and to the relatively generous income supports for unemployed workers. Since the 1980s, these supports and the conditions of their availability have become increasingly restrictive (see below). More important, government and employer efforts have succeeded, if gradually and against much resistance, in making working conditions more "flexible." These developments have intensified employment and labor-market insecurity in the EU, particularly in France.

It has been argued that the hiring of workers was impeded in the EU by legal and administrative difficulties and attendant expense of dismissal. The American employment-at-will doctrine is not acceptable there and could not be enforced. But this difficulty has been widely circumvented by the use of temporary help and of term contracts. Temporary employment in France, Germany, and the Netherlands runs to near 15 percent of total employment and to some 30 percent in Spain. Moreover, there is a tendency to replace permanent employees, as these quit or retire, with temporary workers. It is in part this prospect that caused French youth to revolt against the law (eventually rescinded) that would have permitted employers to fire workers aged twenty-six and under without notice or explanation—thus invalidating part of the protective clauses of existing labor law.

Despite its subsequent rescission, the law exemplifies legislative tendencies in European countries seeking to deregulate or destandardize existing terms of employment and dismissal, thus facilitating a more "flexible" labor market. In Germany, for example, small and newly established firms have been relieved from certain worker protective rules. Part-time workers are excluded in determining the number of employees of a firm, thus "allowing more firms to remain below the size threshold for which protective rules apply." The "social plan that employers must negotiate in case of an economic downturn has been modified so that up to 20 percent of employees may be dismissed before a plan is worked out, rather than only 5 percent.[4] In general, protective statutes are evaded or circumvented. Outsourcing, for example, affects a substantial part of the labor force. Larger companies outsource work to small or semi-independent firms to whom conventional statutory regulations don't apply or don't fully apply. Guy Standing writes that "(T)he current era has seen a regrowth of casualization."[5]

Degrading Unemployment Compensation

In the advanced industrial countries, labor-market security—fundamentally assured by policies of full or near full employment—included the understanding, until the 1980s or 1990s, that income support would be available in case of job loss, and that such support would not be conditional on accepting the first job offered. It was a social right, if somewhat encumbered bureaucratically. It was part of a range of income supports to promote "the decommodification of labor." Now decommodification has turned into its opposite. The conditions for unemployment compensation have become stringent and exacting. Income maintenance programs have been designed to "activate beneficiaries," and the criteria for "suitable work"—which an unemployed person must accept—have been broadened well beyond the occupational status of previous employment. Entry to social protection has been restricted, says Neil Gilbert, and exit has been accelerated.[6] According to the ILO report, income insecurity linked to unemployment has "unquestionably increased." Qualifying periods for benefit eligibility have been lengthened in many countries and the duration of benefits reduced; income replacement ratios have declined.

More generally, social protection in many, perhaps most, countries remains severely inadequate and is becoming even more inadequate under budgetary and privatization pressures. In the absence of reliable quantitative data, the ILO has developed a database derived from descriptive and budgetary information for 102 countries. It concludes that only one in three countries offers schemes covering the conventional social risks—among them, sickness, maternity, old-age disabilities, the plight of survivors, injury, and unemployment. One in six countries covers only one half or fewer of these risks. Only one in two pays unemployment benefits—and even then coverage is sparse, payouts low. Estimates of the adequacy of risk protection or of eligibility allow an evaluation of effectiveness: Only 17 of the 102 countries examined meet ILO criteria satisfactorily; 34 countries, mostly in Africa and Latin America, meet none of the criteria.

Pensions have been under strong privatization pressure. Moreover, there is a significant movement from defined benefits to defined contributions—a shift of investment risks to employees. As a result, income security in old age is in jeopardy. In addition, current earnings of workers bear a greater and greater burden of pension costs. Contribution rates have risen in half the countries surveyed by the ILO; the legal retirement age is being steadily increased; the number of years in which workers must contribute before they are entitled to state pensions is also being increased. Mandatory private insurance schemes (such as the one in Chile) intensify income insecurity.

The ILO report, in an unusually acerbic statement, says, "As income inequality grows, social policy is likely to become regressive. . . . The reality is that in the early years of the 21st century powerful interests are pressing governments all over the world to cut public social spending, and in doing so reduce the income security provided by the State."

The Curse of "Informal Labor"

"Labour relations are being informalized," says the report. Often the majority of working people, or a large minority of them, lack secure employment; they have no status as wage workers; no fixed workplace, such as a shop, factory, or office; and as often as not they lack social protection, such as health insurance or old-age pensions. The ILO estimates that 50 percent to 70 percent of those countries' labor force engages in informal activities—they are self-employed or casual workers or they work with or for their families. "About 40 percent of people in the developing world live in absolute poverty . . . obliged to take on the most rudimentary form of work or labor to ensure a basic subsistence."

Informal workers maintain work or market exchange relationships with semiformal or, indirectly, with formal enterprises. The *New York Times* of May 23, 2006, tells about Teresa Janoras, who scavenges for discarded food from hotels and restaurants in a Manila dump (where 150,000 people rummage through the daily delivery of 6,700 tons of garbage to find articles for recycling). Mrs. Janoras sells her "goods" to a broker as feed for pigs. On a good day (that is, a very long day), she earns three dollars. The relationship between her and the broker is not uncommon. "Informalization" is perpetuated by chains of subcontractors reaching upward from street and garbage dump collectors to, say, paper, plastic, and glass buyers, who have the stuff cleaned and sorted, then sell it to wholesalers, who in turn sell it to a manufacturer who probably employs a formal work force.

Alejandro Portes argues that "a high proportion of the informal labor force is in reality composed of 'disguised' wage workers who toil for modern firms" but have no status as "regular" employees.[7] Protective labor legislation, often modeled on the laws of industrially advanced countries, will not or cannot be enforced. "The fundamental difficulty in the application of protective legislation in Third World nations is the existence of a large mass of surplus labor," Portes writes. Non-enforcement of such legislation, however, is also part of a deliberate policy.

Portes himself has shown that industrialization in a number of Latin American countries increased at one-third again the rate of the gross domestic product, which itself doubled between the 1950s and 1980s even while their informal work force did not decrease; its proportion to the formal work force was unchanged. Furthermore, spokespersons for developing countries have opposed labor-standard clauses written into trade treaties, because such clauses would reduce the "comparative advantage" that plentiful cheap labor presumably bestows on them. Similarly, they justify the nonenforcement of the core ILO standards (for example, the right to free association and union organization). Considering that property and investment rights are stringently guarded under domestic and international laws, there should certainly be an effort to absorb informal workers in a modernizing economy based on a statutory conception of the labor market. This is clearly a political issue.

The conditions under which masses of workers exist recall Alan Greenspan's words about the "reversion in thinking toward nineteenth century liberalism." It might be relevant to quote a passage from E.J. Hobsbawm's *The Age of Capital, 1848–1875*, bearing upon labor market conditions in that century:

> If any single factor dominated the lives of nineteenth-century workers it was *insecurity*. They did not know in the beginning of the week how much they would bring home at the end. They did not know how long their present work would last or, if they lost it, when they would get another job or under what conditions. They did not know when accident or sickness would hit them, and though they knew that sometime in middle age—perhaps in the forties for unskilled labourers, perhaps in the fifties for the more skilled—they would become incapable of

doing a full measure of adult physical labour, they did not know what would happen to them between then and death. . . . There was no certainty of work even for the most skilled: during the slump of 1857–58 the number of workers in the Berlin engineering industry fell by almost a third (Italics in original).

Although Greenspan and others may deny that the passage reflects the "vision" of nineteenth-century liberalism they have in mind, a large literature, including papers by World Bank staffers and the "Eurosclerosis" school, have argued for years, and with some success, about the adverse consequences of protective labor regulations. Standing writes that "there has been a considerable erosion of protective labor regulation in industrial, industrializing and low-income countries, in response to the growing openness to international trade and the changing international division of labor, under pressure from governments pursuing explicit and implicit protective deregulation or as a consequence of enterprise-level restructuring of employment relations towards 'external' labor flexibility."[8]

Attacking Organized Labor

Widespread hostility to unions has further impaired the capacity of workers to improve their conditions. This probably reflects deeper trends, summarized by the labor historian Henry Phelps Brown in the early 1990s: "The dissolution of the labor movement is . . . the counter-revolution of our time."[9]

Neither international competition nor advances in production technology fully explain the pressures on wages and benefits that American workers have been experiencing. In his *State of the Union: A Century of American Labor*, Nelson Lichtenstein points out, "Union labor's most significant difficulties first appeared not in manufacturing but in the construction industry." And the problems faced by municipal labor beginning in the 1970s were likewise "entirely homegrown," with the federal government refusing to relieve the fiscal crisis that older American cities underwent at the time owing to deindustrialization and a stagnant tax base. Regarding construction labor, the big companies using such labor acted in concert to resist wage demands. Contractors hired more and more non-union labor, and "the great exurban construction boom of the late 1980s and mid-1990s has been largely union-free. 'We're paying less than Wal-Mart,' acknowledged the president of a non-union construction group in Alabama."

A more recent example of labor-cost cutbacks unrelated to international competition is the policy of Caterpillar, an otherwise "healthy and profitable company," according to Louis Uchitelle, in the *New York Times* of February 6, 2006. After years of strikes and job actions at the company, the United Auto Workers union was compelled to accept the two-tier wage and benefit arrangements that had become emblematic of collective bargaining since the early 1980s. Newly hired workers would now receive lower rates of compensation and lower increases than their seniors. The average level of labor costs would thus decline as older workers quit or retired. "The long standing presumption that factory workers at successful companies can achieve a secure, relatively prosperous middle class life for themselves and their families," writes Uchitelle, "is evaporating."

Caterpillar imposed what it termed a "market-competitive payscale" in the localities or regions where it operates. Although workers in the lower tiers have a chance to work their way up, "the union mind set" of gaining annual increases doing minimally skilled jobs must be "shed," according to company officials. Uchitelle doesn't say so, but that policy may in time make the union irrelevant.

During the mid-twentieth century, labor in the industrial countries enjoyed rising real wages, a degree of job security, and an extension of its rights—tendencies that Scandinavian social democrats called decommodification—the distancing of labor, however gradual, from "the whip of the market." It was in line with the ILO's 1944 dictum that "labor is not a commodity"—an idea that had originated with John R. Commons and the Wisconsin school of labor relations. Moreover, labor standards were similar among the industrial countries' major trading partners, hence were neutral in regard to international competition. Yet, Lichtenstein rejects the notion that a "social contract" between labor and management existed during the mid-twentieth century, which was presumably abrogated in the 1980s. He points to the steep barrier to organizing in the South erected by the 1947 Taft-Hartley legislation and to the bitter strikes that occurred during the 1950s and 1960s. Beginning with Taft-Hartley, labor was forced onto the political defensive.

S tanding similarly holds that there was no "Golden Age." The economic security of the few decades following the Second World War could not last. Deepening insecurity already lay ahead for large numbers of workers—an erosion of their rights, a recrudescence of commodification—for the supposed Golden Age, writes Standing, "was based on an inequitable and unsustainable international division of labor . . ." That was not the only reason why economic security crumbled. The postwar boom was ending, an era of much-slowed growth and productivity began. Worker demands for better conditions were resisted more strongly. Welfare-state budgets became

harder to finance and met increasing opposition. But the fundamental event that brought about the end of the era of economic security was the transformation of the international division of labor.

The older division of labor was based, roughly speaking, on the manufacturing preeminence of the West and the agricultural and raw-materials economies of the South. With the end of colonialism and of Western dominance after the Second World War, this dependency relationship was no longer tolerable. The steady reduction of tariffs and import restrictions that industrial countries negotiated with one another in the postwar period (but which applied universally under the most-favored-nation principle) promised trading opportunities to some industrializing poorer countries.

Export- or trade-based economic growth, urged by the International Monetary Fund and the World Bank, spelled intensified global competition based on low labor costs. Low labor costs were enforced by repressive wage and worker association policies, as in Korea, until the late 1980s and other Southeast Asian countries. In China such policies have not abated. Even where such repressiveness has eased, labor cost differentials persist and keep attracting foreign capital—though, as product upgrading requires some skill improvement and as internal markets develop, such cost differentials will probably diminish to some degree.

T he inequality of the international division of labor that marked the nineteenth and much of the twentieth centuries has undoubtedly lessened. This has been in large measure the result of an expanding world market—an expansion driven by capitalist enterprise, financial interests, reduction of trade barriers, and not least, since the 1960s, increasing pressures by developing countries. This same world market, however, has been the arena of widespread deprivation of fundamental labor rights and standards. The "liberalization context of insecurity" described in the ILO report has embraced efforts by international financial institutions to break down the collective bargaining power of labor as part of their deregulation project. These efforts have probably perpetuated the "informalization" of much of the working-age population in developing countries—the more so as the privatizing of public services and enterprises has inevitably meant layoffs.

"Liberalization" doesn't refer only to a pattern of regressive social policies; it is linked to powerful political forces that have material and ideological interests in privatizing public assets and services, and whose influence extends worldwide. There is little likelihood that these regressive forces will be overcome any time soon. Nor does a party of social democracy exist that appears capable of producing or enforcing a new vision of social justice—or, more particularly, of eliminating global poverty. The struggle for social justice will not cease, but, as yet, it cannot count on more than marginal success.

References

1. Roger Plant, *Labour Standards and Structural Adjustment.* (International Labour Office: Geneva, 1994), p. 9.
2. Alan Greenspan, "Opening Remarks—Global Integration: Opportunities and Challenges," in a symposium sponsored by the Federal Reserve Bank of Kansas City (Jackson Hole, WY, August 24–26, 2000).
3. Raymond Hogler, *Employment Relations in the United States: Law, Policy and Practice.* (Sage Publications, 2004), p. 162.
4. G. Bosch and W. Sengenberger, "Employment Policy, the State and the Unions in the Federal Republic of Germany," in *The State and the Labor Market*, Samuel Rosenberg, ed. (Plenum Press, 1989), p. 96.
5. Guy Standing, *Global Labor Flexibility: Seeking Distributive Justice* (St. Martin's Press, 1999), p.107.
6. Neil Gilbert, *Transformation of the Welfare State: The Silent Surrender of Public Responsibility* (Oxford University Press: New York, 2004), p. 66.
7. Alejandro Portes, "When More Can be Less: Labor Standards, Development, and the Informal Economy." In *Labor Standards and Development in the Global Economy* (U.S. Department of Labor: Washington, 1990), p. 28.
8. Guy Standing, "Structural adjustment and labour market policies: Towards social adjustment?" in *Towards Social Adjustment*, Guy Standing and Victor Tokman, eds. (International Labour Office: Geneva, 1991), p. 36.
9. Quoted in *Global Labour Flexibility*, op. cit., p. 2.2

HORST BRAND writes on economics for *Dissent*.

Collaboration Is Key to Effective Outsourcing

STEPHEN MILLER

S uccess in today's complex outsourcing marketplace depends primarily on a highly collaborative client-service provider relationship, according to a 2007 PricewaterhouseCoopers (PwC) Global Outsourcing study, *Outsourcing Comes of Age: The Rise of Collaborative Partnering.*

The study explores a key issue raised by chief executive officers in PricewaterhouseCoopers' Annual CEO Survey as well as insights garnered from outsourcing clients and providers in 19 countries.

A key finding: Many top global executives say they gain major competitive advantages from outsourcing. The CEOs, in particular, described the growing importance of collaboration with suppliers and service providers as a way to mitigate complexity, reduce transaction costs and gain competitive advantages.

Overall, the survey identified functions now being comprehensively outsourced, including human resources, information technology, production, logistics and distribution, sales, and finance.

A large majority of clients—87 percent—say outsourcing delivers the benefits projected in the original business plans. Outsourcing is perceived as such an essential business practice that 91 percent of clients, whether completely happy or not, said they will outsource again.

"Outsourcing is still very much the game, but the rules have changed," says Pat McArdle, global outsourcing partner at PwC. "The lightning pace of growth in outsourcing is only matched by the transformation of the market as traditional models are gradually being replaced by multi-sourcing, joint ventures and 'best of breed' arrangements."

Managing this extended network of relationships, McArdle adds, "requires more transparency, better communication, greater trust and genuine reciprocity. In a nutshell, success in this environment will heavily hinge on shifting the client-service provider relationship from adversarial to collaborative, from one based on procurement to one grounded in partnership."

Collaboration Pays Off

Collaborative partnering and an openness to business model innovation become more important as clients start to look at "second wave" outsourcing of functions being streamlined within shared service centers, such as HR and finance or accounting.

Collaborative partnering and an openness to business model innovation become more important as clients start to look at 'second wave' outsourcing.

Companies identified as "expert outsourcers" (those that met their business plan goals completely) measured their service providers as better collaborators than "learners" (companies for whom outsourcing only partly met business goals), with 81 percent of experts stating that they have honest and transparent dealings with providers (vs. 62 percent of learners).

Clients defined as "high collaborators," based on rating their providers the highest overall on the key indicators of collaboration such as "business dealings being honest and transparent," experienced the most mutual engagement with their outsourcing providers.

These high collaborators embrace innovative outsourcing business models:

- 51 percent of high collaborators plan to increase their joint ventures, vs. 44 percent of other respondents.
- 46 percent expect their use of open, collaborative business models to grow, vs. 32 percent of other respondents.

Moreover, high collaborators have significantly greater outsourcing growth plans with regard to core products and services (often assumed to be "off limits" when it comes to outsourcing) and in other strategic areas, including:

- Innovation and research and development.
- Customer call centers.
- Information technology.
- HR services.

Other characteristics of high collaborators include:

- Greater likelihood of being open-minded, enabling them to manage better around barriers to outsourcing.

- Tendency to support multi-sourcing (many suppliers or providers) over limited sourcing (few suppliers or providers) far more than other respondents.
- Tendency to support shared risk and reward over traditional commercial terms.

Preventing Disconnects

But the continued growth and significance of outsourcing doesn't mean that the path is without pitfalls. For instance, one clear trend from survey data is the frequent disconnect between the needs and expectations of clients and service providers. While a quarter of clients think that "many suppliers or providers" work better than "few suppliers or providers," only 10 percent of service providers think so. And while 52 percent of service providers recommend offshore outsourcing, only 20 percent of clients say that this works best in real-life outsourcing.

Furthermore, 66 percent of clients say that social and environmental issues will have a significant impact on their offshoring decisions, but providers remain skeptical, with 52 percent claiming that they do not feel that these issues will be significant to their clients.

However, clients and providers agree that labor and employment standards at potential offshore locations are a key concern.

The Real Cost of Offshoring

Michael Mandel and Pete Engardio

Whenever critics of globalization complain about the loss of American jobs to low-cost countries such as China and India, supporters point to the powerful performance of the U.S. economy. And with good reason. Despite the latest slow quarter, official statistics show that America's economic output has grown at a solid 3.3% annual rate since 2003, a period when imports from low-cost countries have soared. Similarly, domestic manufacturing output has expanded at a decent pace. On the face of it, offshoring doesn't seem to be having much of an effect at all.

But new evidence suggests that shifting production overseas has inflicted worse damage on the U.S. economy than the numbers show. BusinessWeek has learned of a gaping flaw in the way statistics treat offshoring, with serious economic and political implications. Top government statisticians now acknowledge that the problem exists, and say it could prove to be significant.

The short explanation is that the growth of domestic manufacturing has been substantially overstated in recent years. That means productivity gains and overall economic growth have been overstated as well. And that raises questions about U.S. competitiveness and "helps explain why wage growth for most American workers has been weak," says Susan N. Houseman, an economist at the W.E. Upjohn Institute for Employment Research who identifies the distorting effects of offshoring in a soon-to-be-published paper.

Fly in the Ointment

The underlying problem is located in an obscure statistic: the import price data published monthly by the Bureau of Labor Statistics (BLS). Because of it, many of the cost cuts and product innovations being made overseas by global companies and foreign suppliers aren't being counted properly. And that spells trouble because, surprisingly, the government uses the erroneous import price data directly and indirectly as part of its calculation for many other major economic statistics, including productivity, the output of the manufacturing sector, and real gross domestic product (GDP), which is supposed to be the inflation-adjusted value of all the goods and services produced inside the U.S. (For a detailed explanation of how import price data are calculated and why the methodology is suspect, see page 34.)

The result? BusinessWeek's analysis of the import price data reveals offshoring to low-cost countries is in fact creating "phantom GDP"—reported gains in GDP that don't correspond to any actual domestic production. The only question is the magnitude of the disconnect. "There's something real here, but we don't know how much," says J. Steven Landefeld, director of the Bureau of Economic Analysis (BEA), which puts together the GDP figures. Adds Matthew J. Slaughter, an economist at the Amos Tuck School of Business at Dartmouth College who until last February was on President George W. Bush's Council of Economic Advisers: "There are potentially big implications. I worry about how pervasive this is."

By BusinessWeek's admittedly rough estimate, offshoring may have created about $66 billion in phantom GDP gains since 2003 (page 31). That would lower real GDP today by about half of 1%, which is substantial but not huge. But put another way, $66 billion would wipe out as much as 40% of the gains in manufacturing output over the same period.

It's important to emphasize the tenuousness of this calculation. In particular, it required BusinessWeek to make assumptions about the size of the cost savings from offshoring, information the government doesn't even collect.

Getting Worse

As a result, the actual size of phantom GDP could be a lot larger, or perhaps smaller. This estimate mainly focuses on the shift of manufacturing overseas. But phantom GDP can be created by the introduction of innovative new imported products or by the offshoring of research and development, design, and services as well—and there aren't enough data in those areas to take a stab at a calculation. "As these [low-cost] countries move up the value chain, the problem becomes worse and worse," says Jerry A. Hausman, a top economist at Massachusetts Institute of Technology. "You've put your finger on a real problem."

Alternatively, as Landefeld notes, the size of the overstatement could be smaller. One possible offset: Machinery and high-tech equipment shipped directly to businesses from foreign suppliers may generate less phantom GDP, just because of the way the numbers are constructed.

Depending on your attitude toward offshoring, the existance of Phantom GDP id either testimony to the power of globalization or confirmation of long-held fears. The U.S. economy no longer stops at the water's edge. Global corporations often provide their foreign suppliers and overseas subsidiaries with business knowledge, management practices, training, and all sorts of other intangible exports not picked up in the government data. In return, they get back cheap products.

But the new numbers also require a reassessment of productivity and wages that could add fire to the national debate over the true performance of the economy in President Bush's second term. The official statistics show that productivity, or output per hour, grew at a 1.8% rate over the past three years. But taking the phantom GDP effect into account, the actual rate of productivity growth might be closer to 1.6%—about what it was in the 1980s.

More broadly, it becomes clear that "gains from trade are being measured instead of productivity," according to Robert C. Feenstra, an economist at the University of California at Davis and the director of the international trade and investment program at the National Bureau of Economic Research. "This has been missed."

Pat Byrne, the global managing partner of Accenture Ltd.'s supply-chain management practice, goes even further, suggesting that "at least half of U.S. productivity [growth] has been because of globalization." But quantifying this is tough, he notes, because most companies don't look at how much of their productivity growth is onshore and how much is offshore. "I don't know of any companies or industries that have tried to measure this. Maybe they don't even want to know."

Phantom GDP helps explain why U.S. workers aren't benefiting more as their companies grow ever more efficient. The cost savings that companies are reaping "don't represent increased productivity of American workers producing goods and services in the U.S.," says Houseman. In contrast, compensation of senior executives is typically tied to profits, which have soared alongside offshoring.

Importing Earnings

But where are those vigorous corporate profits coming from? The strong earnings growth of U.S.-based corporations is still real, but it may be that fewer of the gains are coming from improvements in domestic productivity. In fact, holding down costs by moving key tasks overseas could be having a greater impact on corporate earnings than anyone guessed—or measured.

There are investing implications, too, although those are harder to quantify. Companies with their primary focus in the U.S. might suddenly seem less attractive, since underlying economic growth is slower here than the numbers show. But if the statistical systems of other developed countries suffer from the same problem—and they might—then growth in Europe and Japan might be overstated, too.

When Houseman first uncovered the problem with the numbers that is created by offshoring, she was primarily focused on manufacturing productivity, where the official stats show a 32% increase since 2000. But while some of the gains may be real, they also include unlikely productivity jumps in heavily outsourced industries such as furniture and audio and video equipment such as televisions. "In some sectors, productivity growth may be an indicator not of how competitive American workers are in international markets," says Houseman, "but rather of how

cost-uncompetitive they are." For example, furniture manufacturing has been transformed by offshoring in recent years. Imports have surged from $17.2 billion in 2000 to $30.3 billion in 2006, with virtually all of that increase coming from low-cost China. And the industry has lost 21% of its jobs during the same period.

Yet Washington's official statistics show that productivity per hour in the furniture industry went up by 23% and output by 3% between 2000 and 2005. Those numbers baffle longtime industry consultant Arthur Raymond of Raleigh, N.C., who has watched factory after factory close. "And we haven't pumped any money into the remaining plants," says Raymond. "How anybody can say that domestic production has stayed level is beyond me."

Wrenching Process

Paul B. Toms Jr., CEO of publicly traded Hooker Furniture Corp., recently closed his company's last remaining domestic wood-furniture manufacturing plant, in Martinsville, Va. It was the culmination of a wrenching process that started in 2000, when Hooker still made the vast majority of its products in the U.S. Toms didn't want to go overseas, he says, but he couldn't pass up the 20% to 25% savings to be gleaned from manufacturing there.

The lure of offshoring works the same way for large companies. Byrne of Accenture is working with a "major transportation equipment company" that's planning to offshore more than half of its parts procurement over the next few years. Most of it will go to China. "We're talking about 30% to 40% cost reductions," says Byrne.

Yet no matter how hard you look, you can't find any trace of the cost savings from offshoring in the import price statistics. The furniture industry's experience is particularly telling. Despite the surge of low-priced chairs, tables, and similar products from China, the BLS is reporting that the import price of furniture has actually risen 6.7% since 2003.

The numbers for Chinese imports as a whole are equally out of step with reality. Over the past three years, total imports have climbed by 89%, as U.S.-based companies have rushed to take advantage of the enormous cost advantages. Yet over the same period, the import price index for goods coming out of China has declined a mere 2.3%.

Facade of Growth

The import price index also misses the cost cut when production of an item, such as blue jeans, is switched from a country such as Mexico to a cheaper country like China. That's especially likely to happen if the item goes through a different importer when it comes from a new country, because government statisticians have no way of linking the blue jeans made in China with the same pair that had been made in Mexico.

Phantom GDP can also be created in import-dependent industries with fast product cycles, because the import price statistics can't keep up with the rapid pace of change. And it can happen when foreign suppliers take on tasks such as product design without raising the price. That's an effective cost cut for the American purchaser, but the folks at the BLS have no way of picking it up.

The effects of phantom GDP seem to be mostly concentrated in the past three years, when offshoring has accelerated. Indeed, the first time the term appeared in BusinessWeek was in 2003. Before then, China and India in particular were much smaller exporters to the U.S.

The one area where phantom GDP may have made an earlier appearance is information technology. Outsourcing of production to Asia really took hold in the late 1990s, after the Information Technology Agreement of 1997 sharply cut the duties on IT equipment. "At least a portion of the productivity improvement in the late 1990s ought to be attributed to falling import prices," says Feenstra of UC Davis, who along with Slaughter and two other co-authors has been examining this question.

What does phantom GDP mean for policymakers? For one thing, it calls into question the economic statistics that the Federal Reserve uses to guide monetary policy. If domestic productivity growth has been overstated for the past few years, that suggests the nation's long-term sustainable growth rate may be lower than thought, and the Fed may have less leeway to cut rates.

In terms of trade policy, the new perspective suggests the U.S. may have a worse competitiveness problem than most people realized. It was easy to downplay the huge trade deficit as long as it seemed as though domestic growth was strong. But if the import boom is actually creating only a facade of growth, that's a different story. This lends more credence to corporate leaders such as CEO John Chambers of Cisco Systems Inc. who have publicly worried about U.S. competitiveness—and who perhaps coincidentally have been the ones leading the charge offshore.

In a broader sense, though, the problem with the statistics reveals that the conventional nation-centric view of the U.S. economy is completely obsolete. Nowadays we live in a world where tightly integrated supply chains are a reality.

For that reason, Landefeld of the BEA suggests perhaps part of the cost cuts from offshoring are being appropriately picked up in GDP. In some cases, intangible activities such as R&D and design of a new product or service take place in the U.S. even though the production work is done overseas. Then it may make sense for the gains in productivity in the supply chain to be booked to this country. Says Landefeld: "The companies do own those profits." Still, counters Houseman, "it doesn't represent a more efficient production of things made in this country."

What Landefeld and Houseman can agree on is that the rush of globalization has brought about a fundamental change in the U.S. economy. This is why the methods for measuring the economy need to change, too.

China: Land of Opportunity and Challenge

HR professionals at U.S. companies in China have to work fast to attract, develop and retain employees in this booming economy.

ADRIENNE FOX

"When good fortune finally comes, no one can ever stop it." This Chinese proverb accurately describes the current mood in the world's most populous country.

After three decades of economic reforms and promises of prosperity, China is enjoying an economic bonanza. That translates into record annual growth rates near 10 percent a year for the past decade and the foreseeable future. In less tangible terms, this translates into overwhelming optimism among Chinese people: Seven in 10 believe that five years from now they will stand on the top rungs of the ladder of life, according to the Pew Research Center.

They are moving up the ladder with the help of hordes of multinational companies seeking to capitalize on the country's unprecedented growth. After a steady stream of foreign direct investment began in the late 1970s, the trend has accelerated. The country's accession to the World Trade Organization (WTO) in 2001 made it more amenable for foreign companies to operate securely and profitably.

By 2004, the WTO required China to allow foreign owners to distribute goods without state-owned Chinese partners. Such partners often siphoned profits and stole technology, according to the American Chamber of Commerce in China. Since then, the percentage of American Chamber members operating joint ventures in China slid from 78 percent in 1999 to 27 percent in 2005.

Another measure of growth comes from the Chinese Ministry of Commerce, where foreigners must sign contracts before investing. U.S. contracts increased 44 percent since the WTO accession to 3,741 in 2005, according to the U.S.-China Business Council (USCBC).

China's economic shift up the value chain—from parts manufacturing to research and development—represents another change. With that shift toward higher-end manufacturing, innovation and services comes greater need—and competition—for experienced and skilled labor.

"Local managers are shifting their expertise away from the traditionally heavy emphasis on technical skills to skills that are more business-focused," says Nick Chang, a management consultant in Beijing who leads Accenture's Human Performance practice in China.

HR professionals in China face the challenge of finding, training and retaining skilled employees who can thrive in Western-style multinational corporate cultures.

That's the flip side of enormous growth. Many HR professionals in China face the significant challenge of finding, training and retaining skilled employees who can thrive in Western-style multinational corporate cultures. In 2006, USCBC members ranked human resources as their No. 1 concern—the first time the top reason was not a regulatory issue. In particular, members cited the ability to attract and retain talented employees, especially mid-level managers.

But U.S. companies in China are having some success attracting and retaining local managers, mainly through development and other upward career-planning initiatives. However, HR professionals must stay several steps ahead of this fast-moving market to retain the talented people they train. It requires flexibility and creativity to manage Chinese employees' steep expectations for career growth.

Scarcity in a Sea of Plenty

Despite China's population of 1.3 billion and a workforce of 800 million, only a small percentage of workers is considered skilled and experienced enough to work in multinational companies (MNCs). The McKinsey Global Institute estimates that of 4.9 million college graduates in 2006, only 10 percent had skills necessary to work in MNCs. Language, basic education and interpersonal skills, and attitudes toward teamwork and flexible working hours were lacking.

"The shortage exists primarily because the Chinese educational system has not yet evolved to teach the range of skills that MNCs are looking for," notes Chang. "Cultural differences also continue to play a role." China's Ministry of Education estimates that 350 million Chinese are studying English.

What's more, the mid- and high-level managers in short supply are usually 40- to 50-year-olds in the generation affected by the Cultural Revolution, the period between 1966 and 1976 when the educational system was brought to a halt.

Of the talent paradox, Tom Petersen, director of the University of Southern California Global E-MBA program in Shanghai, notes, "This is a result of the fast economic expansion combined with a shortage of educated personnel in this age range."

Enormous demand and short supply create a seller's market for managers. Those with skills can demand high salaries and expect fast upward mobility. If one MNC does not meet the seller's demand, there are plenty of other buyers.

Furthermore, state- or privately owned Chinese companies have joined in the fierce competition for high-caliber talent, according to Patrick Ran, GPHR, chief representative for the Society for Human Resource Management (SHRM) in Beijing. "As more Chinese companies seek to expand overseas, they are also looking for talent with MNC experience," he says.

The 2007 *Flight* of *Human Talent* survey of HR professionals and Chinese employees by SHRM and Development Dimensions International (DDI) found that 38 percent of HR professionals said turnover has increased in the past 12 months, and 53 percent said it had remained the same, with no sign of relief.

Online Resources

For more information about doing business in China, see the online version of this article at www.shrm.org/hrmagazine/07September for links to:

- An online sidebar on China's regulatory climate.
- A SHRM-DDI study, *2007 Flight of Human Talent*.
- A SHRM webcast on doing business In China.
- A 2007 SHRM study on corporate social responsibility.
- The U.S.-China Business Council's 2006 Member Priorities Survey.
- The American Chamber of Commerce in China.
- A Manpower study on the shortage of mid-level managers in China.
- A Towers Perrin survey that defines strategies for managing global workforces.
- A video Interview with Eric Drummond, GPHR, on hiring local managers and developing an employment brand.

Nearly three-fourths (73 percent) of employees surveyed had resigned previous jobs, and 22 percent said they were likely to leave their positions in the next year. Although higher-level leaders had been employed with their organizations longer than other employees, their average tenures were still only one to two years.

During Chinas boom, "a lot of workers see this as their time to be upwardly mobile," says Rich Wellins, senior vice president of DDI in Bridgeville, Pa.

Skills Needed

Just a few years ago, U.S. companies could rely on workers with basic skills, as the manufacturing processes were not end to end and the services industry was nascent. That changed when Chinas accession to the WTO loosened restrictions on foreign investment in the services and financial sectors.

Two years ago, Beckman Coulter, based in Fullerton, Calif., became first in the health care industry to establish a wholly owned legal entity after China abolished restrictions in 2004. The manufacturer of biomedical testing instrument systems, tests and supplies first invested in a Chinese joint venture 20 years ago. It now has 270 employees working in sales, marketing and services in Shanghai, Guangzhou, Fuzhou and Beijing as well as in a small manufacturing facility in Suzhou.

Developing Managers Keys Retention at All Levels

In China, the manager-employee relationship has become critical to retention at all levels. It's another reason why U.S. companies are investing in developing managers.

If employees have good managers, they are highly unlikely to leave the organization, according to the *2007 Flight of Human Talent* survey by the Society for Human Resource Management (SHRM) and Development Dimensions International (DDI).

Lesley Feinberg, vice president of international HR at Beckman Coulter in Fullerton, Calif., repeatedly stresses the role that managers play in retention on her regular visits to operations in China. Before the company's leadership development program rolled out, she says, "I met with the top managers and said, '[This program] is important because you can make or break this person's motivation and the retention piece if you don't support it.'"

What makes a good leader? "Communication, experience and humility," says Lucille Wu, managing director of Manpower China in Beijing.

Because of Chinese employees' reluctance to admit when they don't understand, Wu explains, "Leaders must not make assumptions that employees know their work. Check their understanding. Be humble. A good leader in China can't order someone to do something because they will do the opposite. You won't get buy-in. You also need to model the behavior you want them to emulate."

Another key to buy-in among employees: Managers should communicate and be open about the company's direction and financial goals. "Leaders need to show how their work relates to the company's direction," says Wu. "That will make employees feel more secure." Employees also need to understand "the expansion plans, the vision."

Respect for elders and those with experience prevails in Chinese culture—so much so that it can be hard to create an environment where employees feel comfortable bringing problems to their managers or to HR. "Going from this hierarchical, top-down model [in China] to a flat, team-oriented, more empowering Western-style multinational corporation is a culture change for these people," says Feinberg. "It's a challenge. You have to respect both sides, but you want the employees to feel empowered and that it's OK [to be critical]."

To those ends, "You have to be open in communication with Chinese employees and be very visible about your follow through" if problems are brought to your attention, says Feinberg. "Building trust and having strong relationships with leaders is key."

—Adrienne Fox

"We are trying to find people who have the experience, the expertise, the contacts, the understanding of the business and the relationships," says Lesley Feinberg, vice president of international HR at Beckman Coulter. "That's a shift. Five years ago, we weren't even interested in that expertise. Now, we're very interested because we're thinking long term."

Similarly, when Springdale, Ark.-based Tyson Foods opened operations in Shanghai during 2001, obtaining talent with technical skills was the higher priority, says Vivian Lee, HR manager. Today, at two operations employing 250 in Shanghai and Shandong, "the main challenge is management skills and [the] people skills of finding qualified local managers. The managers in the key positions are qualified. But in the long run, we need them to train their subordinates. If they fail to do that, we either have to 'buy' talent again or the shortage may affect our operational competitiveness."

Development as a Recruitment Tool

Company officials try to avoid "buying" talent in China. It's a slippery slope. With wage growth of 9 percent to 14 percent annually, luring talented candidates on salary alone does not attract the people companies want to invest in.

Yet Manpower's *The China Talent Paradox* study offers good news: Nearly 75 percent of Chinese employees would prefer to work for wholly owned foreign companies rather than joint-venture companies or wholly owned Chinese companies.

"It's easier for multinational companies with brand names to attract workers," says Wellins. "Chinese workers are very brand conscious. Also, multinationals are more aggressive about wanting to develop people. Their development programs are much more advanced and comprehensive."

Chinese culture calls for learning and growing. A Chinese proverb says, "If you want one year of prosperity, grow grain. If you want 10 years of prosperity, grow trees. If you want 100 years of prosperity, grow people." And, creating opportunities for learning sends a message to potential candidates that the company is in China long term.

"We're trying to show local [People's Republic of China] people that we want to invest and develop them and don't want to rely on expatriates and returnees all the time," says Feinberg.

That's a not-so-subtle message to the workforce at large. Workers have seen many companies come to China, expand too quickly and shut down, leaving many without jobs. Lured with visions of dollar signs, these companies did not take the time and resources—including labor—to make a profit and sustain long-term growth.

Also, if Chinese employees see that a company relies heavily on expatriate managers, they will think its investment in China is short term and not a place of career growth for them. "If you bring more expatriates or hire non-Chinese locals, people will question whether you want to develop local people or not and will look for other companies," says Lucille Wu, managing director of Manpower China in Beijing. "It will hurt your ability to recruit."

Developing Chinese employees also produces coveted word-of-mouth. "Chinese employees like to talk to their friends about what they are learning and what projects they are working on," says Wu. "They need to show [their friends] they are working on something interesting and are upgrading their skills. If they are, they will stay . . . and share that with their friends."

Retention via Leadership Development

Leadership development is also critical to retention. Once you attract Chinese talent with the promise of leadership development and career progression, you had better follow through on those promises—or they will be out the door quickly.

The SHRM-DDI survey asked HR professionals and employees to rank reasons for turnover. The top two reasons for both groups were lack of growth and development, cited by 53 percent of employees and 54 percent of HR professionals, and better career opportunities elsewhere, according to 42 percent of employees and 70 percent of HR professionals.

While company officials recognize the importance of development, they are not always meeting employees' expectations. Fewer than half of the employees surveyed (44 percent) were satisfied with growth opportunities.

"Training and development is a great retention tool that the Chinese employees demand," says Feinberg. "They see this as critical for their careers."

These development plans reach hyper speed—they're not your typical U.S. five-year or longer plans.

"We see a lot of young people with huge expectations," notes Feinberg. "They expect to move so quickly up the organization and if they don't, in a couple of years, they're gone."

Wu agrees: For good performers, "you better have a change in their assignments after the two years or they will look for another company."

Because young managers are promoted quickly, many don't have the skills and experience to lead. This results in turnover at lower levels, since the employee-manager relationship is so critical to retention in China. (See "Developing Managers Keys Retention at All Levels".)

"A middle manager in China is not at the same level as one in the United States," explains Wu. "You often promote or hire people and their skills fit maybe 60 percent to 70 percent of the qualifications."

Leadership Centers

U.S. companies in China are establishing leadership development programs that meet employees' expectations and business needs. For example, San Jose, Calif.-based Cisco Systems Inc. opened its Chinese operation during 1994 and now has sales, research and development, and manufacturing operations employing more than 1,000 workers in nine cities.

Recognizing the need to create its own skilled labor, the company opened Cisco Network Academy in Shanghai during 1998 and now has 220 academies in all provinces with more than 22,000 students enrolled at any time—more than Cisco needs to hire.

"We are developing and nurturing talent, not waiting for the education channels to provide us," says James Jianbo Li, head of human resources in Greater China. "We go to universities that provide good academic skills, and we put in new employee training and coaching and invest in the young people the skills that Cisco believes are important," such as effective communications, project management and teamwork.

Open to all students, not just Cisco employees or candidates, the academies accomplish a twofold strategy: Create a ready source of labor and improve the employment brand with the Chinese government and the workforce. Leadership development centers such as Cisco's are one way U.S. companies use corporate social responsibility efforts to build employment brands and carve a competitive edge.

In 2004, Cisco created an initiative to attract top talent from colleges and "train them as the core of Cisco's next-generation workforce with the mind-set, skills, passion and cultural alignment we needed," Li says.

The program sends about 20 new hires a year to its training center in Raleigh, N.C., for nine months to study Cisco culture, values and skills such as proposal design, presentation, teamwork, and product knowledge and sales. Then, "They come back and have one year of coaching under senior staff," says Li.

Development by Phases

In October, Beckman Coulter plans to launch a leadership development program to work on basic, professional and strategic levels of leadership. "We are initially working with high potentials," says Feinberg. "These people meet the criteria that we've laid out in our talent management strategy, and we want to invest in them."

Led by company executives, the first leadership foundation will contain two sessions of five days each over several months. In addition, external consultants will lead small teams on projects where they take on specific business challenges. At the end, team members will present their findings and solutions.

The second level of the program will roll out next year and focus on participants' business acumen and development as leaders in the company. They will work with customer panels, review financial indicators and learn how they impact the business.

The third series will focus on strategic leadership, organizational change, and how to create and maintain company culture.

"It's a leadership journey over 18 months, with 30 days total of training," notes Feinberg.

After the Development Programs

Formal leadership programs have become important to attract and retain talent in China, and so have on-the-job learning opportunities achieved through mentoring, coaching, succession planning and job rotations.

Formal leadership programs have become important to attract and retain talent in China, and so have on-the-job learning opportunities.

Many companies such as Cisco and Beckman Coulter manage attrition by bringing top talent to headquarters for a period of time or rotating top performers through the organization globally, being mindful to rotate them into jobs that have more responsibility or at least changes in titles, a critical element for this "saving face" culture. Also, establishing formal mentorships or apprenticeships promotes engagement and loyalty.

"Give them access to global or headquarters people for mentorships," advises Wu. "Involve them in global projects. Don't be afraid to give them additional work."

In the SHRM-DDI study, employees ranked "did not find the work interesting" as the No. 4 reason for leaving.

In interviews, several employees described restlessness and boredom resulting from uninteresting jobs, according to the report.

A 2006 Towers Perrin study, *Winning Strategies for a Global Workforce*, also found that only 8 percent of Chinese employees consider themselves "engaged and involved," compared with 20 percent in the United States.

"Give managers more challenging and strategic work and empower them while also making them accountable for specified results," says Accenture's Chang. "Empowerment is among the most motivating ways to develop talent in China."

HR professionals invariably remark on the frenzied pace of retention efforts in China compared to other parts of the world. For an example, look at succession planning: "Every quarter, we identify high potentials, assess them, develop them and rotate them through different levels," says Li.

Beckman Coulter has lower-than-average turnover in China, yet it will not rest in making sure top talent remains happy, learning and progressing, Feinberg says. "We are doing a thorough talent review for the second year in a row and putting plans in place for key players," she adds. "We want to look down the organization at up-and-coming people who aren't ready to take a lead role today but have the potential. We ask ourselves, 'What can we do today to keep them, develop them and motivate them?' We know those young people are looking around."

At Manpower, succession planning is part of the manager's performance appraisal. "I have to ensure I have two or three people to be my successor as managing director, and I'm measured on developing them," notes Wu.

Money Still Talks

No amount of development and opportunity will be enough to retain talent without competitive salaries. "Every year, we check the market on salary, and we have to respond quickly," says Wu. "That's a lot different than every three years or so in the United States."

If your company can't afford to raise rates for the entire workforce every year, at least concentrate on top performers. "We're doing a much more proactive analysis of the best people who, if we lost, would be detrimental to our business," says Feinberg. "We then look at their total compensation, make market adjustments proactively and communicate to [them]." That forestalls "employees coming to us saying they have [other job offers]" that spark rounds of counteroffers. "We do this analysis much more often in China," she adds.

It's an investment worth making. China is "such a dynamic environment," says Feinberg. "That's because of the growth potential and the investment we are making there. We need the fight people to allow us to expand."

Indeed, don't get caught in the accelerated pace in China and the opportunity for expansion without adequate workforce planning. It's something that Cognizant Technology Solutions, an outsourcing firm in Teaneck, N.J., has kept in check.

Cognizant's philosophy "has been to slowly build a strong foundation and then scale it up to meet increased business demand," says Henry Yang, head of China operations in Shanghai. "Because of our moderate growth in China, we have been able to specifically go after the right talent, and, with internal grooming programs, build our next level of managerial professionals."

ADRIENNE FOX, a freelance writer and editor in Alexandria, Va., is a contributing editor and former managing editor of *HR Magazine.*

Test-Your-Knowledge Form

We encourage you to photocopy and use this page as a tool to assess how the articles in *Annual Editions* expand on the information in your textbook. By reflecting on the articles you will gain enhanced text information. You can also access this useful form on a product's book support Web site at *http://www.mhcls.com*.

NAME: DATE:

_____

TITLE AND NUMBER OF ARTICLE:

_____

BRIEFLY STATE THE MAIN IDEA OF THIS ARTICLE:

_____

LIST THREE IMPORTANT FACTS THAT THE AUTHOR USES TO SUPPORT THE MAIN IDEA:

_____

WHAT INFORMATION OR IDEAS DISCUSSED IN THIS ARTICLE ARE ALSO DISCUSSED IN YOUR TEXTBOOK OR OTHER READINGS THAT YOU HAVE DONE? LIST THE TEXTBOOK CHAPTERS AND PAGE NUMBERS:

_____

LIST ANY EXAMPLES OF BIAS OR FAULTY REASONING THAT YOU FOUND IN THE ARTICLE:

_____

LIST ANY NEW TERMS/CONCEPTS THAT WERE DISCUSSED IN THE ARTICLE, AND WRITE A SHORT DEFINITION:

We Want Your Advice

ANNUAL EDITIONS revisions depend on two major opinion sources: one is our Advisory Board, listed in the front of this volume, which works with us in scanning the thousands of articles published in the public press each year; the other is you—the person actually using the book. Please help us and the users of the next edition by completing the prepaid article rating form on this page and returning it to us. Thank you for your help!

ANNUAL EDITIONS: Human Resources 09/10

ARTICLE RATING FORM

Here is an opportunity for you to have direct input into the next revision of this volume.
We would like you to rate each of the articles listed below, using the following scale:

1. **Excellent: should definitely be retained**
2. **Above average: should probably be retained**
3. **Below average: should probably be deleted**
4. **Poor: should definitely be deleted**

Your ratings will play a vital part in the next revision.
Please mail this prepaid form to us as soon as possible.
Thanks for your help!

RATING	ARTICLE	RATING	ARTICLE
	1. Spotlight on Human Resource Management		22. Your Co-Worker, Your Teacher: Collaborative Technology Speeds Peer-Peer Learning
	2. HR Jobs Remain Secure		23. The 40 Best Companies for Diversity
	3. Why We Hate HR		24. The Face of Diversity Is More than Skin Deep
	4. Strange Bedfellows: Could HR Be Marketing's New Best Friend?		25. Philosophizing Compensation
	5. Not the Usual Suspects		26. Do Your Employees Qualify for Overtime?: The Answer May Surprise You
	6. Employers Prepare to Keep, Not Lose, Baby Boomers		27. Pay-for-Performance Plans Should Be Fair and Clear
	7. The Best 4 Ways to Recruit Employees with Disabilities		28. Pay Setters
	8. Making Reasonable Accommodations for Employees with Mental Illness Under the ADA		29. Doc in a Box
			30. Building a Mentally Healthy Workforce
	9. The Wonder of Work		31. Employee Benefits of the Future
	10. The Disability Advantage		32. Benefits and the Bottom Line
	11. Implementing Sexual Harassment Training in the Workplace		33. Setting Up a Disciplinary Procedure
	12. Fighting for Values		34. Poor Performance & Due Process
	13. White Collared		35. How to Investigate Workplace Misconduct & Avoid the HP Syndrome
	14. Managing in the New Millennium: Ten Keys to Better Hiring		36. Working with "Temps" Is Not a Temporary Job
	15. Six Ways to Strengthen Staffing		37. Business Ethics: The Key Role of Corporate Governance
	16. Balancing HR Systems with Employee Privacy		38. Supporting Ethical Employees
	17. Technology Tames Password Overload, Boosts HR Data Security		39. Throwing the Switch
	18. The 'Brain Drain': How to Get Talented Women to Stay		40. Roots of Insecurity: Why American Workers and Others Are Losing Out
	19. Managing in the New Millennium: Interpersonal Skills		41. Collaboration Is Key to Effective Outsourcing
	20. Managing Employee Relations		42. The Real Cost of Offshoring
	21. Banishing Bullying		43. China: Land of Opportunity and Challenge

BUSINESS REPLY MAIL
FIRST CLASS MAIL PERMIT NO. 551 DUBUQUE IA

POSTAGE WILL BE PAID BY ADDRESSEE

McGraw-Hill Contemporary Learning Series
501 BELL STREET
DUBUQUE, IA 52001

NO POSTAGE
NECESSARY
IF MAILED
IN THE
UNITED STATES

ABOUT YOU

Name   Date

Are you a teacher? ❑ A student? ❑
Your school's name

Department

Address   City   State   Zip

School telephone #

YOUR COMMENTS ARE IMPORTANT TO US!

Please fill in the following information:
For which course did you use this book?

Did you use a text with this ANNUAL EDITION? ❑ yes ❑ no
What was the title of the text?

What are your general reactions to the Annual Editions concept?

Have you read any pertinent articles recently that you think should be included in the next edition? Explain.

Are there any articles that you feel should be replaced in the next edition? Why?

Are there any World Wide Web sites that you feel should be included in the next edition? Please annotate.

May we contact you for editorial input? ❑ yes ❑ no
May we quote your comments? ❑ yes ❑ no